Jay Atlas

PLATO'S PHAEDRUS

PLATO'S PHAEDRUS

*Translated with an Introduction
and Commentary by*

R. HACKFORTH, F.B.A.

*formerly Emeritus Professor of Ancient Philosophy
in the University of Cambridge*

CAMBRIDGE
AT THE UNIVERSITY PRESS
1972

Published by the Syndics of the Cambridge University Press
Bentley House, 200 Euston Road, London NW1 2DB
American Branch: 32 East 57th Street, New York, N.Y. 10022

ISBN: 0 521 08459 8   Clothbound
0 521 09703 7   Paperback

First published 1952
Reprinted 1972

First printed in Great Britain
at the University Printing House, Cambridge

Reprinted in the United States of America

CONTENTS

PREFACE

In this book I have slightly altered the form adopted in my earlier work *Plato's Examination of Pleasure* (*Philebus*) by prefixing a brief analysis to each section of the translation, and reserving the whole commentary to the end of the section. This will, I hope, prove a convenience to readers.

No English commentary on the *Phaedrus* has appeared, so far as I know, since that of W. H. Thompson, published in 1868. Of that excellent work I have naturally made much use. Another obvious source of help has been L. Robin's edition (1933) in what is commonly known as the Budé series. Next to these I am probably most indebted to the well-known *Mythes de Platon* of Perceval Frutiger, and to P. Friedländer's *Die Platonischen Schriften* and his earlier volume of essays *Eidos, Paideia, Dialogos*. Specific acknowledgements to these and other works will be found in my footnotes.

I am most grateful to Prof. D. S. Robertson, who read the whole of my typescript, and to Prof. Dorothy Tarrant, who read the translation at the manuscript stage and also checked the proofs. Both these friends have made valuable suggestions and saved me from many mistakes. Some of the central sections were also read in their first draft by Mr W. K. C. Guthrie, whose helpful comments I am also glad to acknowledge. Lastly I am indebted to the late Dr R. G. Bury, that fine scholar and lover of Plato, for advice on a number of points.

Burnet's text has been followed, except where noted.

R. H.

CAMBRIDGE
6 *October* 1951

LIST OF ABBREVIATIONS

Diels-Kranz or DK =*Die Fragmente der Vorsokratiker, griechisch und deutsch*, von H. Diels: fünfte Auflage herausgegeben von W. Kranz (1934).

Hermeias   =*Hermiae Alexandrini in Platonis Phaedrum Scholia* ed. P. Couvreur (1901).

Robin   =Platon, *Phèdre*, texte établi et traduit par L. Robin (Collection des Universités de France, 1933).

Thompson   =*The 'Phaedrus' of Plato*, with English notes by W. H. Thompson (1868).

INTRODUCTION

I. Date of composition

Although it is impossible, and likely to remain impossible, to assign a precise date to the composition of the *Phaedrus*, or even to fix with complete certainty its position in the order of dialogues, there has been an increasing tendency during the present century to consider it a relatively late work. Apart from the patently absurd belief preserved by Diogenes Laertius (III, 38), and echoed by Olympiodorus in the sixth century, that it was the earliest of Plato's writings, the only ancient opinion that has come down to us is that of Cicero (*Orator* XIII, 47), who refers to the compliment paid by Socrates to Isocrates at the very end of the dialogue (279 A) and adds 'at ea de seniore scribit Plato et scribit aequalis, et quidem exagitator omnium rhetorum hunc miratur unum'. This is indeed vague enough; but if we may accept W. H. Thompson's belief that the word *senior* would not be applied to a man under fifty, it would follow that Plato, being at most eight years younger than Isocrates, was certainly over forty at the time. That few to-day would doubt, but it does not get us very far.

We are therefore thrown back on internal evidence, and more particularly on the relations between the *Phaedrus* and other dialogues. And we may begin by noting that, whereas it is universally recognised nowadays that the *Sophist* is the first of a group of six late dialogues (*Sophist, Statesman, Philebus, Timaeus, Critias, Laws*) which all display a deliberate avoidance of hiatus, the *Phaedrus* stands, on this criterion, outside the group, yet near to it.[1] Although more significance attaches, in the present writer's opinion, to this avoidance of hiatus than to any other of the stylometrists' criteria, it would be unwise to build too much upon it; the relatively low figure of 23·9 may after all be due to accident, or to temporary conformity to a feature of Isocratean style in a work addressed, in a sense, to Isocrates. Still, it can hardly be wholly accidental that, on the general results of the stylistic examination by Ritter and others, our dialogue, together with the *Theaetetus* and *Parmenides*, is placed between the *Republic* and the late six.[2]

An exhaustive investigation with the object of confirming this

---

[1] The figures are given by Ritter, *Platon* I, p. 238. In the six dialogues the average occurrence of hiatus varies between 0·61 per page in *Sophist* and 5·85 in *Laws*; the remaining dialogues vary between 23·9 (*Phaedrus*) and 45·97 (*Lysis*).
[2] See the table in Ritter I, p. 254.

position was undertaken by H. von Arnim,[1] who moreover finds reasons for putting the *Phaedrus* after the *Theaetetus* and *Parmenides*. Although some of his arguments are much less cogent than others, their cumulative evidence is strong, at least in so far as a post-*Republic* dating is maintained. He seems to me to show convincingly that there are a number of passages, particularly in Socrates's second speech, which would be unintelligible or barely intelligible to readers unacquainted with the *Republic*. Allowing that the comparison of the soul to a charioteer with two winged horses might be understood without a knowledge of *Rep.* IV, we must nevertheless, in my opinion, agree with von Arnim that it is unlikely that Plato would have put the tripartition doctrine before the public for the first time in this symbolic form. This argument might seem to be weakened by the objection, put forward by A. E. Taylor, that the doctrine was already familiar as 'a piece of fifth century Pythagoreanism';[2] but although this is recorded[3] on the authority of Posidonius, it has been discredited by Wilamowitz[4] and others, and certainly the exposition in the *Republic* has every appearance of being Plato's own original doctrine, without any hint of indebtedness. And even if we accept its Pythagorean origin, the balance of probability still seems to me in favour of the priority of the *Republic* exposition.

One of von Arnim's points of detail concerns the passage (249 B) in which the words ἀφικνούμεναι ἐπὶ κλήρωσίν τε καὶ αἵρεσιν τοῦ δευτέρου βίου seem to allude to the curious mixture of determination by lot and choice with which souls are confronted in the myth of Er (*Rep.* X, 617 D ff.). I find his argument[5] on this irresistible, and regard it as one of the strongest evidences of the priority of the *Republic*.

It is well known that the proof of the soul's immortality given in our dialogue (245 C–E) differs from those of the *Phaedo* and *Rep.* X, and rests on a conception of the soul's nature, as that which moves itself, which is preserved in Plato's latest work (*Laws* X), but is apparently unknown to the *Phaedo* and *Republic*. This point too is dealt with by

---

[1] *Platos Jugenddialoge und die Entstehungszeit des Phaidros* (1914). Some of his points had been already made by H. Raeder, *Platos Philosophische Entwickelung*, pp. 245–79.

[2] *Plato, the Man and his Work*, p. 300.

[3] Galen, *de Hippocratis et Platonis placitis* IV, 425 (Kühn).

[4] *Platon* I, p. 395.

[5] *op. cit.* pp. 172–3: the concluding words are 'Es ist also zu schliessen, dass P. die κλήρωσις nur deshalb erwähnte, weil er eben rekapitulierte und den Leser an seine eigene Darstellung des Gegenstandes in *Rep.* X erinnern wollte'.

von Arnim thoroughly and convincingly; in particular one may ask why the very unsatisfactory proof of immortality in *Rep.* x should have been preferred to that of the *Phaedrus* if the *Phaedrus* had already been written.

The post-*Republic* position is accepted—largely, I think, as the result of von Arnim's investigations, by Taylor[1] (with a certain measure of doubt), Frutiger,[2] Stenzel,[3] Wilamowitz[4] and Jaeger.[5] On the other side the most important name—indeed the only important name, so far as I know, in the present century—is that of Pohlenz.[6] His arguments are chiefly directed towards discrediting the results of the stylometrists, and are not without force; for the rest his principal, indeed almost his only, argument is of a very subjective and unconvincing character: 'the general manner in which Plato here speaks of Eros, and in particular his portrayal of the passion of sensual love, does not suggest assigning the composition of the *Phaedrus* to a date when Plato was in his later fifties.'[7]

Dr R. G. Bury, in his edition of the *Symposium* (1909), is inclined[8] to put the *Phaedrus* before the *Symposium*, and to date the former about 388–386 B.C. But he does not examine the question in detail, nor seek to determine the position of these two dialogues relatively to the *Republic*; and of course he wrote before von Arnim's investigation.

M. Robin, though without reference to von Arnim by name, seems to accept his general conclusions, though he would put our dialogue at approximately the same date as the *Theaetetus*, whereas von Arnim puts it after both *Theaetetus* and *Parmenides*. I do not myself think that anyone has brought forward any decisive arguments on this further point; there are of course numerous features which connect *Phaedrus* with *Sophist*, *Statesman*, *Timaeus* and *Laws* x; Robin's introduction (pp. v–ix) makes it unnecessary for me to recapitulate them; but they are compatible with any position relatively to the *Theaetetus* and *Parmenides*; and Robin seems to me to exaggerate the closeness of *Phaedrus* to *Theaetetus*.

In a paper in *Classical Quarterly* XXXI (1937) entitled 'The Attack on Isocrates in the *Phaedrus*', Mr R. L. Howland seeks to date the dialogue by finding in it an allusion to the oration (II) *ad Nicoclem*. This Cypriot

---

[1] *op. cit.* p. 300. [2] *Les Mythes de Platon*, p. 80.
[3] *Studien zur Entwick. der plat. Dialektik*, p. 108 n.
[4] *Platon* I, p. 459. [5] *Paideia* III, p. 193.
[6] *Aus Platos Werdezeit*, pp. 355–64.
[7] *op. cit.* p. 341, repeated in much the same words at p. 355.
[8] p. lxvii.

prince succeeded his father Evagoras in 374 B.C. and the oration is
believed to be not more than a few years later in date. Further, 'The
Nicocles (III), published a few years later, opens with a long attack on
those who decry oratory, and this may be Isocrates's attempt to reply
to the *Phaedrus*. The date of the *Phaedrus* would then fall between the
dates of these two works of Isocrates, that is approximately between
372 and 368.'

I should make it clear that the words just quoted are from a footnote,
and that it is not Mr Howland's primary object to date the dialogue:
hence he must not be taken to wish to press this point as something
definitely established. The date suggested seems to me very reasonable;
but I cannot accept the argument on which it is based. Setting aside
the suggestion as to the object of the *Nicocles* as no more than con-
jectural, we must ask whether we can in fact find an allusion to *ad
Nicoclem*, and so obtain a *terminus a quo*. I fear that we cannot. The
argument is that in making Phaedrus say (259 E) that he has heard that
the intending orator need not learn τὰ τῷ ὄντι δίκαια ἀλλὰ τὰ δόξαντ'
ἂν πλήθει οἵπερ δικάσουσιν Plato has in mind *ad Nic.* §§ 45–9 (Blass),
particularly the final sentence: τοιούτων οὖν παραδειγμάτων ὑπαρ-
χόντων δέδεικται τοῖς ἐπιθυμοῦσι τοὺς ἀκροωμένους ψυχαγωγεῖν ὅτι
τοῦ μὲν νουθετεῖν καὶ συμβουλεύειν ἀφεκτέον, τὰ δὲ τοιαῦτα λεκτέον
οἷς ὁρῶσι τοὺς ὄχλους μάλιστα χαίροντας. 'Plato interprets this, not
without some justification, as meaning that the function of rhetoric is
to please the audience, and that the successful orator has to know how
to do this rather than to know τἀληθές' (*loc. cit.* p. 156).

It seems to me impossible that Isocrates is here expressing his own
opinion on the function of rhetoric, or that Plato could have believed
him to be doing so. The point he seeks to make, as will appear if we
read on to the end of the oration, is that Nicocles is not a commonplace
person (οὐχ ἕνα τῶν πολλῶν, § 50) who rejects sound advice and
admonition, who judges everything and everyone by the standard of
pleasure: he is one who can profit by the counsel Isocrates will give him.
The words quoted from § 49 are not intended to mean anything more
than what has been already said at the beginning of § 48, namely that
the multitude prefer to be entertained rather than exhorted for their
good, and that one who seeks to please or allure (ψυχαγωγεῖν)
a popular audience has to bear this in mind. No doubt there is a certain
touch of cynical exaggeration in this estimate of the ὄχλος: the
'superiority' of the prince has to be underlined; but Isocrates was the

last man to depreciate the claim of rhetoric νουθετεῖν καὶ συμβουλεύειν the serious-minded: Plato himself might well have said much what he says here about the ὄχλος and could never have so misunderstood him as to miss the point of the present passage. It cannot therefore be Isocrates from whom Phaedrus has 'heard' that the orator need only care for τὰ δόξαντ' ἂν πλήθει.

To sum up, we can, in my judgment, say at least that there is a very strong probability, amounting indeed to virtual certainty, that our dialogue is later in composition than the *Republic*; and a fair probability that it belongs to the same period as those other two dialogues which must intervene between *Republic* and *Sophist*, namely *Parmenides* and *Theaetetus*. It may be added that this will also involve its being later than the other dialogue which is prominently concerned with love, the *Symposium*; and in any case this posteriority is rendered highly probable by the words of Phaedrus at *Symp.* 177C, where he expresses surprise at the neglect of mankind worthily to sing the praises of love. I agree with Robin (*Banquet*, p. iii) that Plato could hardly have put the words Ἔρωτα δὲ μηδένα πω ἀνθρώπων τετολμηκέναι εἰς ταυτηνὶ τὴν ἡμέραν ἀξίως ὑμνῆσαι into the mouth of Phaedrus if he had already composed the dialogue in which he makes Socrates, in the hearing of Phaedrus himself, glorify the god of love as he does; and that Plato does deem his μυθικὸς ὕμνος 'worthy' may be inferred from the sentence with which Socrates concludes it: αὕτη σοι, ὦ φίλε Ἔρως, εἰς ἡμετέραν δύναμιν ὅτι καλλίστη καὶ ἀρίστη δέδοταί τε καὶ ἐκτέτεισται παλινῳδία (257A).

I am disinclined to set down any precise date, even tentatively; but readers may perhaps be helped in placing the dialogue by having one before their minds: I will therefore give as my guess 370 B.C. or thereabouts. This is in accordance with Howland's result, it is implied by Pohlenz's reference to a man in his later fifties, and tallies with Robin's belief that both *Phaedrus* and *Theaetetus* were composed shortly before Plato's second visit to Syracuse.[1]

---

[1] It is probable that the battle of Corinth referred to in the introduction to *Theaetetus* took place in 369, and it is commonly, though perhaps somewhat rashly, assumed that that dialogue was composed soon after this date. Even if we knew the date of *Republic*, as we do not (since *Epistle* VII, 326A, is not necessarily a quotation from it, and so far as I know there is no other evidence of any value), we could not say how long a gap intervened between it and *Phaedrus*. I would hazard the conjecture—it is no more—that the composition of *Republic* occupied the greater part of the decade 380–370.

II. The dramatic date

This is a matter of little importance, and it may be doubted whether Plato was ever at pains to preserve the unity of time in his dialogues, except of course in those which are centred upon the trial and death of Socrates. The scene is essentially 'en dehors de toute histoire' as Robin remarks; nevertheless such marks of date as there are fit the period 411–404 B.C., and an earlier year in this rather than a later. Lysias is living in Athens, and that gives a *terminus a quo*, since he returned from Thurii in 412–411; his brother Polemarchus is still alive, and as he perished at the hands of the Thirty we have the other limiting date. Isocrates is still young (278 E) and would be about twenty-five in 410.

The only circumstance difficult to reconcile with a dramatic date about 410 is the age of Phaedrus. We have virtually no knowledge of him independently of Plato,[1] but in the *Protagoras* (315 C) he is imagined as old enough (say eighteen) to appear in the train of Hippias at the famous gathering of sophists in the house of Callias: and the date of this must be 433–432 at latest. His next appearance is in the *Symposium*, which celebrates Agathon's tragic victory of 416, when he ought to be about thirty-four at least; and in 410 he would be about forty years of age. Yet Socrates calls him a νεανίας at 257C, a παῖς at 267C, and numbers him amongst οἱ νέοι at 275 B.

This however should not trouble us: Robin is surely right in saying that Plato is 'peu soucieux de ces scrupules chronologiques'. He wants a Phaedrus who is young enough still to possess an indiscriminate *Schwärmerei* for rhetoric.

III. Subjects and purposes of the dialogue

Our dialogue has at least one feature in common with its near neighbour, the *Republic*: it is not obvious, at a first reading, what its subject and purpose are, whether there are two or more, and if so how they are connected. Scholars, ancient and modern alike, have been puzzled on the point; Hermeias has a section of some length, before his commentary proper begins, on the δόξαι του σκοποῦ: some, he tells us, say it is Love, some Rhetoric, some the Good, some the πρῶτον καλόν, one—the only one named—Iamblichus περὶ τοῦ παντοδαποῦ καλοῦ φησὶν εἶναι τὸν σκοπόν, and Hermeias himself agrees. There is

---

[1] In Lysias XIX, 15, he is mentioned as impoverished οὐ διὰ κακίαν.

a grain of truth in this, but since the substantiation of it starts with the quite unfounded assertion that Lysias was the ἐραστής (in the primary sense) of Phaedrus, we need not trouble to discuss it.[1]

Instead of attempting to recapitulate and mediate between the views of modern scholars, who necessarily agree with and differ from each other in an infinite variety of combinations, I shall make bold to state my own view baldly and somewhat dogmatically, trusting to the commentary which follows to confirm it. I think it is helpful to ask for the purpose rather than the subject, and I believe there are three purposes, all important but one more important than the others. They are:

(1) To vindicate the pursuit of philosophy, in the meaning given to that word by Socrates and Plato, as the true culture of the soul (ψυχῆς θεραπεία), by contrast with the false claims of contemporary rhetoric to provide that culture. This I regard as the most important purpose.

(2) To make proposals for a reformed rhetoric, which should subserve the ends of philosophy and adopt its method.

(3) To announce a special method of philosophy—the 'dialectic' method of Collection and Division—and to exemplify this both positively (in the two speeches of Socrates) and negatively (in the speech of Lysias).

Of course, these purposes are not independent of each other, nor are they pursued each in a separate part of the dialogue; Plato does not write treatises: he dramatises arguments as they might conceivably be developed by persons actually conversing. Although the first or dominant purpose is most clearly discerned and most directly pursued in the middle part of the work (the second discourse of Socrates), it is present throughout, and is what gives the dialogue its unity. Once this is seen, or rather felt, by the reader, he will no longer think it necessary or helpful to ask whether the main subject is Love or Rhetoric.[2]

The above statement of purposes, however, does not in itself account for the prominence of love in the discussion. Love is of course the subject of all three set discourses, the Lysias speech, the first speech of

---

[1] The reverse relation is asserted at 236B and 279B, but only in jest.

[2] Robin (chapter III of his introduction) has convincingly shown that there are insuperable objections to regarding either Rhetoric or Love as *the* subject; but he seems to me less successful in explaining precisely how the apparent duality is resolved. The comparison to a symphony (p. lviii) with its interweaving of 'subjects'—originally suggested by M. E. Bourguet—is a μετάβασις εἰς ἄλλο γένος which seems to me rather to restate the problem than solve it.

Socrates, and his 'palinode'; nor does it really drop out of sight in the last part of the dialogue, for what Plato there seeks especially to drive home, in the exaltation (274C–278B) of the spoken word over the written, is just this, that the quest of truth must be the joint effort of two minds, the minds of teacher (or guide) and disciple, whose love for one another is rooted in their common love of truth, beauty, and goodness, their common pursuit of φιλοσοφία. This we have in fact already been told more directly in the great μυθικὸς ὕμνος to Ἔρως, in which Socrates uses the pregnant phrase παιδεραστεῖν μετὰ φιλοσοφίας (249A), a phrase whose full meaning we are brought to see in the picture of lover and beloved regrowing together those wings of the soul which fell from them on their incarceration in the body.

For to Plato philosophy *is* love, that is to say the whole-hearted passionate devotion to a quest in which the soul's deepest need finds its fulfilment. The knowledge of true Being, of all those Forms in which the supreme Form, the Form of the Good, is manifested, is the goal of that part of the soul which Plato calls νοῦς in the *Phaedo*, the object of that faculty which he calls νόησις in *Rep.* VI–VII, even as in the present dialogue he tells us that ἡ ἀχρώματός τε καὶ ἀσχημάτιστος καὶ ἀναφὴς οὐσία ὄντως οὖσα is μόνῳ θεατὴ νῷ (247C). But νοῦς in Plato is not mere intellect divorced from passion and desire, as a superficial reading of *Phaedo* and *Republic* might perhaps lead us to suppose; it is reason or thought moved by desire, by the desire of the soul for that which is akin to it, the desire to know and enjoy its object in that complete union which the great mystics have sought to describe, and which Plato himself so often describes in terms of sexual imagery, not only in the *Phaedrus* but also in the other two works where the mystical aspect of his philosophy is prominent, *Symposium* and *Republic*.[1]

Plato's dissatisfaction with rhetoric is at bottom due to his conviction that it knows nothing of all this. Purporting to be a means of education, it has no conception of what education is; to use the symbolism of the myth (248B), its teachers and its pupils feed on τροφὴ δοξαστή: as indeed the foremost among them, Isocrates, had loudly proclaimed when he rejected the useless and unattainable 'knowledge'

---

[1] See e.g. *Rep.* 490A–B, especially the closing words: ᾧ πλησιάσας καὶ μιγεὶς τῷ ὄντι ὄντως, γεννήσας νοῦν καὶ ἀλήθειαν, γνοίη τε καὶ ἀληθῶς ζῴη καὶ τρέφοιτο, καὶ οὕτω λήγοι ὠδῖνος, πρὶν δ' οὔ. The *Phaedo*, be it noted, despite its condemnation of the ἔρωτες and ἐπιθυμίαι with which the body fills us (66C), speaks of φρόνησις as that οὗ ἐπιθυμοῦμέν τε καί φαμεν ἐρασταὶ εἶναι (66E).

of the Socratics in favour of useful 'opinion' about practical affairs.[1]
But what he stresses in our dialogue is the indifference of rhetoric to
truth, which involves indifference to right and wrong, just and unjust.
Unless a man recognises that there is a reality behind sense-appearances,
that there are absolute moral standards behind or above our shifting,
inconsistent and vaguely conceived notions of what is just and fair
and honourable; unless, having recognised this, he seeks by the
discipline of his appetitive nature—the lusts of the flesh—to foster
that higher self which is akin to the Forms and whose driving force is
the love of those Forms; unless, in short, he loves truth and righteous-
ness, and hates falsehood and iniquity, his claim to teach ἀρετή (as most
of the Sophists claimed), his claim to fit men to play a part in the affairs
of their πόλις, more particularly in assembly and lawcourt (as most of
the teachers of rhetoric claimed), is inadmissible. The blind cannot lead
the blind.

In so far as the *Phaedrus* is much concerned with rhetoric it is natural
to compare it with the *Gorgias*. The difference of standpoint between
the two dialogues, which are separated probably by some seventeen
years, is that whereas in the earlier Plato is content merely to contrast
rhetoric and philosophy, in the later he seeks to harness rhetoric in the
service of philosophy. Rhetoric as it is actually practised and the
principles (or lack of principles) on which it is actually based are
condemned as vigorously as ever: it is still no τέχνη, no true art, for
it knows nothing of dialectic, the sovereign method of philosophy;
but it can, Plato suggests, become a τέχνη by basing itself on dialectic
and psychology.[2]

Are Plato's suggestions for a reformed rhetoric merely theoretical
and visionary, or did he conceive of them bearing fruit in his own
time? It is not easy to say: but if he did, he must have believed there
was a chance of winning over Isocrates, whose school had by now
stood over against the Academy, with no little success, for something
like twenty years. It is not necessary here to enlarge upon the profound
difference in spirit between the two educationalists; it is clear enough
that to Isocrates Plato seemed an unpractical visionary and a hair-
splitting eristic; it is harder to say what Isocrates seemed to Plato;

---

[1] *Helen* § 5 (Blass).
[2] We may believe that it is a reformed rhetoric that is allotted an honourable
function in the state at *Pol.* 304 D: καὶ τοῦτο μὲν ἔοικε ταχὺ κεχωρίσθαι πολιτικῆς τὸ
ῥητορικόν, ὡς ἕτερον εἶδος ὄν, ὑπηρετοῦν μὴν ταύτῃ.

Plato must, I think, have recognised the sincerity of the man's aims as a humanist and an exponent of enlightened pan-Hellenism, even while he deplored his indifference to the mathematical sciences which 'draw us towards true Being' (*Rep.* 521 D) and his disbelief in absolute moral standards. I do not find it difficult to believe that the ascription of φιλοσοφία τις (279 A) to Isocrates is, as Cicero took it, seriously meant and contains no lurking sarcasm, though the τις no doubt limits the amount of φιλοσοφία.

Our knowledge does not permit us to estimate the chances of converting Isocrates and his school: but it is difficult to think they were more than slender. In any case I am strongly of opinion that a conciliatory attitude towards Isocrates himself is not incompatible with the uncompromising criticism of rhetoric—which must include rhetoric as expounded in the school of Isocrates—that has preceded. To suppose that Isocrates is the individual target throughout seems to me incompatible with that superiority to Lysias which is so emphatically accorded to him at the end;[1] so far as any individual is taken to represent rhetoric it is not the living Isocrates, but the dead Lysias.[2]

IV.   The characters

The dialogue has only two characters, Socrates and Phaedrus. This can hardly be called unusual, since except for the *Protagoras* and *Symposium* it is Plato's practice to work with three characters at most in the body of the dialogue (e.g. Socrates, Simmias and Cebes in *Phaedo*; Socrates, Glaucon, Adimantus in *Republic*; Socrates, Theodorus, Theaetetus in *Theaetetus*) though there are often a number of others in the introductory scenes, or 'chipping in' occasionally later on. In our dialogue Lysias may be regarded as in effect a third character.[3] The scene, however, almost necessitates a duologue: it would be unconvincing to have a number of people accompanying Socrates on

---

[1] δοκεῖ μοι ἀμείνων ἢ κατὰ τοὺς περὶ Λυσίαν εἶναι λόγους τὰ τῆς φύσεως (279 A).

[2] Robin (p. clxxiii) comes to the conclusion that 'le *Phèdre* dans ses deux dernières parties et, par conséquent, dans son ensemble puisque c'est un tout solidaire, m'apparaît donc comme un réquisitoire contre la rhétorique d'Isocrate'. It is perhaps unfair to quote this sentence by itself, for M. Robin cannot think that the *Phaedrus* is nothing more than this. The truth, as I see it, is that the dialogue *includes* an attack on contemporary rhetoric, and thereby hits Isocrates; but that there is no personal attack is made plain by what amounts to a conciliatory overture at the end.

[3] cf. παρόντος δὲ καὶ Λυσίου (228 E).

his unusual country walk, or casually turning up in the secluded spot on the bank of the Ilissus; and if *mutae personae* are wanted they are supplied by the 'divinities of the place' (262D).

Phaedrus is not painted in strong colours, partly no doubt because he is sufficiently familiar to Plato's readers from the *Symposium*; from the *Protagoras* (315C) too they knew that he kept company with the Sophist Hippias. He is plainly an intelligent person, alive to the movement of thought in his day; no stranger to Socrates, but clearly not of his 'circle'. 'Toujours', writes Robin,[1] 'il apparaît comme un fervent partisan des Sophistes, totalement incapable par là même de communier avec la pensée de Socrate.' These last words go perhaps rather too far: no doubt they are true of the early pages of the work, but they seem to become less so later on, and I am inclined to think that Phaedrus is converted to philosophy in the end.[2] This may or may not be true[3] of the historical Phaedrus. For the rest I cannot do better than quote Robin's admirable sketch[4] drawn from the two (or three) dialogues: 'Préoccupé de sa santé, attentif à son hygiène, plein de foi dans les théoriciens de la médecine et aussi bien de la rhétorique ou de la mythologie, curieux de savoir mais dépourvu de jugement, superficiel dans ses curiosités et.naïf dans l'expression de ses sentiments, admirateur fervent des réputations dûment cataloguées et consacrées.'

Socrates has many of the familiar features of the Platonic portrait. He is poor, goes barefoot, is given to self-depreciation and mock-respect for persons of repute, urbane and lively, prone to word-play (235E, 238C, 244C, 252B), eager for discussion but conscious of his own ignorance, even on the subject of Love (235C)[5] on which elsewhere (*Symp.* 177D, 198D) he proclaims himself an expert. His serenity or cheerfulness is a feature emphasised by Ivo Bruns and Wilamowitz as specially marked in our dialogue, though I am not sure that it is not equally manifest elsewhere; no doubt Plato deliberately avoids letting the shadow of 399 darken the 'glücklicher Sommertag' of some ten years earlier.

[1] p. xiii.   [2] See pp. 111-12 *infra*.
[3] Nothing can safely be built on the 'philosophising' put into his mouth by the comic poet Alexis (frag. 245, Kock; cf. Robin, *Banquet*, p. xxxviii). Nor does any value attach to the anonymous statement (*D.L.* III, 29) that Plato was his ἐραστής or to the epigram (*Anth. Pal.* VII, 100=*D.L.* III, 31) ascribed to Plato in which the name Phaedrus occurs. The Phaedrus that we know must have been some twenty years older than Plato.   [4] *Banquet*, p. xxxvii.
[5] Yet at the end of the 'palinode' he admits what he has previously disclaimed, the possession of ἐρωτικὴ τέχνη (257A).

But there is one new feature, or more exactly perhaps one feature which hitherto has been only faintly suggested but now becomes prominent, namely a susceptibility to the influence of external Nature felt as a power lifting him out of his normal rational self into a state of 'possession' (ἐνθουσιασμός). His recognition of this influence is for the most part expressed, *more suo*, in a light, bantering fashion: θεῖος ἔοικεν ὁ τόπος εἶναι, ὥστε ἐὰν ἄρα πολλάκις νυμφόληπτος προϊόντος τοῦ λόγου γένωμαι, μὴ θαυμάσῃς (238 D); ἆρ' οἶσθ' ὅτι ὑπὸ τῶν Νυμφῶν...σαφῶς ἐνθουσιάσω; (241 E); φεῦ, ὅσῳ λέγεις τεχνικώτερος Νύμφας τὰς Ἀχελῴου καὶ Πᾶνα τὸν Ἑρμοῦ Λυσίου τοῦ Κεφάλου πρὸς λόγους εἶναι (263 D).

What degree of seriousness in this matter we ought to ascribe to the dramatic character 'Socrates' (leaving aside for the moment the question of historicity) is doubtful; but more important is Plato's purpose in making him speak as he does. I cannot doubt that he wishes thereby to make the substance of Socrates's great second speech less startling in his mouth. The exaltation of 'divine madness' over rational prudence, and indeed the whole splendid apparatus of the μυθικὸς ὕμνος, are hardly in character with the Socrates whom we know from the 'Socratic' dialogues.[1] The mystical side of the Platonic Socrates has indeed appeared to some extent in the early part of the *Phaedo*, in *Rep.* VI, and more clearly in the *Symposium*, though in the last-named dialogue Plato has adopted the device of making him learn τὰ τέλεα καὶ ἐποπτικά from the wise woman Diotima, and actually puts the exposition thereof into Diotima's mouth, doubtless in order to minimise the shock of the rationalist suffering a sea-change.

The taking of Socrates away from his customary haunts in the gymnasia and the market-place, the choice of the country scene so beautifully described, the still atmosphere of the shady retreat beside the Ilissus, so different from the urban bustle and matter-of-fact *milieu* of most of the dialogues—all this contributes to the same end.

But we cannot avoid asking whether the picture is true to life. Had Socrates in fact this non-rational, mystical side to counterbalance his rationalism and intellectualism? The question is not of course to be answered simply by saying that Plato had these two sides to his

---

[1] At *Phaedo* 61 B Socrates says αὐτὸς οὐκ ἦ μυθολογικός, and the great myth at the end of the dialogue is introduced by the words λέγεται δ' οὕτως (107 D); similarly with the myth of *Gorgias* ἃ ἐγὼ ἀκηκοὼς πιστεύω ἀληθῆ εἶναι (524 A) and the myth of Er. Amongst the eschatological myths that of *Phaedrus* is exceptional in being attributed directly to Socrates: the palinode is 'all his own work' (257 A).

nature; though indeed it is surely undeniable that he had: for, apart from clear hints in the seventh *Epistle*,[1] nobody could have written of the ὑπερουράνιος τόπος as he does (247 C–E) who had not known the mystic's experience.[2] But the same might be true of Socrates also. It seems to me impossible strictly to prove that it was not; but if it were, it would be puzzling that the feature in question is not, to my knowledge, hinted at in any dialogue earlier than *Symposium* and *Phaedo*;[3] and the numerous references to Socrates's 'queerness' (ἀτοπία) do not seem to point in this direction: many people have been no less eccentric, yet wholly devoid of mystical experience.

The 'divine sign' or 'voice', which is vouchsafed to Socrates in the present dialogue (242 B) amongst others, is sometimes appealed to in this connexion. It was of course not the voice of conscience, having nothing to do with right and wrong; it was always inhibitory, according to Plato, and sometimes concerned with quite trivial matters (πάνυ ἐπὶ σμικροῖς ἐναντιουμένη, *Apol.* 40 A), though on one occasion at least it determined a most important matter, namely Socrates's abstention from politics (*ibid.* 31 D). We may call it a 'mystical' experience if we choose, for the term is vague in its connotation; but to Socrates himself, if we may believe Plato's account, it was no more than a *communication* from a divine source: there is no suggestion of 'possession' or of a *mystica unio*; so that it is unwarrantable to appeal to it as evidence for a mysticism in the historical Socrates of the kind which the *Phaedrus* presents.

In two passages of the *Symposium* (175 A–B and 220 C–D) Socrates is recorded as having fits of abstraction, the latter lasting for twenty-four hours: and these are sometimes given a mystical interpretation. Thus Robin writes[4] of them as 'ces extases dans lesquelles Socrate, absorbé par ses méditations, se détache de la vie sensible et corporelle pour entrer en communication par la pensée avec un autre monde'; and Burnet[5] writes in a similar vein. But what reason is there to suppose that Plato meant us to read this between his lines? On the second occasion, at least, the more striking occasion, the word σκοπῶν and the

---

[1] Especially the famous passage 341 C with its mention of φῶς ἀπὸ πυρὸς πηδήσαντος ἐξαφθέν, a passage which Plotinus (VI, ix, 4) rightly interprets in a mystical sense (see E. R. Dodds, *Proclus's Elements of Theology*, p. 311).

[2] A fine study of this side of Plato and Platonism is to be found in A. J. Festugière, *Contemplation et vie contemplative selon Platon* (1936).

[3] Xenophon's silence of course proves nothing: he was not the man to understand such things or record them, even if he had heard of them.

[4] *Banquet*, p. cvi.   [5] *Greek Philosophy* I, p. 140.

clause ἐπειδὴ οὐ προὔχώρει αὐτῷ suggest nothing more than puzzling out some problem, and are perversely misleading on the mystical interpretation. No doubt it is unusual to concentrate on any problem for twenty-four hours on end: but Socrates was unusual on any showing, and unusual in many ways.[1]

V. Lysias and his speech

Early in the dialogue (230E–234C) we have a long speech attributed to Lysias, the famous Attic orator, and though not appearing as a character he plays a prominent part throughout the dialogue. He is represented as enjoying a very high reputation (δεινότατος τῶν νῦν γράφειν, 228A), a reputation due, it would seem from Plato, equally to the epideictic speeches which he composed as a professor of rhetoric (of which that read out by Phaedrus purports to be an example) and to those which, as a λογογράφος, he wrote for plaintiffs or defendants in the courts. It is uncertain which of these two occupations was the earlier: Cicero (*Brutus* § 48) says that he started as a teacher of rhetoric, but that later, recognising his inferiority to Theodorus of Byzantium, he turned to writing for the courts. On the other hand, the single surviving epideictic speech[2] (leaving that of the *Phaedrus* out of account), his Olympic oration, belongs to 388 B.C., quite late in his lifetime.[3] But the point[4] is of little moment for the student of the *Phaedrus*: for whatever the facts were, Plato, writing in all probability after Lysias's death,[5] thinks of the two sorts of literary occupation as concurrent, or at all events has not cared to discriminate them in time.

It has always been a puzzle that Plato should criticise as unfavourably as he does a writer whose name, both in ancient times (as attested among others by Cicero and Quintilian) and in modern, stands in such high repute. I find it difficult to accept any of the explanations that have been offered, for example that Plato thought the Olympic oration,

---

[1] Paul Shorey (*What Plato said*, pp. 189, 197) describes both occasions as 'meditating on a problem'. In a note on p. 542 he adds: 'Plato never represents this Socratic self-absorption as a *méditation extatique*.' I agree. Wilamowitz, though he refers to the two stories in his chapter on *Symposium*, is wholly silent about the mystical interpretation. Bertrand Russell (*History of Western Philosophy*, p. 109) suggests that Socrates was subject to cataleptic trances.

[2] The surviving Funeral Oration is probably spurious (see Jebb, *Attic Orators* I, 201 ff.).   [3] The date of his birth is uncertain; he died about 379.

[4] It is fully discussed by Robin, pp. xiv–xviii.

[5] I agree with Robin (p. xix) and Wilamowitz (*Platon* I, p. 259) that the severity of Plato's attack makes this probable.

with its attack on Dionysius of Syracuse, tactless and mischievous, or that he was offended by Lysias's *Defence of Socrates*, or that Lysias had been behind the scenes in instigating Socrates's prosecution.[1] We must, I submit, believe that Plato's literary judgments rest on literary, not on extraneous grounds: they may be unfair or misguided; Plato may have singled out one unfortunate composition, not a fair sample of its author's work in the field of epideictic oratory;[2] more probably, as I think, the speech read by Phaedrus and criticised by Socrates is not in fact Lysias's work at all, but Plato's own invention, to which the name of Lysias is attached chiefly because he wants to have a precise target at which to aim his criticism of the rhetorical culture of his own and the preceding age and Lysias's name is the obvious one to fix upon in a dialogue of this dramatic date. No doubt such a procedure seems to us grossly unfair and even stupid; but he could doubtless count upon his readers knowing what he was doing, and forgiving the unfairness in their delight in a clever caricature; for caricature or parody I think it must be: that is to say, Plato has accumulated the mannerisms[3] and exaggerated the shortcomings of Lysias's epideictic speeches, or maybe of one particular epideictic speech. If this is so, what we have before us is from one point of view a bit of semi-malicious fun—in bad taste by our tenderer standards—and from another, more important point of view a construction intended as a vivid dramatic representation of the errors, both of substance and form—errors not peculiar to Lysias[4]—which its author desired to expose. We need not, of course, doubt that Plato disagreed with the current estimate of Lysias's actual compositions, or at least those in the epideictic style.

In making these suggestions I am venturing, perhaps imprudently, to take sides in an age-long dispute. 'The debate', wrote Shorey[5] in 1933, 'on the authenticity of the speech attributed to Lysias in the *Phaedrus* long since reached a deadlock, the one side arguing that Plato could imitate any style, the other affirming that he would not have

---

[1] The two former suggestions are made by Wilamowitz, the third by Robin, whose argument here (pp. xix–xxii) seems to me far from convincing.

[2] In any case it is on his forensic speeches that his reputation, both in later antiquity and in modern times, rests.

[3] As suggested by Shorey (*Class. Phil.* XXIII (1933), p. 131) who instances the fivefold repetition of καὶ μὲν δή. Cf. Denniston, *Greek Particles*, p. 396.

[4] Although the name of Lysias constantly recurs throughout the dialogue, it has been noted that certain expressions, such as those at 277D (Λυσίας ἤ τις ἄλλος), 278C, 258D, may be intended as hints that it is general tendencies rather than a single individual that Plato is criticising.   [5] *loc. cit.*

exercised his criticism of Lysias upon an invention of his own.' Shorey's own mind appears to have been made up on the strength of a single point, which I have just quoted in a footnote. M. Robin is more cautious: after an admirably fair discussion, citing the ancient evidence (such as it is, and it is woefully meagre) and summarising modern arguments, he writes:[1] 'Sur un terrain aussi mal connu il est sage de ne pas avancer avec trop d'assurance', adding finally: 'Jusqu'à ce que les partisans de l'authenticité aient apporté des preuves qui ne soient pas au fond de simples opinions, on sera en droit à ces opinions d'en opposer d'autres qui du moins ne prétendent pas à être rien de plus, attendu que, dans l'état actuel de notre information, rien de plus ne semble permis et possible.'

And so, I agree, the case stands. It should be added that the partisans of Lysian authorship include Diogenes Laertius (III, 25) and Hermeias[2] in antiquity, and such modern scholars as Vahlen, Blass, A. E. Taylor, Wilamowitz and Hude; on the other side are A. Croiset, Diès, Shorey and H. Weinstock. Conscious of siding with the minority, I may confess that I am to some extent influenced by the 'simple opinion' that Plato would thoroughly enjoy exercising his powers of imitation, and would have disliked incorporating extensive material from another's pen.[3] Though it is not possible to support this opinion by any precise parallel, we may reasonably point to the myth of Protagoras in the dialogue bearing his name. It is commonly recognised[4] that Plato is there drawing freely from the Sophist's work περὶ τῆς ἐν ἀρχῇ καταστάσεως: it is likely that in places Protagoras's actual words are used; yet, though literal transcription would have adequately served his purpose, Plato has, it would seem,[5] renounced it.

[1] p. lxiii.

[2] p. 35.20 (Couvreur): εἰδέναι δὲ δεῖ ὅτι αὐτοῦ Λυσίου ὁ λόγος οὗτός ἐστι, καὶ φέρεται ἐν ταῖς ἐπιστολαῖς ταῖς ἐκείνου καὶ αὕτη ἡ ἐπιστολή. The first clause implies that the matter was in doubt already in Neoplatonic times; as to the collection of letters, they are also mentioned by Ps.-Plutarch (*Lives of Ten Orators*, III = *Moralia* 836B), but they do not survive, and we may suspect that like most ancient collections of letters they were spurious; the collector might well have included our speech as the nearest approach to a real letter that he could find.

[3] Plato has admittedly taken great pains (228A–E) to convince us that the speech is authentic; the question is whether he has not taken too great pains. As Robin excellently remarks, 'ce n'est pas en niant le principe propre du pastiche qu'on prouvera que le discours de Lysias n'est pas un pastiche'.

[4] cf. Apelt's edition of the dialogue, pp. 22–6, and Adam's edition, p. 108.

[5] It is no doubt impossible to prove that it is not transcribed; I follow Diels-Kranz in assuming it is not, and indeed I know of no one who maintains that it is: it is fair to say that the *onus probandi* would rest with the believer in transcription.

TRANSLATION & COMMENTARY

I

Socrates meets Phaedrus, who is about to take a walk outside the city wall, after spending the whole morning listening to a speech by Lysias and studying it. Socrates expresses great interest in the speech, and is told that he may well do so, for its subject was love; it took the form of an address to a boy by one who was not his lover, but claimed his favour for that very reason. Phaedrus, entreated to repeat the discourse, professes his inability to do so; but before long it transpires that he has the actual manuscript with him, and he agrees to read it.

The two turn their steps along the bank of the Ilissus, and pass the spot reputed to be the scene of the rape of Oreithuia by Boreas. Phaedrus mentions a rationalised version of the legend, but Socrates professes indifference to such 'scientific' interpretations: his time is better spent in 'knowing himself'. Finally a cool shady spot is reached, hard by a sanctuary of the Nymphs. Socrates grows enthusiastic over the delightful scene, and Phaedrus rallies him on his unfamiliarity with the countryside. Fields and trees, replies Socrates, have nothing to teach him; yet Phaedrus has discovered the way to lure him out: to hear a literary composition he would be ready to go anywhere.

Socrates. Where do you come from, Phaedrus my friend, and where 227 are you going?

Phaedrus. I've been with Lysias, Socrates, the son of Cephalus, and I'm off for a walk outside the wall, after a long morning's sitting there. On the instructions of our common friend Acumenus[1] I take my walks on the open roads; he tells me that is more invigorating than walking in the colonnades.

Soc. Yes, he's right in saying so. But Lysias, I take it, was in town. B

Ph. Yes, staying with Epicrates, in that house where Morychus used to live, close to the temple of Olympian Zeus.

Soc. Well, how were you occupied? No doubt Lysias was giving the company a feast of eloquence.

Ph. I'll tell you, if you can spare time to come along with me and listen.

---

[1] A well-known physician, father of Eryximachus, the physician who is one of the speakers in the *Symposium*.

Soc. What? Don't you realise that I should account it, in Pindar's words,[1] 'above all business' to hear how you and Lysias passed your time?

C   *Ph.* Lead on then.

Soc. Please tell me.

Ph. As a matter of fact the topic is appropriate for your ears, Socrates; for the discussion that engaged us may be said to have concerned love. Lysias, you must know, has described how a handsome boy was tempted, but not by a lover: that's the clever part of it: he maintains that surrender should be to one who is not in love rather than to one who is.

Soc. Splendid! I wish he would add that it should be to a poor man rather than a rich one, an elderly man rather than a young one, and, in

D   general, to ordinary folk like myself. What an attractive democratic theory that would be! However, I'm so eager to hear about it that I vow I won't leave you even if you extend your walk as far as Megara, up to the walls and back again as recommended by Herodicus.[2]

228   *Ph.* What do you mean, my good man? Do you expect an amateur like me to repeat by heart, without disgracing its author, the work of the ablest writer of our day, which it took him weeks to compose at his leisure? That is far beyond me; though I'd rather have had the ability than come into a fortune.

Soc. I know my Phaedrus; yes indeed, I'm as sure of him as of my own identity. I'm certain that the said Phaedrus didn't listen just once to Lysias's speech: time after time he asked him to repeat it to him, and

B   Lysias was very ready to comply. Even that would not content him: in the end he secured the script and began poring over the parts that specially attracted him; and thus engaged he sat there the whole morning, until he grew weary and went for a walk. Upon my word, I believe he had learnt the whole speech by heart, unless it was a very long one; and he was going into the country to practise declaiming it. Then he fell in with one who has a passion for listening to discourses; and when he saw him[3] he was delighted to think he would have someone to share his frenzied enthusiasm; so he asked him to join him on

C   his way. But when the lover of discourses begged him to discourse, he

---

[1] *Isthm.* I, 2.

[2] Another physician, mentioned in *Protag.* 316D as a Megarian who afterwards settled at Selymbria in Thrace.

[3] I follow Oxyrynchus Papyrus 1016 and Robin in excising the second ἰδών.

became difficult, pretending he didn't want to, though he meant to do so ultimately, even if he had to force himself on a reluctant listener. So beg him, Phaedrus, to do straightway what he will soon do in any case.

Ph. Doubtless it will be much my best course to deliver myself to the best of my ability, for I fancy you will never let me go until I have given you some sort of a speech.

Soc. You are quite right about my intention.

Ph. Then here's what I will do: it really is perfectly true, Socrates, D that I have not got the words by heart; but I will sketch the general purport of the several points in which the lover and the non-lover were contrasted, taking them in order one by one, and beginning at the beginning.

Soc. Very well, my dear fellow: but you must first show me what it is that you have in your left hand under your cloak; for I surmise that it is the actual discourse. If that is so, let me assure you of this, that much as I love you I am not altogether inclined to let you practise your E oratory on me when Lysias himself is here present. Come now, show it me.

Ph. Say no more, Socrates; you have dashed my hope of trying out my powers on you. Well, where would you like us to sit for our reading?

Soc. Let us turn off here and walk along the Ilissus:[1] then we can 229 sit down in any quiet spot you choose.

Ph. It's convenient, isn't it, that I chance to be bare-footed: you of course always are so. There will be no trouble in wading in the stream, which is especially delightful at this hour of a summer's day.

Soc. Lead on then, and look out for a place to sit down.

Ph. You see that tall plane-tree over there?

Soc. To be sure.

Ph. There's some shade, and a little breeze, and grass to sit down on, B or lie down if we like.

Soc. Then make for it.

Ph. Tell me, Socrates, isn't it somewhere about here that they say Boreas seized Oreithuia from the river?

Soc. Yes, that is the story.

Ph. Was this the actual spot? Certainly the water looks charmingly

---

[1] For an excellent discussion of the route taken see Robin, pp. x–xii (with sketch-map).

pure and clear; it's just the place for girls to be playing beside the stream.

C   *Soc.* No, it was about a quarter of a mile lower down, where you cross to the sanctuary of Agra:[1] there is, I believe, an altar dedicated to Boreas close by.

Ph. I have never really noticed it; but pray tell me, Socrates, do you believe that story to be true?

Soc. I should be quite in the fashion if I disbelieved it, as the men of science do: I might proceed to give a scientific account of how the maiden, while at play with Pharmaceia, was blown by a gust of Boreas down from the rocks hard by, and having thus met her death was said

D to have been seized by Boreas: though it may have happened on the Areopagus, according to another version of the occurrence. For my part, Phaedrus, I regard such theories as no doubt attractive, but as the invention of clever, industrious people who are not exactly to be envied, for the simple reason that they must then go on and tell us the real truth about the appearance of Centaurs and the Chimaera, not to mention a whole host of such creatures, Gorgons and Pegasuses and

E countless other remarkable monsters of legend flocking in on them. If our sceptic, with his somewhat crude science, means to reduce every one of them to the standard of probability, he'll need a deal of time for it. I myself have certainly no time for the business: and I'll tell you

230 why, my friend: I can't as yet 'know myself', as the inscription at Delphi enjoins; and so long as that ignorance remains it seems to me ridiculous to inquire into extraneous matters. Consequently I don't bother about such things, but accept the current beliefs about them, and direct my inquiries, as I have just said, rather to myself, to discover whether I really am a more complex creature and more puffed up with pride than Typhon,[2] or a simpler, gentler being whom heaven has blessed with a quiet, un-Typhonic nature. By the way, isn't this the

B tree we were making for?

Ph. Yes, that's the one.

Soc. Upon my word, a delightful resting-place, with this tall, spreading plane, and a lovely shade from the high branches of the agnus: now that it's in full flower, it will make the place ever so fragrant. And what a lovely stream under the plane-tree, and how cool

---

[1] An Attic *deme* or district.

[2] Socrates connects the name of this hundred-headed monster with the verb τύφω, *to smoke*, and perhaps also with the noun τῦφος, *vanity, humbug*.

to the feet! Judging by the statuettes and images I should say it's consecrated to Achelous and some of the Nymphs. And then too, isn't the c freshness of the air most welcome and pleasant: and the shrill summery music of the cicada-choir! And as crowning delight the grass, thick enough on a gentle slope to rest your head on most comfortably. In fact, my dear Phaedrus, you have been the stranger's perfect guide.

Ph. Whereas you, my excellent friend, strike me as the oddest of men. Anyone would take you, as you say, for a stranger being shown the country by a guide instead of a native: never leaving town to cross D the frontier nor even, I believe, so much as setting foot outside the walls.

Soc. You must forgive me, dear friend; I'm a lover of learning, and trees and open country won't teach me anything, whereas men in the town do. Yet you seem to have discovered a recipe for getting me out. A hungry animal can be driven by dangling a carrot or a bit of green stuff in front of it: similarly if you proffer me volumes of speeches I don't doubt you can cart me all round Attica, and anywhere else you E please. Anyhow, now that we've got here I propose for the time being to lie down, and you can choose whatever posture you think most convenient for reading, and proceed.

Ph. Here you are then.

The opening pages of our dialogue, like those of many others, show Plato's power of presenting his scene vividly, and of leading up naturally and easily to his subject. Since the dialogue is not narrated but direct, Phaedrus cannot be fully and formally characterised: but there is the less need for this inasmuch as Plato's readers know him sufficiently from the *Symposium*; that he should be eagerly interested in a discourse on love is only to be expected from one who in the earlier work had been represented as the πατὴρ τοῦ λόγου (177D), the originator of the theme and the first speaker upon it; and the mention of the physician Acumenus in the first lines here may be meant to recall memories of the intimacy between Phaedrus and Acumenus's son Eryximachus, a physician like his father.

It will appear later that Phaedrus's admiration of Lysias's speech is almost exclusively on account of its form: its matter concerns him little, save that it is paradoxical and 'clever' (αὐτὸ δὴ τοῦτο καὶ κεκόμψευται, 227C). Whether Lysias[1] bases his discourse on a true conception of love he has doubtless not asked himself: and the reader will reflect that if he had he might have found it difficult to reconcile Lysias's views with his

[1] As stated in the Introduction, I do not accept the speech as authentic; but it is convenient to refer to its author as Lysias.

own encomium on Eros as θεῶν καὶ πρεσβύτατον καὶ τιμιώτατον καὶ κυριώτατον εἰς ἀρετῆς καὶ εὐδαιμονίας κτῆσιν ἀνθρώποις καὶ ζῶσι καὶ τελευτήσασιν (*Symp.* 180B).

What purpose is served by making Phaedrus keep the manuscript hidden, and suggest giving a summary (ἐν κεφαλαίοις ἕκαστον ἐφεξῆς, 228D) of the speech? No doubt it was customary for rhetorical teachers to encourage their pupils to make such summaries, and it is natural enough for Phaedrus to complain that Socrates, by detecting the manuscript, has cheated him of an opportunity for doing so. At the same time the episode serves to bring out Phaedrus's youthful vanity: he would dearly like to be complimented by Socrates on his ability to present Lysias's arguments in his own words, despite the fact that just before (228A) he had disclaimed such ability: he would enjoy that even more than eliciting from Socrates an encomium on his teacher.

Of the significance of the rural scene in which the dialogue is set I have spoken in the Introduction. It remains here to consider the discussion of the Boreas myth. Has this any organic connexion with the rest of the introductory conversation or with the dialogue as a whole? Or is it merely a natural tilt, *en passant*, at the allegorical school of poetical interpretation, which had become prominent before the time of Plato, and perhaps of Socrates too?

Plato's attitude to the 'allegorists' is well discussed by Prof. J. Tate in *C.Q.* XXIII (1929) and XXIV (1930). He shows that there is no ground for thinking that Plato simply denied 'hidden meanings': but since a diversity of such meanings was possible in every case, and no principle could be found for deciding between them, it was to little purpose to devote one's energy to excogitating them. Moreover (though this does not directly concern the present passage) the existence of a ὑπόνοια is no adequate ground for permitting morally offensive poetry to be accessible, particularly to children. A man's time, then, can be better occupied as Socrates's was, in 'knowing himself';[1] and if a myth be inoffensive[2] he will be content to take it at its face value.

If the Boreas myth episode has any organic significance, I would suggest that it is inserted in order to preclude any questions that might arise later on about the local divinities who inspire Socrates: Phaedrus, and the reader too, are not to attempt to rationalise what Plato makes Socrates say about them any more than they should rationalise the rape of Oreithuia.

[1] cf. Xen. *Mem.* I, i, 12, for a similar explanation of Socrates's unconcern with physics and cosmology. With γνῶναι ἐμαυτόν (229E) cf. *Apol.* 28E, φιλοσοφοῦντα... ζῆν καὶ ἐξετάζοντα ἐμαυτὸν καὶ τοὺς ἄλλους.

[2] I agree with Thompson, in spite of Prof. Tate's dissent, that the Boreas myth is inoffensive, or that at all events Socrates regards it as so. His standards of literary morality are perhaps rather less austere than in *Rep.* II.

II

The speech, the purport of which has already been announced, consists mainly in adducing a large number of prudential considerations. In every way it will be to a boy's good—to his material advantage, his security, his good repute, and even his moral improvement—to yield not to a lover, that is to one who feels genuine passion for him, but to one who is moved by physical desire and nothing else. The lover's passion is a malady, precluding him from all self-restraint, and no permanent satisfaction can be expected from him. Moreover, there is a far wider field of choice from amongst non-lovers, though it is of course not all such that should be favoured.

You know how I am situated, and I have told you that I think it to 230 E our advantage that this should happen. Now I claim that I should not be refused what I ask simply because I am not your lover. Lovers, 231 when their craving is at an end, repent of such benefits as they have conferred: but for the other sort no occasion arises for regretting what has passed; for being free agents under no constraint, they regulate their services by the scale of their means, with an eye to their own personal interest. Again, lovers weigh up profit and loss accruing to their account by reason of their passion, and with the extra item of labour expended decide that they have long since made full payment B for favours received; whereas the non-lovers cannot allege any consequential neglect of their personal affairs, nor record any past exertions on the debit side, nor yet complain of having quarrelled with their relatives; hence, with all these troubles removed, all they have left to do is to devote their energies to such conduct as they conceive likely to gratify the other party.

Again, it is argued that a lover ought to be highly valued because c he professes to be especially kind towards the loved one, and ready to gratify him in words and deeds while arousing the dislike of everyone else. If this is true, however, it is obvious that he will set greater store by the loved one of to-morrow than by that of to-day, and will doubtless do an injury to the old love if required by the new.

And really, what sense is there in lavishing what is so precious[1] upon one labouring under an affliction which nobody who knew anything D

[1] I propose τοσοῦτον for τοιοῦτον, in view of 232c 1.

of it would even attempt to remove? Why, the man himself admits that he is not sound, but sick; that he is aware of his folly, but cannot control himself; how then, when he comes to his senses, is he likely to approve of the intentions that he formed in his aberration?

And observe this: if you are to choose the best of a number of lovers, your choice will be only amongst a few; whereas a general choice of the person who most commends himself to you gives you a wide field, E so that in that wide field you have a much better prospect of finding someone worthy of your friendship.

Now maybe you respect established conventions, and anticipate odium if people get to hear about you; if so, it may be expected that 232 a lover, conceiving that everyone will admire him as he admires himself, will be proud to talk about it and flatter his vanity by declaring to all and sundry that his enterprise has been successful; whereas the other type, who can control themselves, will prefer to do what is best rather than shine in the eyes of their neighbours.[1]

Again, a lover is bound to be heard about and seen by many people, consorting with his beloved and caring about little else; so that when B they are observed talking to one another, the meeting is taken to imply the satisfaction, actual or prospective, of their desires; whereas, with the other sort, no one ever thinks of putting a bad construction on their association, realising that a man must have someone to talk to by way of friendship or gratification of one sort or another.

And observe this: perhaps you feel troubled by the reflection that it is hard for friendship to be preserved, and that whereas a quarrel arising from other sources will be a calamity shared by both parties, one that C follows the sacrifice of your all will involve a grievous hurt to yourself;[2] in that case it is doubtless the lover who should cause you the more alarm, for he is very ready to take offence, and thinks the whole affair is to his own hurt. Hence he discourages his beloved from consorting with anyone else, fearing that a wealthy rival may overreach him with his money, or a cultured one outdo him with his intelligence: and he is perpetually on guard against the influence of D those who possess other advantages. So by persuading you to become estranged from such rivals he leaves you without a friend in the world;

---

[1] There is a pleasant irony in this twisting of a Socratic precept—τὸ βέλτιστον ἀντὶ τῆς δόξης τῆς παρὰ τῶν ἀνθρώπων αἱρεῖσθαι—into propaganda for the sensualist; it is almost the devil quoting scripture, and might well throw doubt on the authenticity of the speech.

[2] In c 2 σοί should be accented.

alternatively, if you look to your own interest and show more good sense than your lover, you will find yourself quarrelling with him. On the other hand, one who is not a lover, but has achieved what he asked of you by reason of his merit, will not be jealous of others who seek your society, but will rather detest those who avoid it, in the belief that the latter look down on him, whereas the former are serving his turn.[1] Consequently the object of his attentions is far more likely to E make friends than enemies out of the affair.

And observe this: a lover more often than not wants to possess you before he has come to know your character or become familiar with your general personality; and that makes it uncertain whether he will still want to be your friend when his desires have waned; whereas in 233 the other case, the fact that the pair were already friends before the affair took place makes it probable that instead of friendship diminishing as the result of favours received, these favours will abide as a memory and promise of more to come.

And observe this: it ought to be for your betterment to listen to me rather than to a lover; for a lover commends anything you say or do even when it is amiss, partly from fear that he may offend you, partly because his passion impairs his own judgment. For the record of B Love's achievement is, first that, when things go badly, he makes a man count that an affliction which normally causes no distress: secondly that, when things go well, he compels his subjects to extol things that ought not to gratify them: which makes it fitting that they should be pitied far more than admired by the objects of their passion. On the other hand, if you listen to me,[2] my intercourse with you will be a matter of ministering not to your immediate pleasure but to your future advantage; for I am the master of myself, rather than the victim C of love; I do not bring bitter enmity upon myself by resenting trifling offences: on the contrary it is only on account of serious wrongs that I am moved, and that but slowly, to mild indignation, pardoning what is done unintentionally, and endeavouring to hinder what is done of intent: for these are the tokens of lasting friendship. If however you are disposed to think that there can be no firm friendship save with a lover, you should reflect that in that case we should not set store by D sons, or fathers, or mothers, nor should we possess any trustworthy

---

[1] The meaning seems to be that the non-lover counts it to his own advantage that the boy should be admired by others and so kept in good humour.

[2] In B 6 ἐὰν δ' ἐμοὶ πείθῃ seems necessary in place of ἐὰν δέ μοι πείθῃ.

friends: no, it is not to erotic passion that we owe these, but to conduct of a different order.

Again, if we ought to favour those who press us most strongly, then in other matters too[1] we should give our good offices not to the worthiest people but to the most destitute; for since their distress is the greatest, they will be the most thankful to us for relieving them. And E observe this further consequence: when we give private banquets, the right people to invite will be not our friends but beggars and those in need of a good meal: for it is they that will be fond of us and attend upon us and flock to our doors: it is they that will be most delighted and most grateful and call down blessings on our heads. No: the proper course, surely, is to show favour not to the most importunate but to those most able to make us a return; not to mere beggars, but to the 234 deserving; not to those who will regale themselves with your youthful beauty, but to those who will let you share their prosperity when you are older; not to those who, when they have had their will of you, will flatter their vanity by telling the world, but to those who will keep a strict and modest silence; not to those who are devoted to you for a brief period, but to those who will continue to be your friends as long as you live; not to those who, when their passion is spent, will look for an excuse to turn against you, but to those who, when your beauty is past,[2] will make that the time for displaying their own goodness.

B   Do you therefore be mindful of what I have said and reflect that, while lovers are admonished by their friends and relatives for the wrongness of their conduct, the other sort have never been reproached by one of their family on the score of behaving to the detriment of their own interest.

Perhaps you will ask me whether I recommend you to accord your favours to all and sundry of this sort. Well, I do not suppose that even a lover would bid you to be favourable towards all and sundry lovers; C in the first place a recipient would not regard it as meriting so much gratitude, and in the second you would find it more difficult if you wished to keep your affairs concealed; and what is wanted is that the business should involve no harm, but mutual advantage.

And now I think I have said all that is needed; if you think I have neglected anything, and want more, let me know.

---

[1] Reading κἀν τοῖς ἄλλοις with Badham in D 6.
[2] Reading παυσαμένῳ in A 8, as suggested to me by Dr R. G. Bury.

This tedious piece of rhetoric deserves little comment. It is a flat, monotonous, repetitive composition, a 'mosaic' as Robin has said, in which little or no plan is discernible, the arguments being tacked or 'glued' together (cf. Socrates's expression πρὸς ἄλληλα κολλῶν, 278D) by formulas of mechanical connexion such as ἔτι δέ (four times) and καὶ μὲν δή (five times).[1] And the flatness of the style is matched by the banality of the sentiment; the speaker's attitude is one of cold, prudential calculation, of respect indeed for conventions but of utter oblivion of the existence of true affection or unselfishness, or even of a romantic sentiment which might do something to palliate the grossness of the relation in question. There is, it is true, a gleam of something less ignoble at one point (233A), where he says that to yield to him will make the other 'better' (βελτίων), following this up a little later (233B) by a contrast between 'immediate pleasure' and 'future advantage' (παροῦσαν ἡδονήν, μέλλουσαν ὠφέλειαν); but it is a delusive gleam, for the argument substantiating this claim to confer moral betterment adduces no positive action by the non-lover, but merely his abstention from the lover's indiscriminate praise and flattery; while as to the second point, it is difficult either to accept the words οὐ τὴν παροῦσαν ἡδονήν as true to fact, or to find any real ground for the promise of ὠφέλεια. Nevertheless the passage does betray some faint consciousness of the desirability of appealing to moral sentiment, however unreal the appeal may be; so that I think it is going rather too far to say, with Prof. Taylor: 'It is throughout an appeal to "utility" in the most sordid sense of the word.'

Yet the author—whether Lysias or Plato—has the merit of 'getting inside' his character. The formlessness, the mosaic-like character of the discourse, the mechanical piling up of disconnected points—these are due to the fact that the imaginary speaker is posing, without any real belief in his thesis, and therefore unable to give it life or do more than string together conventional sentiments, racking his brains to excogitate this, that and the other. The one merit which Socrates will recognise is of the sort that such a man in such a situation might in fact achieve: it is all σαφῆ and στρογγύλα (234E), each point is clearly expressed and neatly turned.

So much for the speech taken by itself. But more important is its function as an organic part of the dialogue; and from this standpoint the fault to be stressed is the speaker's assumption that love is simply a name for unrestrained sexual desire, and is therefore a malady (νοσεῖν, 231D). If this were so, there would doubtless be some truth at least in the negative aspect of the speech, the recommendation μὴ χαρίζεσθαι τῷ ἐρῶντι. As the dialogue proceeds the falsity of this assumption will be fully brought out.

---

[1] Robin has attempted to find a formal structure of four parts and a conclusion, or fifteen κῶλα in all.

*Phaedrus is full of admiration for the speech, but Socrates professes doubt
as to the correctness of its substance, while in point of style he finds it clear
and polished, but repetitive. He fancies he has heard the subject better
dealt with, though he cannot remember by whom—possibly by Sappho or
Anacreon; and this emboldens him to offer a speech of his own, with the
proviso that, if he is to support Lysias's thesis, he cannot be wholly original
but must adopt Lysias's basic assumptions. Phaedrus agrees that this is
reasonable, but Socrates now appears reluctant; after some banter, however,
and a playful threat by Phaedrus to use physical force, he submits, calling
upon the Muses for aid and veiling his face to avoid embarrassment.*

234 C   *Ph.* What do you think of the speech, Socrates? Isn't it extra-
ordinarily fine, especially in point of language?

D   *Soc.* Amazingly fine indeed, my friend: I was thrilled by it. And it
was you, Phaedrus, that made me feel as I did: I watched your apparent
delight in the words as you read. And as I'm sure that you understand
such matters better than I do, I took my cue from you, and therefore
joined in the ecstasy of my right worshipful companion.

  Ph. Come, come! Do you mean to make a joke of it?

  Soc. Do you think I am joking, and don't mean it seriously?

E   *Ph.* No more of that, Socrates: tell me truly, as one friend to another,
do you think there is anyone in Greece who could make a finer[1] and
more exhaustive speech on the same subject?

  Soc. What? Are you and I required to extol the speech not merely
on the score of its author's lucidity and terseness of expression, and his
consistently precise and well-polished vocabulary, but also for his
having said what he ought? If we are, we shall have to allow it only
on your account, for my feeble intelligence failed to appreciate it; I was
235 only attending to it as a piece of rhetoric, and as such I couldn't think
that even Lysias himself would deem it adequate. Perhaps you won't
agree with me, Phaedrus, but really it seemed to me that he said the
same things several times over: maybe he's not very clever at expa-

---

[1] I accept ἀμείνω (H. Richards) in place of μεῖζω in E 3, in view of 235 B 5 and
D 6.

tiating at length on a single theme, or possibly he has no interest in such topics. In fact it struck me as an extravagant performance, to demonstrate his ability to say the same thing twice, in different words but with equal success.

Ph. Not a bit of it, Socrates: the outstanding feature of the discourse B is just this, that it has not overlooked any important aspect of the subject, so making it impossible for anyone else to outdo what he has said with a fuller or more satisfactory oration.

Soc. If you go as far as that I shall find it impossible to agree with you; if I were to assent out of politeness, I should be confuted by the wise men and women who in past ages have spoken and written on this theme.

Ph. To whom do you refer? Where have you heard anything C better than this?

Soc. I can't tell you off-hand; but I'm sure I have heard something better, from the fair Sappho maybe, or the wise Anacreon, or perhaps some prose writer. What ground, you may ask, have I for saying so? Good sir, there is something welling up within my breast, which makes me feel that I could find something different, and something better, to say. I am of course well aware it can't be anything originating in my own mind, for I know my own ignorance; so I suppose it can only be that it has been poured into me, through my ears, as into a vessel, from D some external source; though in my stupid fashion I have actually forgotten how, and from whom, I heard it.

Ph. Well said! You move me to admiration. I don't mind your not telling me, even though I should press you, from whom and how you heard it, provided you do just what you say: you have undertaken to make a better speech than that in the book here and one of not less length[1] which shall owe nothing to it; I in my turn undertake like the nine Archons[2] to set up at Delphi a golden life-size statue, not only of E myself but of you also.

Soc. How kind you are, Phaedrus, and what a pattern of golden-age

---

[1] Socrates had not in fact said anything about length: but to Phaedrus no doubt length is important.

[2] The archons' oath, as given by Ar. *Ath. Pol.* VII, 1, was ἀναθήσειν ἀνδριάντα χρυσοῦν, ἐάν τινα παραβῶσι τῶν νόμων: there is no mention of the statue being life-sized, or set up at Delphi. In Plut. *Solon* 25, however, both these points are added; doubtless they are later insertions intended to bring the terms of the oath into conformity with our present passage; but in fact ἰσομέτρητον and ἐν Δελφοῖς should be taken as belonging to Phaedrus's individual undertaking only. (See Sandys on *Ath. Pol. ad loc.*)

simplicity,[1] in supposing me to mean that Lysias has wholly missed the mark and that another speech could avoid all his points! Surely that couldn't be so even with the most worthless of writers.[2] Thus, as regards the subject of the speech, do you imagine that anybody could argue that the non-lover should be favoured, rather than the lover, without praising the wisdom of the one and censuring the folly of the 236 other? That he could dispense with these essential points, and then bring up something different? No, no: surely we must allow such arguments, and forgive the orator for using them; and in that sort of field what merits praise is not invention, but arrangement; but when it comes to non-essential points, that are difficult to invent, we should praise arrangement and invention too.

Ph. I agree: what you say seems fair enough. For my part, this is B what I will do: I will allow you to take it for granted that the lover is less sane than the non-lover: and for the rest, if you can replace what we have here by a fuller speech of superior merit, up with your statue in wrought gold beside the offering of the Cypselids at Olympia.

Soc. Have you taken me seriously, Phaedrus, for teasing you with an attack on your darling Lysias? Can you possibly suppose that I shall make a real attempt to rival his cleverness with something more ornate?

Ph. As to that, my friend, I've got you where I can return your C fire.[3] Assuredly you must do what you can in the way of a speech, or else we shall be driven, like vulgar comedians, to capping each other's

---

[1] χρυσοῦς echoes Phaedrus's χρυσῆν εἰκόνα, but with altered meaning, viz. 'as simple as a man of the Golden Age', Κρονίων ὄζων (to quote Aristophanes's coarser expression, *Clouds* 398).

[2] Mr R. L. Howland (*C.Q.* XXXI, p. 154) suspects an allusion here to Isocrates, *Helen*, § 15, where the author promises a new treatment of his subject παραλιπὼν ἅπαντα τὰ τοῖς ἄλλοις εἰρημένα. It may be so; but would Plato have thought it worth while to make this covert 'dig' at a slight work written probably some fifteen to twenty years earlier, with little chance of his readers detecting the allusion?
There is much difference of opinion as to the date of *Helen*; E. Brémond, the Budé editor of Isocrates, puts it later than *Phaedrus* but still before 380. Münscher, in Pauly-Wissowa, *RE*, s.v. Isocrates, not long before 380; Jebb (*Attic Orators* II, p. 99) probably about 370 (on very slender grounds). Blass and Christ-Schmidt put it much earlier, and perhaps the most recent pronouncement is by Jaeger (*Paideia* III, p. 67): 'The exact date of its composition is unknown, but it was obviously written soon after the speech *Against the Sophists*, namely while Isocrates's school was yet new.' This view seems to me most probable, but it should be confessed that the establishment of chronological relations between Plato's dialogues and the works of Isocrates is *periculosae plenum opus aleae*.

[3] Phaedrus, having been compelled to read Lysias's speech, can now compel Socrates to make one of his own.

remarks. Beware:[1] do not deliberately compel me to utter the words 'Don't I know my Socrates? If not, I've forgotten my own identity', or 'He wanted to speak, but made difficulties about it'. No: make up your mind that we're not going to leave this spot until you have delivered yourself of what you told me you had within your breast. We are by ourselves in a lonely place, and I am stronger and younger than you: for all which reasons 'mistake not thou my bidding'[2] and D please don't make me use force to open your lips.

Soc. But, my dear good Phaedrus, it will be courting ridicule for an amateur like me to improvise on the same theme as an accomplished writer.

Ph. Look here, I'll have no more of this affectation; for I'm pretty sure I have something to say which will compel you to speak.

Soc. Then please don't say it.

Ph. Oh, but I shall, here and now; and what I say will be on oath. I swear to you by—but by whom, by what god? Or shall it be by this E plane-tree?[3] I swear that unless you deliver your speech here in its very presence, I will assuredly never again declaim nor report any other speech by any author whatsoever.

Soc. Aha, you rogue! How clever of you to discover the means of compelling a lover of discourse to do your bidding!

Ph. Then why all this twisting?

Soc. I give it up, in view of what you've sworn. For how could I possibly do without such entertainment?

Ph. Then proceed.   237

Soc. Well, do you know what I'm going to do?

Ph. Do about what?

Soc. I shall cover my head before I begin: then I can rush through my speech at top speed without looking at you and breaking down for shame.[4]

Ph. You can do anything else you like, provided you make your speech.

---

[1] I retain εὐλαβήθητι in c 3, putting a full stop before it.
[2] Pindar, *frag.* 94 (Bowra).
[3] For such euphemistic oaths (ἵνα μὴ κατὰ θεῶν οἱ ὅρκοι γίγνωνται, *Schol.* on *Apol.* 22 A) see Burnet's note on that passage. The commonest was νὴ τὸν κύνα.
[4] To Phaedrus Socrates's words here doubtless express apprehension that he will disgrace himself by an inferior performance, but the shame that Socrates really feels is, as transpires later (243 B), due to his having been forced to adopt an unworthy conception of Eros.

Soc. Come then, ye clear-voiced Muses, whether it be from the nature of your song, or from the musical people of Liguria that ye came to be so styled,[1] 'assist the tale I tell' under compulsion by my good friend here, to the end that he may think yet more highly of one B dear to him, whom he already accounts a man of wisdom.

The reader who is familiar with the Socratic self-depreciation (εἰρωνεία) will readily understand that this suggestion of inspiration by Sappho or Anacreon or some prose writer is not to be taken seriously. When Socrates says that he has stupidly forgotten the exact source of inspiration (235 D), even Phaedrus seems to see through the fiction.

But there is probably more behind Socrates's words here: they are meant to prepare us for his serious recognition later on of inspiration from a divine source, from 'the divinities of the place' (262 D), from 'Pan and all the other gods here present' (279 B). As yet he is only beginning to feel inspired or possessed, and while conscious of something 'welling up within his breast' casts about for a purely rational account of its origin. But the reader may discern even at this early stage that something more than a 'rationalistic' treatment of love is to be expected from him.

For the rest, this section is directed (apart from some typically Platonic by-play) to bringing out two main points. First, the coming (first) speech of Socrates will be concerned mainly, if not exclusively, with τὰ ἀναγκαῖα (236 A), the 'necessary' or inevitable, obvious points which any defender of Lysias's thesis must make; all that can be really original is the arrangement (διάθεσις) of these. The points 'difficult to invent' will emerge in the second speech, and when we reach it we shall be in no doubt of its author's inventive power. Thus the reader is warned what to look for and what not to look for; and indeed it is true that the speech, though not confined to a repetition of Lysias's points, will move within the orbit of commonplace conventional morality, accepting in particular the 'necessary' principle that the rational must always be praiseworthy and the irrational always deserve censure (235 E)—a principle to be discarded in the 'palinode'; it is true also that the διάθεσις will be incomparably superior to that of Lysias.

But if this is what the promised discourse is to be, what has become of Socrates's inspiration? Can he mean that his memories of Sappho and Anacreon inspire him merely to a superior presentation of Lysias's theme? Assuredly not: it would be absurd to think of these poets as

---

[1] The suggested connexion between λιγύς (*clear-voiced*) and the Ligurian people is one of those etymological jests in which Plato often, and sometimes rather pointlessly, indulges.

upholding Lysias's thesis. The explanation must be that whereas Socrates means that he has something 'better' to say, because truer, Phaedrus assumes that he is promising merely a better treatment of the same thesis; he misinterprets Socrates' παρὰ ταῦτα ἕτερα μὴ χείρω (235 C) as meaning not a contradiction of the thesis but a fresh set of arguments in support of it; all he expects is that Socrates will 'keep away from the arguments in the book' (τῶν ἐν τῷ βιβλίῳ ἀπεχόμενος, 235 D). And Socrates silently accepts the misinterpretation, which thereby fulfils its function in the economy of the dialogue: for it enables Plato to do what he wants, namely to heighten the effect of the really important discourse—the discourse which reveals his deepest thoughts on love and philosophy—by making it the recantation of a discourse forced on Socrates by Phaedrus, in defence of a thesis repugnant to him.

And this brings us to the second main point brought out in this section, namely that the speech is extorted from Socrates.[1] Ostensibly his reluctance is due to modesty: he would not vie with the 'wisdom' of the famous orator; really of course it is due to repugnance. In his last words here (237A) Socrates, besides underlining the compulsion, calls for the aid of the Muses; and this creates a real difficulty, for it would naturally imply that the substance of his first speech is truly inspired; and yet we shall find that it will later be disowned as false, and requiring a recantation.

The explanation, I think, is this: Socrates will not, when it comes to the point, fully yield to the compulsion which Phaedrus seeks to put upon him: he will only uphold the Lysian thesis in so far as it condemned unrestrained sexual passion; he will not speak in support of τὸ τῷ μὴ ἐρῶντι χαρίζεσθαι.[2] Hence the coming speech is complementary to the great second speech in the sense that it condemns the false—or what is afterwards (266A) called the left-hand (σκαιός)—Eros, in preparation for extolling the true; and qua complementary it shares in that inspiration by the Muses which is more fully characteristic of the second speech. The blasphemy (242 C ff.), the aspect of the first speech which calls for its recantation, consists only in the assumption—taken over from Lysias and dictated by Phaedrus's misunderstanding—that the false Eros is the true.

---

[1] Later (244A) it is called the speech of Phaedrus.
[2] Except indeed for the generalising assertion at 241 E 5, on which see below p. 53.

237B–238C SOCRATES BEGINS HIS SPEECH.
A DEFINITION OF LOVE

The speaker begins by insisting that in any deliberation the first essential is to understand clearly the nature of the subject on which we are deliberating: otherwise confusion must result. He therefore proceeds to determine the nature of love, which is found to be a form of irrational desire, or of wantonness (ὕβρις), directed towards physical beauty; and the definition is so worded as to reveal an etymological connexion between love (ἔρως) and the strength (ῥώμη) of uncontrolled passion.

237 B   *Soc.*   Well then, once upon a time there was a very handsome boy, or rather young man, who had a host of lovers; and one of them was wily, and had persuaded the boy that he was not in love with him, though really he was, quite as much as the others. And on one occasion, in pressing his suit he actually sought to convince him that he ought to favour a non-lover rather than a lover. And this is the purport of what he said:

My boy, if anyone means to deliberate successfully about anything,
C there is one thing he must do at the outset: he must know what it is he is deliberating about; otherwise he is bound to go utterly astray. Now most people fail to realise that they don't know what this or that really is: consequently when they start discussing something, they dispense with any agreed definition, assuming that they know the thing; then later on they naturally find, to their cost, that they agree neither with each other nor with themselves. That being so, you and I would do well to avoid what we charge against other people; and as the question before us is whether one should preferably consort with a lover or a non-lover, we ought to agree upon a definition of love which shows its nature and its effects, so that we may have it before our
D minds as something to refer to while we discuss whether love is beneficial or injurious.

Well now, it is plain to everyone that love is some sort of desire; and further we know that men desire that which is fair without being lovers. How then are we to distinguish one who loves from one who does not? We must go on to observe that within each one of us there are two sorts of ruling or guiding principle that we follow: one is an innate desire for pleasure, the other an acquired judgment that aims at what is best. Sometimes these internal guides are in accord, sometimes at variance: now one gains the mastery, now the other. And E when judgment guides us rationally towards what is best, and has the mastery, that mastery is called temperance; but when desire drags us 238 irrationally towards pleasure, and has come to rule within us, the name given to that rule is wantonness. But in truth wantonness itself has many names, as it has many branches or forms,[1] and when one of these forms is conspicuously present in a man it makes that man bear its name, a name that it is no credit or distinction to possess. If it be in the matter of food that desire has the mastery over judgment of what is for the best, and over all other desires, it is called gluttony, and the person B in question will be called a glutton; or again if desire has achieved domination in the matter of drink, it is plain what term we shall apply to its subject who is led down that path; and no less plain what are the appropriate names in the case of other such persons and of other such desires, according as this one or that holds sway.[2]

Now the reason for saying all this can hardly remain in doubt; yet even so a statement of it will be illuminating. When irrational desire, pursuing the enjoyment of beauty, has gained the mastery over judgment that prompts to right conduct, and has acquired from other c desires, akin to it, fresh strength to strain towards bodily beauty, that very strength provides it with its name: it is the strong passion called Love.[3]

The stress here laid upon the need for defining the subject of discourse is of course characteristic of Socrates and Plato, and will appear again at 263 C–D. We may also recall that in the *Symposium* (195 A) Agathon promises that, unlike the previous speakers, he will praise the nature of Eros before praising his gifts—in other words, he

[1] I retain πολυειδές in A3 in place of Burnet's πολυμερές: it better suits ἰδεῶν which follows.

[2] The text of B 4–5 is probably correct, though difficult. I take it to stand for καὶ τἆλλα δὴ τὰ τούτων (masculine) ἀδελφὰ ὀνόματα, ᾗ προσήκει καλεῖσθαι, καὶ ᾗ τὸ τῆς ἀδελφῶν ἐπιθυμιῶν ἀεὶ δυναστευούσης ὄνομα (sc. προσήκει καλεῖσθαι), πρόδηλον. ἀδελφῶν ἐπιθυμιῶν is either partitive genitive or the genitive regular with verbs of ruling.

[3] In this difficult passage, where the suggested etymological connexion of ἔρως (love) with ῥώμη (strength) and the cognate words ἐρρωμένως and ῥωσθεῖσα (ῥώννυμι) cannot be reproduced in English, I have bracketed νικήσασα as a gloss on ῥωσθεῖσα and taken ἀγωγῇ closely with ἐπὶ σωμάτων κάλλος. I am by no means sure that ἀγωγῇ should not be deleted also: if it were, the above translation might still stand.

will say what love is before describing its effects: for which Socrates commends him (199 c).

Why does Socrates put his speech into the mouth of αἱμύλος τις, of one who only pretends not to be a lover? Prof. Taylor answers: 'This gives Socrates a double advantage over Lysias. He safeguards his own character by abstaining from even a playful defence of a morally disgraceful thesis, and he leaves himself free, if he pleases, to urge subsequently that the apparent reasonability of the speech is only the simulated rationality of a madman, since the client into whose mouth it is put is really inspired all the time by "romantic" unreason.'[1]

I should prefer a simpler explanation. The whole attitude of the speaker, unlike that of Lysias's speaker, shows a real concern for the welfare, especially the moral welfare, of the boy, a concern which it would have been unconvincing to attribute to a genuine cold-blooded sensualist. When, for example, it is argued that the jealous lover will debar the boy from associations likely to make a man of him, and in particular from divine philosophy (239 B), we see the lover peeping through the disguise—not indeed the σκαιὸς ἐραστής but the true lover as conceived by Socrates and Plato; in fact we get a glimpse of the ἐραστής par excellence, Socrates himself. We should note also the stress laid on ψυχῆς παίδευσις at the end (241 c).

The method by which the definition of love is here arrived at partly, but only partly, exemplifies the method of dialectic which will be described later (265 D ff.). Socrates starts by subsuming ἔρως under the generic term ἐπιθυμία: this first step, not reached by argument nor by the process called Collection (συναγωγή) but by simple observation (ἅπαντι δῆλον), might be expected to be followed by a series of dichotomies, a formal divisional scheme such as those elaborated in the later dialogues *Sophist* and *Statesman*. But this does not happen, because Socrates is anxious to show not only what species of ἐπιθυμία constitutes love, but also that it involves a state of disharmony in the soul, a discord which is improperly resolved by the victory of the lower, irrational part of soul. It is through this account of psychical discord that we arrive at the concept of ὕβρις: and ὕβρις now takes the place of ἐπιθυμία as the genus to be divided.

From this point onwards the division into kinds is straightforward, though not dichotomous: ὕβρις has many co-ordinate kinds, of which ἔρως will be found to be one. It is not said that ὕβρις is a kind of ἐπιθυμία: rather it is the name of that psychical state which results from the victory of irrational desire for pleasure over rational belief, which aims at good; nevertheless the connexion of ὕβρις with ἐπιθυμία is so close that the speaker treats the species of the one as species of the other, and in the end arrives at a definition of love which, as we were

---

[1] *Plato, the Man and his Work*, p. 303.

led to expect at the outset, makes it a kind of desire, and carefully states its specific difference.

It will of course be realised that this definition of love is not really accepted by Socrates or Plato: the restriction to physical beauty (ἐπὶ σώματος κάλλος) is enough to indicate that; it is only put forward because Socrates is adopting, under compulsion, the principle of Lysias that τὸν ἐρῶντα τοῦ μὴ ἐρῶντος μᾶλλον νοσεῖν. Yet it is perfectly satisfactory as a definition of the σκαιὸς ἔρως.

The section, however, presents a problem in psychology. Instead of the three parts of soul recognised in the *Republic*, reason, 'spirit' and desire, between which there may or may not be harmony, and any of which[1] may exercise the rule, we have here 'two sorts of ruling or guiding principle', ἡ μὲν ἔμφυτος οὖσα ἐπιθυμία ἡδονῶν, ἄλλη δὲ ἐπίκτητος δόξα ἐφιεμένη τοῦ ἀρίστου. There are however other cases in the dialogues of bipartition of soul: in the *Republic* itself there is that of a rational and an irrational part (604–5), while in the *Timaeus* the primary division is into the immortal and mortal parts, the latter being then subdivided into a better part and a worse (69 E), corresponding to the two lower parts of *Rep.* IV.

More difficult is the use of the word δόξα. Normally it is used in contrast to ἐπιστήμη or νοῦς or νόησις and dissociated from a reasoning process. Thus in *Rep.* 476–8 δόξα is intermediate between knowledge and ignorance, and its object intermediate between Being and Not Being. At *Timaeus* 51 E we are told that δύο δὴ λεκτέον ἐκείνω (sc. νοῦς and δόξα ἀληθής) διότι χωρὶς γεγόνατον ἀνομοίως τε ἔχετον. τὸ μὲν γὰρ αὐτῶν διὰ διδαχῆς τὸ δ' ὑπὸ πειθοῦς ἡμῖν ἐγγίγνεται, καὶ τὸ μὲν ἀεὶ μετ' ἀληθοῦς λόγου, τὸ δὲ ἄλογον. These passages may be said to represent Plato's normal doctrine. What then are we to make of the δόξα of our present passage, which is described not only as ἐφιεμένη τοῦ ἀρίστου, but as ἐπὶ τὸ ἄριστον λόγῳ ἄγουσα?

It seems probable that Plato is here using non-technical language, and that the antithesis of ἐπιθυμία and ἐπίκτητος δόξα is popular rather than philosophical. We should remember that Socrates is not speaking *in propria persona*, but as the mouthpiece of an imaginary ἐραστὴς αἱμύλος: we should therefore not attach much importance to discrepancy with Plato's normal psychological and epistemological terms. What we have is a broad contrast, simple enough to be drawn by the average man, between unreflective desire for immediate pleasure and the reflective condition of mind which tends to run counter to that desire, though of course a harmony may be established. To call such a condition δόξα is perfectly natural; but it is not δόξα in the common Platonic sense of 'opinion' or 'belief' as distinct from knowledge, nor

[1] This is true of τὸ θυμοειδές no less than of the other two: *Rep.* 550B.

yet has it quite the later Platonic meaning of 'conclusion of a process of thought' (διανοίας ἀποτελεύτησις, *Soph.* 264A), though it is nearer to this. It is not a deciding or judging,[1] for these are mental *acts*: it is rather the condition of mind in which a man takes thought, reflects and weighs alternatives instead of thoughtlessly obeying the promptings of desire; and its aim is a satisfaction deeper than the fulfilment of unreflective desire. This is what is intended in the phrase δόξης ἐπὶ τὸ ἄριστον λόγῳ ἀγούσης, a phrase which we should read without the Platonic overtones which it inevitably carries to our ears. As for ἐπίκτητος, the word is well suited to convey that such δόξα is not innate, but comes only with riper years and mental growth.

In the substance of all this there is nothing un-Socratic or un-Platonic; indeed we may see in it the popular germ of Platonic psychology, which, whatever it may owe to Pythagorean or other philosophical sources, is firm-rooted in common human experience.

[1] I have adopted Prof. Taylor's 'judgment' in my translation, as perhaps the nearest we can get with a single English word. Robin has 'une façon de voir'.

Having thus defined love, Socrates pauses to comment on the dithyrambic style of his last words, feeling that it points to a supernatural influence. He then proceeds to consider the evil effect of love so conceived on the mind of the beloved, on his body, and on his 'estate' (κτῆσις), the last of these being interpreted in a wide sense to include relatives and friends. In the latter half of the section he turns to the boy's feelings towards his importunate lover, and finally to the desertion and betrayal which will ensue when his passion is spent, emphasising towards the end the harm done in the matter of the 'education of the soul' (ψυχῆς παίδευσις) in terms that remind us of Socrates's famous account of his mission in the Apology. *The section ends with a hexameter line, declaring the lover to be like a wolf devouring a lamb.*

Soc. Well, Phaedrus my friend, do you think, as I do, that I am 238 C divinely inspired?

Ph. Undoubtedly, Socrates, you have been vouchsafed a quite unusual eloquence.

Soc. Then listen to me in silence. For truly there seems to be a divine presence in this spot, so that you must not be surprised if, as D my speech proceeds, I become as one possessed; already my style is not far from dithyrambic.

Ph. Very true.

Soc. But for that you are responsible. Still, let me continue; possibly the menace may be averted. However, that must be as God wills: our business is to resume our address to the boy:—

Very well then, my good friend: the true nature of that on which we have to deliberate has been stated and defined; and so, with that definition in mind, we may go on to say what advantage or detriment E may be expected to result to one who accords his favour to a lover and a non-lover respectively.

Now a man who is dominated by desire and enslaved to pleasure is of course bound to aim at getting the greatest possible pleasure out of his beloved; and what pleases a sick man[1] is anything that does not thwart him, whereas anything that is as strong as, or stronger than, himself gives him offence. Hence he will not, if he can avoid it, put up

[1] cf. 231 D, 236 A.

239 with a favourite that matches or outdoes him in strength, but will always seek to make him weaker and feebler: and weakness is found in the ignorant, the cowardly, the poor speaker, the slow thinker, as against the wise, the brave, the eloquent, the quick-minded. All these defects of mind and more in the beloved are bound to be a source of pleasure to the lover: if they do not exist already as innate qualities, he will cultivate them, for not to do so means depriving himself of immediate pleasure. And of course he is bound to be jealous, constantly

B debarring the boy not only, to his great injury, from the advantages of consorting with others, which would make a real man of him, but, greatest injury of all, from consorting with that which would most increase his wisdom; by which I mean divine philosophy: no access to that can possibly be permitted by the lover, for he dreads becoming thereby an object of contempt. And in general he must aim at making the boy totally ignorant and totally dependent on his lover, by way of securing the maximum of pleasure for himself, and the maximum of damage to the other.

C   Hence in respect of the boy's mind it is anything but a profitable investment to have as guardian or partner a man in love.

After the mind, the body; we must see what sort of physical condition will be fostered, and how it will be fostered, in the boy that has become the possession of one who is under compulsion to pursue pleasure instead of goodness. We shall find him, of course, pursuing a weakling rather than a sturdy boy, one who has had a cosy, sheltered upbringing instead of being exposed to the open air, who has given himself up to a soft unmanly life instead of the toil and sweat of manly

D exercise, who for lack of natural charm tricks himself out with artificial cosmetics, and resorts to all sorts of other similar practices which are too obvious to need further enumeration; yet before leaving the topic we may sum it up in a sentence: the boy will be of that physical type which in wartime, and other times that try a man's mettle, inspires confidence in his enemies and alarm in his friends, aye and in his very lovers too.

E   And now let us pass from these obvious considerations and raise the next question: what advantage or detriment in respect of property and possessions shall we find resulting from the society and guardianship of a lover? Well, one thing is plain enough to anyone, and especially to the lover, namely that his foremost wish will be for the boy to be bereft of his dearest possessions, his treasury of kindness and ideal affection: father and mother, kinsmen and friends—he will want him to be robbed of them all, as likely to make difficulties and raise objec- 240 tions to the intercourse which he finds so pleasant. If however the boy possesses property, in money or whatever it may be, he will reckon that he will not be so easy to capture, or if captured to manage; hence a lover is bound to nurse a grudge against one who possesses property, and to rejoice when he loses it. Furthermore he will want his beloved to remain as long as possible without wife or child or home, so as to enjoy for as long as may be his own delights.

There are, to be sure, other evils in life, but with most of them heaven has mixed some momentary pleasure: thus in the parasite, B a fearsome and most pernicious creature, nature has mingled a dash of pleasing wit or charm; a courtesan may well be branded as pernicious, not to mention many other similar creatures with their respective callings, yet in everyday life they can be very agreeable; but a lover, besides being pernicious, is the most disagreeable of all men for a boy to spend his days with. There's an old saying about 'not matching May C with December', based, I suppose, on the idea that similarity of age tends to similarity of pleasures and consequently makes a couple good friends: still even with such a couple the association is apt to pall. Then again, in addition to the dissimilarity of age, there is that compulsion which is burdensome for anybody in any circumstances, but especially so in the relations of such a pair.

The elderly lover will not, if he can help it, suffer any desertion by his beloved by day or by night; he is driven on by a compelling, D goading power, lured by the continual promise of pleasure in the sight, hearing, touching or other physical experience of the beloved; to minister unfailingly to the boy's needs is his delight. But what pleasure or what solace will he have to offer to the beloved? How will he save him from experiencing the extremity of discomfort in those long hours at his lover's side, as he looks upon a face which years have robbed of its beauty, together with other consequences which it is unpleasant E even to hear mentioned, let alone to have continually to cope with in stark reality. And what of the suspicious precautions with which he is incessantly guarded, with whomsoever he associates, the unseasonable fulsome compliments to which he has to listen, alternating with reproaches which when uttered in soberness are hard to endure, but coming from one in his cups, in language of unlimited, undisguised coarseness, are both intolerable and disgusting?

To continue: if while his love lasts he is harmful and offensive, in later days, when it is spent, he will show his bad faith. He was lavish with promises, interspersed amongst his vows and entreaties, regarding those later days, contriving with some difficulty to secure his partner's
241 endurance of an intercourse which even then was burdensome, by holding out hopes of benefits to come. But when the time comes for fulfilling the promises, a new authority takes the place within him of the former ruler: love and passion are replaced by wisdom and temperance: he has become a different person. But the boy does not realise it, and demands a return for what he gave in the past, reminding him of what had been done and said, as though he were talking to the same person; while the erstwhile lover, who has now acquired wisdom and temperance, cannot for very shame bring himself to declare that
B he has become a new man, nor yet see his way to redeeming the solemn assurances and promises made under the old régime of folly; he fears that if he were to go on acting as before he would revert to his old character, his former self. So he runs away from his obligations as one compelled to default; it's 'tails' this time instead of 'heads',[1] and he has to turn tail and rush away. But the boy must needs run after him, crying indignantly to high heaven: though from start to finish he has never understood that he ought not to have yielded to a lover inevitably devoid of reason, but far rather to one possessed of reason
C and not in love. He should have known that the wrong choice must mean surrendering himself to a faithless, peevish, jealous and offensive captor, to one who would ruin his property, ruin his physique, and above all ruin his spiritual development, which is assuredly and ever will be of supreme value in the sight of gods and men alike.[2]

Let that then, my boy, be your lesson: be sure that the attentions of a lover carry no goodwill: they are no more than a glutting of his appetite, for
D   As wolf to lamb, so lover to his lad.[3]

---

[1] An allusion to the game called ὀστρακίνδα in which a shell was thrown into the air between two opposing sides, and according as it fell white or dark side uppermost one side had to run and the other to catch them.

[2] cf. *Apol.* 29E, 30A–B.

[3] Probably the singular ἄρνα should be read, with Hermeias, who takes the line to be an adaptation of *Iliad* XXII, 263, οὐδὲ λύκοι τε καὶ ἄρνες ὁμόφρονα θυμὸν ἔχουσι. This seems doubtful.

There, I knew I should,[1] Phaedrus. Not a word more shall you have from me: let that be the end of my discourse.

In the transitional passage (238 C–D) Socrates remarks on his 'dithyrambic' style (he is no doubt referring to the deliberately high-flown diction of his last sentence), and to the possibility of his becoming 'possessed'. This 'menace', however, he thinks may possibly be averted. We see here the rationalist becoming gradually conscious of an influence which he feels to be irrational, or supra-rational, half unwilling to yield, yet knowing that if a god does come to possess him it will be for the best: ταῦτα θεῷ μελήσει.

The 'menace' will be averted for a time yet: that is to say, the remainder of Socrates's first speech will be no more suggestive of ἐνθουσιασμός than was the definitory first section; yet it ends with a break into epic verse, which the speaker, at the opening of the next section, professes to regard as marking a further stage in his 'irrationality': ἤδη ἔπη φθέγγομαι ἀλλ' οὐκέτι διθυράμβους (241 E). It is only when we reach the myth of the great second speech that Socrates becomes fully possessed; but Plato has been at pains to mark his progress step by step.

The orderly arrangement of the speech, in contrast to the formlessness of its predecessor, is at once apparent. It falls, as Robin says, into two main parts: in the first (down to 240 A 8) the speaker reveals the harmful effect of the lover on the boy's mind, his body and his estate successively; in the second he describes the boy's feelings (a) while the lover's passion lasts, and (b) afterwards.

Of the genuine concern of this pretended non-lover for the boy's welfare I have spoken already. Some of the points are substantially identical with those of the previous speech; that is only to be expected, and Socrates had disarmed criticism by giving warning of this beforehand (235 E–236 A). We may agree with Thompson's verdict that 'his arguments, like those of his predecessor, professedly appeal to self-interest, but to a self-interest more enlightened, comprehensive, and far-sighted'.

At 241 A Socrates speaks of the lover whose passion is spent as letting a new authority, νοῦς καὶ σωφροσύνη, replace within him the rule of ἔρως καὶ μανία: and the words are echoed a little later by νοῦν ἤδη ἐσχηκὼς καὶ σεσωφρονηκώς (241 B 1), and again by νοῦν ἔχοντι (C 1).

This may cause some surprise, for it looks at first sight as though the mere dying out of passion automatically involved moral goodness and that highest level of cognition or intelligence which Plato normally —or at all events frequently—calls νοῦς. But this is so incredible that

---

[1] Socrates had feared that he would break out into inspired verse, 238 D.

we are forced either to take the remark as purely ironical or to interpret νοῦς and σωφροσύνη at what may be called the popular level. Irony here would, I think, be inappropriate and pointless, and the second alternative is much to be preferred. As to νοῦς, the phrase νοῦν ἔχειν meant in common parlance no more than 'to be sensible'; similarly the adverb νουνεχόντως means 'sensibly' (cf. the quasi-comic ἐχόντως ἑαυτόν used of a personified νοῦς at *Philebus* 64A). The reformed lover has, as we say, 'come to his senses', but no more than that. And as to σωφροσύνη, no doubt the man in question would commonly be said to have become σώφρων, and to have come to be ruled by σωφρο-σύνη: but for Plato it would be no more than that spurious σωφροσύνη mentioned alongside of a spurious courage at *Phaedo* 68E; there are those, says Socrates there, who are ἀκολασίᾳ τινὶ σώφρονες, in the sense that they renounce one pleasure in order to retain another. In our present case there is no reason to suppose a change of heart, nor an increase in wisdom; the man has become ostensibly σώφρων περὶ τὰ ἀφροδίσια, but (to revert to the previous account of the two ruling principles) he is no more likely to have a δόξα ἐπὶ τὸ ἄριστον λόγῳ ἄγουσα now than before; and in default of that his desires will drag him to other pleasures and other forms of ὕβρις—gluttony, drink or what not. And though it may not be the case that he renounces the one sort of pleasure in order to retain the others, it may fairly be said that his so-called σωφροσύνη involves no renunciation of the others. Hence we should probably regard not only the terms νοῦς and σωφροσύνη but also the phrase μεταβαλὼν ἄλλον ἄρχοντα ἐν αὐτῷ καὶ προστάτην as representing the popular standpoint.

That Plato should thus momentarily adopt the ethical position of the ordinary man will surprise us the less when we remember that the whole standpoint of the present speech is in a sense unreal. The ἔρως that Socrates is condemning is not what Plato conceives to be the true ἔρως, the μανία of which he speaks in this very sentence (241 A 4) is not the μανία in which true ἔρως consists: it is the popular, 'Lysian' ἔρως, the popular 'Lysian' μανία: hence the σωφροσύνη commended over against it may well be the popular, not the Platonic virtue.

It has been noted by Thompson (in his Appendix I) and others that the speech includes passages similar to passages in the address of Socrates to Callias in Xenophon's *Symposium*, chapter VIII; and Thompson thinks the parallels are so close as to 'make it very probable that in both [sc. discourses] we have the actual sentiments of Socrates represented—we may even say reproduced—by his rival disciples'; while Robin allows that the passages 'strangely resemble one another'.[1]

The suggestion is incapable of disproof, but to my mind the resemblances in thought and expression are not greater than might be

[1] p. lxxiv.

due to the common topic of the two writers—true and false (or celestial and earthly) love. And in particular it seems to me that the last of Thompson's three parallels[1] is illusory: for though the word πλησμονή occurs in both passages, in Xenophon it means satiety (κόρος), and in Plato satisfaction of appetite; in fact Xenophon's point is that a lover gets as 'fed up' with his indulgence as a gourmand with his, while Plato's is that the lover resembles the wolf in that each aims at satisfying his appetite.

[1] Quoted on his p. 150: Xen. *Symp.* VIII, 33; *Phaedrus* 241 C.

VI

*Excusing himself from fulfilling Phaedrus's expectation that he would
continue with an encomium of the non-lover, Socrates is about to depart,
when Phaedrus suggests that they should stay awhile to discuss the two
speeches. Socrates however now announces that he has just been checked
by his 'divine sign': he is forbidden to go until he has atoned for his offence
against Eros: his speech, like that of Lysias, had spoken evil of a god. He
must imitate the poet Stesichorus, who recanted his defamation of Helen
in the famous Palinode.*

*After enlarging on the shamefulness of the two speeches Socrates suggests
that Lysias ought to write another speech to contradict his former one, and
Phaedrus says that he will see that this is done. All is now ready for the
speech of recantation.*

241 D   *Ph.* Why, I thought you were only half-way through[1] and would
have an equal amount to say about the non-lover, enumerating his good
points and showing that he should be the favoured suitor. Why is it,
Socrates, that instead of that you break off?

E   *Soc.* My dear good man, haven't you noticed that I've got beyond
dithyramb, and am breaking out into epic verse, despite my fault-
finding? What do you suppose I shall do if I start extolling the other
type? Don't you see that I shall clearly be possessed by those nymphs
into whose clutches you deliberately threw me? I therefore tell you,
in one short sentence, that to each evil for which I have abused the one
party there is a corresponding good belonging to the other. So why
waste words? All has been said that needs saying about them both.
And that being so, my story[2] can be left to the fate appropriate to it,
242 and I will take myself off across the river here before you drive me to
greater lengths.

Ph. Oh, but you must wait until it gets cooler, Socrates. Don't you
realise that it's just about the hour of 'scorching noonday', as the
phrase goes? Let us wait and discuss what we've heard; when it has
got cool perhaps we will go.

---

[1] Reading σε μεσοῦν αὑτοῦ (Hermann).

[2] μῦθος, because Socrates had thrown his speech into the form of a narrative
(ἦν οὕτω δὴ παῖς etc., 237B).

Soc. Phaedrus, your enthusiasm for discourse is sublime, and really moves me to admiration. Of the discourses pronounced during your lifetime no one, I fancy, has been responsible for more than you, B whether by delivering them yourself or by compelling others to do so by one means or another—with one exception, Simmias of Thebes: you are well ahead of all the rest. And now it seems that once more you are the cause of my having to deliver myself.

Ph. It might be a lot worse! But how so? To what do you refer?

Soc. At the moment when I was about to cross the river, dear friend, there came to me my familiar divine sign—which always checks me when on the point of doing something or other—and all at once C I seemed to hear a voice, forbidding me[1] to leave the spot until I had made atonement for some offence to heaven. Now, you must know, I am a seer; not a very good one, it's true, but, like a poor scholar, good enough for my own purposes; hence I understand already well enough what my offence was. The fact is, you know, Phaedrus, the mind itself has a kind of divining power; for I felt disturbed some while ago as I was delivering that speech, and had a misgiving lest I might, in the words of Ibycus[2]

By sinning in the sight of God win high renown from man. D

But now I realise my sin.

Ph. And what is it?

Soc. That was a terrible theory, Phaedrus, a terrible theory that you introduced and compelled me to expound.

Ph. How so?

Soc. It was foolish, and somewhat blasphemous; and what could be more terrible than that?

Ph. I agree, if it merits your description.

Soc. Well, do you not hold Love to be a god, the child of Aphrodite?

Ph. He is certainly said to be.

Soc. But not according to Lysias, and not according to that discourse of yours which you caused my lips to utter by putting a spell on E them. If Love is, as he is indeed, a god or a divine being, he cannot be an evil thing: yet this pair of speeches treated him as evil. That then was their offence towards Love, to which was added the most exquisite

---

[1] Reading εἶα for ἐῷ with Richards in c 2.
[2] Frag. 51 (Bergk).

folly of parading their pernicious rubbish as though it were good sense
243 because it might deceive a few miserable people and win their applause.

And so, my friend, I have to purify myself. Now for such as offend
in speaking of gods and heroes there is an ancient mode of purification,
which was known to Stesichorus, though not to Homer. When
Stesichorus lost the sight of his eyes because of his defamation of Helen,
he was not, like Homer, at a loss to know why: as a true artist he
understood the reason, and promptly wrote the lines:

> False, false the tale:
> Thou never didst sail in the well-decked ships
> Nor come to the towers of Troy.

B

And after finishing the composition of his so-called Palinode he straightway recovered his sight. Now it's here that I shall show greater wisdom
than these poets: I shall attempt to make my due palinode to Love
before any harm comes to me for my defamation of him, and no longer
veiling my head for shame, but uncovered.

Ph. Nothing you could say, Socrates, would please me more.

C   *Soc.* Yes, dear Phaedrus: you understand how irreverent the two
speeches were, the one in the book and that which followed. Suppose
we were being listened to by a man of generous and humane character,
who loved or had once loved another such as himself: suppose he
heard us saying that for some trifling cause lovers conceive bitter
hatred and a spirit of malice and injury towards their loved ones;
wouldn't he be sure to think that we had been brought up among the
scum of the people and had never seen a case of noble love? Wouldn't
D he utterly refuse to accept our vilification of Love?

Ph. Indeed, Socrates, he well might.

Soc. Then out of respect for him, and in awe of Love himself,
I should like to wash the bitter taste out of my mouth with a draught of
wholesome discourse; and my advice to Lysias is that he should lose
no time in telling us that, other things being equal, favour should be
accorded to the lover rather than to the non-lover.

Ph. Rest assured, that will be done. When you have delivered your
E encomium of the lover, I shall most certainly make Lysias compose
a new speech to the same purport.

Soc. I'm sure of that, so long as you continue to be the man you
are.[1]

---

[1] Lysias will not be able to resist Phaedrus, so long as his enthusiasm for
rhetoric endures.

Ph. Then you may confidently proceed.

Soc. Where is that boy I was talking to? He must listen to me once more, and not rush off to yield to his non-lover before he hears what I have to say.

Ph. Here he is, quite close beside you, whenever you want him.[1]

It has been thought that the reason why Socrates abstains from giving what Phaedrus expects, namely a complementary account of the advantages of yielding to the non-lover, is to be found in his moral repugnance to doing so: he could bring himself to lend at least ostensible support to the negative side of Lysias's thesis, but not to the positive side, ὡς τῷ μὴ ἐρῶντι δεῖ χαρίζεσθαι.

That may be so; but it must be observed that at 241 E 5 Socrates says, apparently without irony, that to each evil for which he has abused the one party there corresponds a good belonging to the other. This compactly provides the complement expected by Phaedrus, and the mere absence of its elaboration, point by point, is no evidence of Socrates's repugnance. His real position I take to be this: on the hypothesis that the boy must yield to one or the other, he ought rather (μᾶλλον) to yield to the non-lover than to the 'lover' as hitherto conceived;[2] but that hypothesis is not Socrates's own: his own (and Plato's) view, to be developed later in the dialogue, is that true ἔρως, though based on physical desire, transcends it, and hence οὐδετέρῳ δεῖ χαρίζεσθαι in the sense that χαρίζεσθαι is commonly understood.

Phaedrus's wish to discuss what has been said (242 A 5)—that is to say the two speeches together—is interpreted by Socrates as an invitation to pursue the topic further by a second speech of his own (242 B). That was not, it seems, quite what Phaedrus expected, and perhaps not quite what the reader expects: instead of a discussion (διαλεχθῆναι) we are to have a third discourse. Why that must be so, Socrates goes on to explain. But although Phaedrus is a little surprised, he is by no means displeased: οὐ πόλεμόν γε ἀγγέλλεις, he remarks— a humorous understatement to express his delight. The reader has moreover been prepared for his readiness to accept Socrates's proposal by a renewed allusion to his fondness for λόγοι, in a passage which is

---

[1] P. Friedländer (*Die Platonischen Schriften*, p. 485) thinks this shows that Socrates's second speech is 'unmistakably addressed to Phaedrus himself', and sees in this an indication that 'auch hier wieder der Kampf zwischen sophistischen Rhetorik und Philosophie um die Seele der Jugend gekämpft wird'. While fully agreeing with this view of the dialogue, I do not think that Socrates's veiled suggestion that Phaedrus himself is 'the boy', and Phaedrus's acceptance of it, are anything more than playful. Phaedrus has not been shown as disposed χαρίζεσθαι τῷ μὴ ἐρῶντι in practice, whatever he may think of it in theory.

[2] cf. 241 C 1.

doubtless intended by Plato to recall once more the *Symposium*, where the whole series of speeches (including of course his own) sprang from Phaedrus's suggestion.

The mention of Simmias as the one man who excelled Phaedrus in fondness for discourses may be an allusion to the *Phaedo*, where his determination to thrash out the subject under discussion to the bitter end is forcibly expressed (85 c): but of course it may well be that in Socratic and Platonic circles the φιλολογία of Simmias was proverbial.

The mention by Socrates at this point of his 'divine sign' is dramatically admirable, for he is about to make a *volte-face*, and this is a happy means of making him do so in a dramatically convincing way. It should be noticed that here, as in *Apol.* 31 D (the *locus classicus* for the Sign) its function is exclusively inhibitory, as against Xenophon's account (φάσκοντος αὐτοῦ τὸ δαιμόνιον ἑαυτῷ προσημαίνειν ἅτε δέοι καὶ ἃ μὴ δέοι ποιεῖν, *Mem.* IV, viii, 1). Yet the action of the Sign is here only formally inhibitory: it forbids him to depart without making an atonement, but in effect it commands him to make one. I do not think that the introduction of the Sign here has any deeper significance; and in particular I cannot accept Robin's suggestion that the inspiration which Socrates has acknowledged earlier, the inspiration of the local deities, is hereby repudiated and replaced by another and a higher one.[1] Nowhere do we find Socrates regarding himself as inspired by the Sign, in the sense of being possessed by the deity from whom it emanated; and on the other hand, the renewed mention of the Nymphs and Pan at 263 D and, even more, the final prayer to 'Pan and the other gods of this place' (279 B) surely make it impossible to believe that their inspiration comes 'from below' and is abandoned at this point.

That Socrates should compare his recantation to the famous Palinode of Stesichorus, in which that poet had adopted the legend of the phantom Helen, so well known to us from the play of Euripides, is very natural, one might almost say inevitable.[2] There is, however, another sort of palinode, or apparent retractation, on the part of Socrates which demands some comment. In the *Symposium* he had firmly denied, through the mouth of Diotima, that Eros is a god: he is only a δαίμων, a being intermediate between gods and men, and therewith a mediator and messenger between them (202 D–E). But now his divinity is asserted with no less emphasis: εἰ δ᾽ ἔστιν, ὥσπερ οὖν

---

[1] Robin, p. xxxiv: 'C'est l'admonition démonique qui a vraiment permis à Socrate de prendre enfin pleine conscience de son péché. Il est donc difficile de ne pas voir là une coupe significative dans le développement du dialogue: à une inspiration qui vient d'en bas s'en substitue désormais une autre, qui vient d'en haut.'

[2] Here again (cf. p. 34 above) Mr R. L. Howland (*C.Q.* XXXI, p. 154) detects a covert allusion, of a malicious sort, to Isocrates's *Helen*.

ἔστι, θεὸς ἤ τι θεῖον ὁ Ἔρως (242E). The question is, why did Plato choose to approach the exposition of his own view of Eros from two different standpoints? Why does he start (or rather make Socrates-Diotima start) in the *Symposium* by denying that Eros is a god? Only, I think, because he feels that to call him a god is to obscure what he wants to bring out, namely that 'loving' is essentially the soul's effort to satisfy a want, to attain to the eternal possession of the good and the beautiful. The 'daemonic' or intermediate nature of Eros is simply the mythical way of expressing that to love is to make a progress from want to satisfaction, from misery to bliss, from ignorance to knowledge or wisdom.

In the *Phaedrus*, however, Plato does not start from the conception of a progress—though that conception is fully present at a later stage of Socrates's second speech—but (as we are about to find) from that of *possession*, the divine madness by which the lover is seized. That being so, he must necessarily postulate a personal deity as its source. Hence he naturally makes Socrates here accept the common belief that Eros is θεὸς ἤ τι θεῖον.[1]

The discrepancy, then, between the two dialogues may fairly be said to be due to the fact that in order to bring out two complementary (not contradictory) aspects of love it seemed natural to Plato to employ two different personifications of it, the 'daemon' with his function as intermediary, and the god filling his worshipper with his own super-human, super-rational power.[2]

Near the end of the section (243D) Phaedrus remarks that, when Socrates has delivered his encomium on the lover, he will have to make Lysias write another speech to the same purport. This serves to remind us of what we have noticed before, that Phaedrus is concerned not with truth but with rhetoric. That Lysias (or anyone else) should maintain two opposite theses seems to Phaedrus perfectly in order: all that matters is the eloquence.

[1] It is just possible that ἤ τι θεῖον is a verbal concession—it can be no more—to the δαίμων-Eros view.

[2] We may notice that when Socrates resumes his speech *in propria persona* (*Symp.* 212B) he uses language which seems to imply the full godhead of Eros; the 'intermediate' conception has served its purpose, and is in effect dropped.

VII

In allusion to his resolve to sing a palinode, Socrates declares that whereas his former speech was the work of Phaedrus, this will be the work of Stesichorus. The thesis of Lysias was a 'false tale', since it assumed that madness is in all cases an evil. In reality it may be a divine boon. There are three types of divine madness, (1) that of divination or prophecy, such as belongs to the priestess at Delphi: this must be distinguished from the inferior practice of rational augury, and etymology helps us to maintain the distinction; (2) that which heals the sick by means of purifications and rites revealed to a frenzied sufferer; (3) poetical frenzy, which gives rise to far truer poetry than the art of the sane composer.

We have now to show that love is a fourth type of divine madness, and to that end we must discern the nature of soul, both human and divine.

243 E   *Soc.* Now you must understand, fair boy, that whereas the preceding
244   discourse was by Phaedrus, son of Pythocles, of Myrrinous, that which I shall now pronounce is by Stesichorus, son of Euphemus, of Himera.[1] This then is how it must run:

'False is the tale' that when a lover is at hand favour ought rather to be accorded to one who does not love, on the ground that the former is mad, and the latter sound of mind. That would be right if it were an invariable truth that madness is an evil: but in reality, the greatest blessings come by way of madness, indeed of madness that is heaven-
B sent. It was when they were mad that the prophetess at Delphi and the priestesses at Dodona achieved so much for which both states and individuals in Greece are thankful: when sane they did little or nothing. As for the Sibyl and others who by the power of inspired prophecy have so often foretold the future to so many, and guided them aright, I need not dwell on what is obvious to everyone. Yet it is in place to appeal to the fact that madness was accounted no shame nor disgrace by the men of old who gave things their names: otherwise they would

---

[1] Thompson and, as we should expect, Hermeias before him, regard all these proper names as significant. Doubtless the last two are so: the speech will be εὔφημος, as opposed to κακήγορος, and Ἱμέραιος anticipates the 'flood of passion' (ἵμερος) of 251 C. But to find significance in the other four is a task best left to Neoplatonic subtlety.

not have connected that greatest of arts, whereby the future is discerned, c with this very word 'madness', and named it accordingly. No, it was because they held madness to be a valuable gift, when due to divine dispensation, that they named that art as they did, though the men of to-day, having no sense of values, have put in an extra letter, making it not *manic* but *mantic*. That is borne out by the name they gave to the art of those sane prophets who inquire into the future by means of birds and other signs: the name was 'oionoistic', which by its components[1] indicated that the prophet attained understanding and information by a purely human activity of thought belonging to his own intelligence; though a younger generation has come to call it 'oionistic', lengthening the quantity of the *o* to make it sound impressive. You see D then what this ancient evidence attests: corresponding to the superior perfection and value of the prophecy of inspiration over that of omen-reading, both in name and in fact, is the superiority of heaven-sent madness over man-made sanity.

And in the second place, when grievous maladies and afflictions have beset certain families by reason of some ancient sin,[2] madness has appeared amongst them, and breaking out into prophecy has secured E relief by finding the means thereto, namely by recourse to prayer and worship; and in consequence thereof rites and means of purification were established, and the sufferer[3] was brought out of danger, alike for the present and for the future. Thus did madness secure, for him that was maddened aright and possessed, deliverance from his troubles.

There is a third form of possession or madness, of which the Muses 245 are the source. This seizes a tender, virgin soul and stimulates it to rapt passionate expression, especially in lyric poetry, glorifying the countless mighty deeds of ancient times for the instruction of posterity. But if any man come to the gates of poetry without the madness of the Muses, persuaded that skill alone will make him a good poet, then shall he and his works of sanity with him be brought to naught by the poetry of madness, and behold, their place is nowhere to be found.

[1] Namely οἴομαι, νοῦς, and the first syllable of ἱστορία.

[2] Although there is probably a reminiscence here of Eur. *Phoen.* 934, Κάδμου παλαιῶν Ἄρεος ἐκ μηνιμάτων, the absence of a verb in the relative clause is hardly tolerable, and we should read either ποθὲν ⟨ἦν⟩ ἐν or ποθὲν ἐνῆν.

[3] The MSS. have τὸν ἑαυτῆς ἔχοντα, which is impossible. Burnet brackets ἑαυτῆς as a corruption of ἔξω ἄτης, a gloss on ἐξάντη. τὸν ἔχοντα will then have to mean 'the sufferer', τὸν τὴν νόσον ἔχοντα. This is hardly satisfactory, but the general sense is not in doubt. H. Richards proposed τὸν ⟨εὖ⟩ ἑαυτῆς ἔχοντα, which is not convincing.

B Such then is the tale, though I have not told it fully, of the achieve-
ments wrought by madness that comes from the gods. So let us have
no fears simply on that score; let us not be disturbed by an argument
that seeks to scare us into preferring the friendship of the sane to that
of the passionate. For there is something more that it must prove if it
is to carry the day, namely that love is not a thing sent from heaven for
the advantage both of lover and beloved. What we have to prove is the
C opposite, namely that this sort of madness is a gift of the gods, fraught
with the highest bliss. And our proof assuredly will prevail with the
wise, though not with the learned.

Now our first step towards attaining the truth of the matter is to
discern the nature of soul, divine and human, its experiences and its
activities. Here then our proof begins.

The idea of 'divine madness' or ἐνθουσιασμός is no Platonic
invention: it belongs in origin to the religion of Dionysus, which was
introduced into Greece many centuries before Plato's day; in literature
its most splendid embodiment is of course the *Bacchae* of Euripides.
Whether any previous philosopher, other than Democritus, had used
it is doubtful: M. Delatte[1] has detected it in Heraclitus and Empedocles,
but his arguments have not wholly convinced me; to Empedocles he
attributes the conception of an ἔνθεος ποιητής, and if we could
accept this it would be a most interesting anticipation of the third kind
of madness in our present section. But it seems impossible to deduce
this from the fragments of Empedocles themselves: indeed the chief
evidence for it is a sentence from a very late medical writer.[2] The
earliest use of the noun ἐνθουσιασμός is, as Delatte says, in a passage
of Democritus to be presently noticed.

The first form of divine madness here extolled is divination (μαντική).
This seems inconsistent with the low estimate of μαντική and μάντεις
that often appears in the dialogues (as also in many passages of
Euripides), e.g. at *Rep.* 364B where μάντεις are contemptuously
coupled with ἀγύρται ('begging-friars'), or in the *Euthyphro* where
the μάντις of that name is a stupid and conceited person; in the
Phaedrus itself the μαντικὸς βίος has only fifth place in the order of
merit of lives (248D). In all such passages, however, Plato is doubtless
thinking of a practice which was commonly called μαντική, but which
he here contrasts with μαντική and calls οἰωνιστική. The matter is

[1] In his monograph *Les Conceptions de l'Enthousiasme chez les philosophes
présocratiques* (1934).
[2] Caelius Aurelianus (fifth century A.D.) quoted in Diels-Kranz, *Vors.* 1
(31 A 98).

clearly and concisely explained by Jebb in his note on Soph. *O.T.* 708:
'In the Greek view the μάντις might be (1) the god himself speaking
through a divinely frenzied being in whom the human reason was
temporarily superseded... (2) a man who reads signs from birds, fire,
etc. by rule of mystic science: it was against this τέχνη that scepticism
most readily turned: Eur. *Electra* 399, Λοξίου γὰρ ἔμπεδοι | χρησμοί,
βροτῶν δὲ μαντικὴν χαίρειν λέγω.'[1]

In the *Timaeus* (71A–72B) divination by means of dreams and
visions is extolled, to all appearance quite seriously, as 'God's gift to
human folly', though the account involves a curiously fanciful theory
of the function of the liver. Plainly this refers to the first of the two
kinds of μαντική distinguished above, though it is said that the madness
or irrationality of the diviner is only sometimes, not always, due to
divine possession.[2]

With regard to the etymologies here, it is doubtless true that Plato
is sometimes serious, sometimes playful in this matter, and that
particularly in the *Cratylus* it is not always easy to be sure which he is.
Apparent absurdity is an unsafe criterion, for contemporary notions
about etymology were mostly absurd to our thinking. But in the
present case I believe that he has hinted playfulness clearly enough by
the word ἀπειροκάλως in the first case, and the phrase τῷ ω σεμνύνοντες
in the second. He cannot seriously have believed, or expected his
readers to believe, that the change of μανική into μαντική was due to
modern philistinism, or lack of a proper sense of values;[3] or again that
the long vowel in οἰωνιστική was due to pomposity. It may be
added that he was unlikely to have forgotten the existence of the word
οἰωνός, or the fact (noted by Thompson) that the word μάντις, so
far from being due to 'moderns', was used by Homer. If the παιδιά
needs justification, these 'etymologies' serve the purpose of fixing in
the reader's mind the point that augury is inferior to divination proper.[4]

The second type of θεία μανία is that which effects the care of
sickness by means of 'purifications and rites' discovered by, or rather
revealed to, the sufferer; the frenzy is conceived as at once the climax of
the malady and the source of healing. This is really a particular sort of
divination, as Socrates indicates by the words ἡ μανία...προφητεύσασα.

---

[1] cf. Rohde, *Psyche* (Engl. trans.), pp. 287–9, and W. K. C. Guthrie, *Orpheus
and Greek Religion*, p. 67. Plutarch (*de soll. animalium*, 975 A) says πολὺ καὶ
παμπάλαιον μαντικῆς μόριον οἰωνιστικὴ κέκληται, but the word is very rare, and doubtless the generic name was commonly used for both μόρια.

[2] οὐδεὶς γὰρ ἔννους ἐφάπτεται μαντικῆς ἐνθέου καὶ ἀληθοῦς, ἀλλ᾽ ἢ καθ᾽ ὕπνον τὴν τῆς
φρονήσεως πεδηθεὶς δύναμιν ἢ διὰ νόσον, ἢ διά τινα ἐνθουσιασμὸν παραλλάξας (*Tim.* 71 E).

[3] By ἀπειροκάλως I take him to mean that the 'moderns' failed to realise that
μανία might be καλόν.

[4] I should not have laboured this point but for Thompson's suggestion that
'the derivation of μαντική may have been seriously intended'.

It was specially associated with Orphism: cf. Aristophanes, *Frogs* 1033, where Aeschylus says Ὀρφεὺς μὲν γὰρ τελετάς θ' ἡμῖν κατέδειξε φόνων τ' ἀπέχεσθαι | Μουσαῖος δ' ἐξακέσεις τε νόσων καὶ χρησμούς, and the Scholiast *ad loc.* (quoted in Diels-Kranz, *Vors.* I, 21, 23) οὗτος δὲ παραλύσεις (? λύσεις) καὶ τελετὰς καὶ καθαρμοὺς συνέθηκεν. In the passage before us it is restricted to the special case of curing the 'maladies and afflictions' which arise from an inherited curse, such as that in the families of the Pelopidae or Labdacidae, and Plato may have in mind some well-known legend, possibly a modification of the Orestes story as known to us.

The third type is poetical inspiration. It was of course the traditional Greek belief that poets are inspired by Apollo or the Muses, but the assimilation of their condition to that of the Pythian priestess, of a Sibyl or a Cassandra with their delirious ravings, seems due to Plato himself, unless indeed he is borrowing from Democritus, who is quoted as saying 'all that a poet writes when possessed and divinely inspired is truly excellent'.[1] As E. E. Sikes writes,[2] 'Homer and Hesiod acknowledge inspiration, but neither poet would have cared to be thought ecstatic or "possessed" in the Pythian or Sibylline way. Their inspiration, it is true, came direct from heaven, but they sang "well and with understanding" and had full knowledge of what they sang.... So in later times Pindar might be a "prophet of the Muses" (*frag.* 90), but he was fully conscious of his message—not, as Plato was to argue, a medium for divine outpourings.'

This is not the first time that Plato has written on this theme. In the *Ion*, an early work, he has developed at some length the notion of a chain (ὁρμαθός) of inspiration descending from Muse through poet and rhapsode to audience; poet, interpreter and listener are all alike οὐκ ἔμφρονες, ἐνθουσιάζοντες, κατεχόμενοι: the poet is 'a light winged holy creature, who cannot compose until he becomes possessed (ἔνθεος) and out of his mind (ἔκφρων) and reason no longer dwells within him' (534B); of the rhapsode *qua* interpreter the phrase θεία μοῖρα, 'divine grace', is used: οὐ γὰρ τέχνῃ οὐδ' ἐπιστήμῃ περὶ Ὁμήρου λέγεις ἃ λέγεις, ἀλλὰ θείᾳ μοίρᾳ καὶ κατοκωχῇ (536C). In the *Meno* (98Bff.) the notion of θεία μοῖρα becomes prominent; it is the source both of the truths uttered by the poet and the soothsayer and of the successful

---

[1] *Frag.* 18 (Diels-Kranz); cf. also frag. 21 and Horace, *A.P.* 296: *excludit sanos Helicone poetas | Democritus.* Wilamowitz (*op. cit.* I, p. 483) is inclined to think that the two philosophers reached this view independently. But if we accept the words of *Apol.* 22B, ἔγνων οὖν αὖ καὶ περὶ τῶν ποιητῶν ἐν ὀλίγῳ τοῦτο, ὅτι οὐ σοφίᾳ ποιοῖεν ἃ ποιοῖεν, ἀλλὰ φύσει τινὶ καὶ ἐνθουσιάζοντες ὥσπερ οἱ θεομάντεις καὶ οἱ χρησμῳδοί, or their substance, as coming from Socrates himself, it may be that he is the common source of Democritus and Plato. (For Democritus's knowledge of Socrates see Diog. Laert. IX, 36).

[2] *The Greek View of Poetry*, p. 20.

acts of good statesmen, whose goodness however rests on true opinion, not on knowledge.

In both these dialogues the negative aspect of ἐνθουσιασμός (or, as the *Phaedrus* calls it, of θεία μανία) is emphasised, the fact that it is not knowledge (ἐπιστήμη) but excludes knowledge. The same is true of the brief reference in the *Apology* (22 B–C) where Socrates finds that poets οὐ σοφίᾳ ποιοῖεν ἃ ποιοῖεν ἀλλὰ φύσει τινὶ καὶ ἐνθουσιάζοντες ὥσπερ οἱ θεομάντεις καὶ οἱ χρησμῳδοί. It is in the *Phaedrus* alone that we find unqualified commendation of the poet's μανία, commendation which almost goes to the length of saying that the inspired poet is all the better for his lack of knowledge.

I should be inclined to explain this feature of our present section by the fact, which is universally recognised, that Plato himself is a compound of rationalist and poet, and that whereas in the other dialogues mentioned above his estimate of poets and poetry reflects both elements of the compound in fairly equal degrees, in the *Phaedrus* the poet definitely gets the upper hand. It must be remembered that the motif of inspiration does not make its first appearance in the present section; on the contrary, Plato has been gradually bringing it more and more into the foreground ever since Socrates and Phaedrus reached their resting-place beside the river. It is clear that Plato is in this dialogue quite exceptionally[1] conscious of the value of the imaginative, as against the rational, power of the human soul; and that consciousness finds expression both in the 'inspired' Socrates himself and in his exaltation of inspired divination and poetry.

Every reader of the *Republic* will have been struck by the contrast between the severely critical attitude towards poetry there adopted, terminating in the exclusion of everything except hymns to the gods and praises of good men (607 A), and our present passage. The *Republic* has not a word to say of poetical 'possession', although earlier works, *Apology*, *Ion* and *Meno*, had recognised it. That is perhaps because Plato did not clearly see how to reconcile the appearance in one and the same poet of πολλὰ καὶ καλά, due to ἐνθουσιασμός, and of πολλὰ καὶ αἰσχρά. This is indeed a question to which he never gives a clear answer, and one on which commentators are for the most part strangely silent.[2] Perhaps we should be content to believe that he always thought of inspiration as a matter of degree, so that there would be no hard and fast distinction between the inspired poet and the uninspired; this would indeed be difficult to reconcile with a literal acceptance of

---

[1] cf. Wilamowitz I, p. 459: 'So etwas hatte er nie zuvor geäussert; er wird es auch nie wieder tun, weil er nie wieder so fühlen wird.'

[2] It is indeed faced by Prof. J. Tate in *C.Q.* XXIII (1929), but I cannot feel satisfied with his suggestion (p. 148) that 'the inspired poet when wrong has the symptoms of inspiration without the reality'.

ἐνθουσιασμός—we can hardly think of the deity constantly flashing in and out; but in any case such literal interpretation can hardly be insisted upon: Plato's indwelling deities are not the Stoics' air-currents.

However this may be, it should be realised that our passage does not imply indiscriminate admiration of all poetry; indeed the words 'glorifying the countless mighty deeds of ancient times for the instruction of posterity' confine that admiration to the second type of admissible poetry mentioned at *Rep.* 607A. The poet who is ἔνθεος is, it would seem, the instrument of a divine παιδεία.

The proof that love is a fourth type of θεία μανία will, says Socrates, be δεινοῖς μὲν ἄπιστος, σοφοῖς δὲ πιστή (245 c). By δεινοῖς Hermeias thinks he means Eristics; more probably he means all those who hold materialist and mechanist views of the universe and man, for to them the things of the supra-celestial region, and the soul's vision thereof—in fact the whole substance of the μυθικὸς ὕμνος (265 c) soon to be sung—will be as foolishness. The σοφοί are all those who recognise an immaterial reality, in other words Platonists and some fellow-Socratics and Pythagoreans.

Already in his first speech Socrates had recognised that love could only be explained by reference to the nature of the soul, and had spoken of its two alternative ruling principles, ἔμφυτος ἐπιθυμία and ἐπίκτητος δόξα (237D). Lysias's speaker had of course felt no such explanation necessary. That divine as well as human soul must be taken into account (245 c) would be obvious to the σοφοί, and is no surprise to readers who know the *Phaedo* with its doctrine of the liberation of the human soul and the restoration of its divine nature.[1]

---

[1] See especially *Phaedo* 80B, τῷ μεν θείῳ καὶ ἀθανάτῳ...ὁμοιότατον (συμβαίνει) εἶναι ψυχή, and the whole passage down to 80E 7.

VIII

245 C–246 A THE IMMORTALITY OF SOUL

The immortality of 'all Soul' (ψυχὴ πᾶσα) is established by consideration of its function of moving itself and also being the principle of movement (ἀρχὴ κινήσεως) for all bodies. Soul is both ungenerated and indestructible.

All soul is immortal; for that which is ever in motion is immortal. 245 C But that which while imparting motion is itself moved by something else can cease to be in motion, and therefore can cease to live; it is only that which moves itself that never intermits its motion, inasmuch as it cannot abandon its own nature; moreover this self-mover is the source and first principle of motion for all other things that are moved. Now a first principle cannot come into being: for while anything that comes D to be must come to be from a first principle, the latter itself cannot come to be from anything whatsoever: if it did, it would cease any longer to be a first principle.[1] Furthermore, since it does not come into being, it must be imperishable: for assuredly if a first principle were to be destroyed, nothing could come to be out of it, nor could anything bring the principle itself back into existence, seeing that a first principle is needed for anything to come into being.

The self-mover, then, is the first principle of motion: and it is as impossible that it should be destroyed as that it should come into being: were it otherwise, the whole universe, the whole of that which comes to be,[2] would collapse into immobility, and never find another E source of motion to bring it back into being.

And now that we have seen that that which is moved by itself is immortal, we shall feel no scruple in affirming that precisely that is the essence and definition of soul, to wit self-motion. Any body that has an external source of motion is soulless; but a body deriving its

---

[1] I retain Burnet's reading (after Buttmann) οὐκ ἂν ἔτι ἀρχὴ γίγνοιτο, which is presumably what Cicero (*Tusc.* I, 54) had before him in translating *nec enim esset id principium quod gigneretur aliunde.* The other reading, οὐκ ἂν ἐξ ἀρχῆς γίγνοιτο (*B, T,* Simplicius, Stobaeus), seems to me impossible: the thing in question (τὸ γιγνόμενον) would still come into being from *an* ἀρχή, though not from what would otherwise have been its ἀρχή.

[2] I retain the γένεσιν of the MSS. and Hermeias in E 1, taking it as equivalent to τὰ γιγνόμενα. For οὐρανός=*universe,* cf. *Tim.* 28 B, 92 C; and for the collocation of οὐρανός and γένεσις cf. *Tim.* 29 E, γενέσεως καὶ κόσμου ἀρχήν.

motion from a source within itself is animate or *besouled*, which implies that the nature of soul is what has been said.

And if this last assertion is correct, namely that 'that which moves 246 itself' is precisely identifiable with soul, it must follow that soul is not born and does not die.

At the end of the last section Socrates said 'Here then our proof begins'; and it is with proof, ἀπόδειξις, that he does begin; though he will continue with something else, namely Platonic myth. The immortality of soul is established by an argument which, though not in dialogue, is essentially dialectical,[1] and regarded by Plato as incontrovertible; but the mode of its existence whether incarnate or discarnate can only be told in terms of myth, in figures and allegories and imaginative descriptions; as Socrates says at the opening of our next section, he cannot tell what attributes the soul has (οἷον ἔστι), but only what it resembles (ᾧ ἔοικε, 246A).

What is the precise meaning of ψυχὴ πᾶσα in the first sentence, ψυχὴ πᾶσα ἀθάνατος? Scholars both ancient and modern are divided between 'all soul' and 'every soul'. Frutiger, who has examined the question at some length[2] and has rightly observed that an examination of the usage of πᾶς with and without the article leads us nowhere, decides in favour of the second or distributive meaning; but his decision is largely due to the facts (1) that he wishes to use the present section to rebut those who deny that Plato seriously believed in the immortality of the individual soul, and (2) that at 246B the phrase recurs with the article (πᾶσα ἡ ψυχή in the manuscript *B*, ἡ ψυχὴ πᾶσα in *T*), and the collective sense there is obvious. But, apart from the fact that the reading in the latter passage is rendered doubtful by the varying position of the article, and by its absence from Oxy. Papyrus 1017 and from the citation by Simplicius, it results from Frutiger's own examination of linguistic usage that Plato might have varied his expression without intending two different meanings. My own belief is that the distinction between collective and distributive senses is not here before his mind, any more than it need be in the case of πᾶν σῶμα at 245 E 4, where either sense is equally appropriate.[3] It is true that the argument of our present section cannot be regarded as a direct argument for the immortality of individual souls; but it is reasonable to believe—and indeed, since it is the individual soul that Socrates will be concerned with in the myth, we cannot avoid believing—that Plato

---

[1] For 'dialectic' not in dialogue see Frutiger, *Mythes de Platon*, pp. 24–6.
[2] *op. cit.* pp. 130–4.
[3] But in translating the distinction must be made, and I have accordingly rendered ψυχὴ πᾶσα ἀθάνατος by 'all soul is immortal', because the collective sense is that primarily demanded by the logic of the argument.

regarded any demonstration of the immortality of 'soul' in general as applicable to individual souls. His position seems to be well stated by R. K. Gaye:[1] 'So far as personal immortality is concerned it [sc. our present section] supplies at most a negative argument; that is to say, it creates a certain presumption in favour of personal immortality in so far as it tends to invalidate the popular view of the finality of death. There is certainly a sense in which the soul survives the death of the individual ἔμψυχον, but whether this soul continues to exist as a conscious personality is of course a different question, and there is nothing in the proof of immortality which we have been considering that can be said to furnish a direct argument in favour of it....From whatever source he may have derived his justification for believing in personal immortality, there can be no doubt that he did believe in it, and moreover that he considered the proof that "all soul is immortal" to give some support to the belief.'

Before we examine the argument further it is necessary to defend the reading ἀεικίνητον in the next sentence, 'for that which is ever in motion is immortal'. I submit that the reading of the papyrus (Oxy. 1017), αὐτοκίνητον, though accepted by Robin, cannot outweigh the argument from the logic of the passage as a whole. What we require in this second sentence is the statement of an axiom or, if the term be preferred, an ἔνδοξον, by way of major premiss. Now τὸ αὐτοκίνητον ἀθάνατον is not an ἔνδοξον, nor is it so regarded by Socrates; if it were, he would not need to establish the point that τὸ αὐτὸ κινοῦν οὔποτε λήγει κινούμενον as he does, partly by the words ἅτε οὐκ ἀπολεῖπον ἑαυτό, partly by the identification of τὸ αὐτὸ κινοῦν with ἀρχὴ κινήσεως and the corollaries drawn from that identification.[2]

Taking then as our premiss τὸ ἀεικίνητον ἀθάνατον[3] we ask 'Then

---

[1] *The Platonic Conception of Immortality*, p. 39. I have omitted one sentence, in which Gaye says that Plato must have known that he could never prove individual immortality. From this I dissent. I believe that both in *Rep.* x and *Phaedo* he thinks he has proved it; in *Phaedo* particularly the repeated use of ἀποδεικνύναι, λόγον διδόναι and the like (see Frutiger, p. 136), taken together with Socrates's emphatic conclusion at 106E, παντὸς μᾶλλον ψυχὴ ἀθάνατον καὶ ἀνώλεθρον καὶ τῷ ὄντι ἔσονται ἡμῶν αἱ ψυχαὶ ἐν Ἅιδου, seems conclusive, despite Socrates's encouragement of 'honest doubt' at 107B. The final argument of *Phaedo*, no less than *Phaedrus*, appears however to regard personal immortality as a corollary of the immortality of 'soul'.

[2] Skemp (*The Theory of Motion in Plato's Later Dialogues*, p. 3) argues that the sentence τὸ δ' ἄλλο...ζωῆς would be otiose with the reading αὐτοκίνητον. If that means merely that we could do without it, I agree; but I cannot see that it would not be a natural expansion of τὸ αὐτοκίνητον ἀθάνατον by way of antithesis. Robin seems to me to mistake the logic of the section in his note on p. lxxvii.

[3] If Plato had our terminology, he would probably call it an analytic proposition. Deathlessness is implied by eternal movement as a contained notion, and vice versa.

what is ἀεικίνητον;' and discover the answer by means of a dichotomy of τὸ κινητόν. Let us for convenience use the symbols A and B
to denote this dichotomy, A being τὸ ὑπ' ἄλλου κινούμενον, B τὸ
αὐτὸ κινοῦν (τὸ ὑφ' ἑαυτοῦ κινούμενον). Now since A's motion depends on B continuing to move it, and there is no certainty that B
will so continue, A is susceptible of the cessation of movement, and
therefore (if it is a ζῷον) of the cessation of life. But in the case of B
there is nothing to arrest its self-originated and self-maintained motion;
it is in fact part of the notion or essence of B to move itself: to cease
to do so would be ἀπολείπειν ἑαυτό, to abandon its own nature,
which is inconceivable.[1]

Hence when we reach the words οὔποτε λήγει κινούμενον we have
answered the question 'What is ἀεικίνητον;' and nothing more is
needed save to show that ψυχή can properly be substituted for τὸ
ὑφ' ἑαυτοῦ κινούμενον. In other words we might have expected
Socrates to say now what he says at E 2, ἀθανάτου δὲ πεφασμένου τοῦ
ὑφ' ἑαυτοῦ κινουμένου, ψυχῆς οὐσίαν τε καὶ λόγον τοῦτον αὐτόν τις
λέγων οὐκ αἰσχυνεῖται. Instead of this Plato has thought well to
strengthen the argument by considering τὸ αὐτὸ κινοῦν in its aspect
as ἀρχὴ κινήσεως τοῖς ἄλλοις.

What then is the substance of this further argument? It may be
stated briefly: an ἀρχὴ κινήσεως can have neither γένεσις nor φθορά,
it cannot (a) come into being nor (b) pass out of being; for (a) is
a self-contradictory notion, and if (b) were possible there would be an
end of all things, since *ex hypothesi* there is no other ἀρχή from which
either itself or the things whose motion depends on it could be reborn.
In other words, as Socrates forcefully puts it, the whole universe and
all that comes into being would crash into everlasting annihilation. This
last part of the argument—the demonstration that the ἀρχὴ κινήσεως
is ἀδιάφθορον—clearly rests on an assumption, but when we realise
precisely what the assumption is, we may readily understand that
Plato regards it as legitimate. What he assumes to be inconceivable is
not that this universe may cease to be,[2] but that all γένεσις—all
things that could make up any possible universe—might cease to be:
in other words that there should be absolutely nothing at all.[3] That

---

[1] It is implied that for B to cease moving A would not be ἀπολείπειν ἑαυτό.
I do not see how it can be denied that this is arbitrary, but without it the argument
fails.

[2] That indeed is not inconceivable, though in fact it will never happen. In
Timaeus (41 A) we learn that the created gods (the heavenly bodies) are everlasting
because a good creator will not undo his own handiwork, but they are not
intrinsically eternal as the Forms are; τὸ δεθὲν πᾶν λυτόν.

[3] If it be asked, would not the eternal Forms still exist in the absence of all
γιγνόμενα, I think it a sufficient answer to say that Plato would have deemed this
an idle question. As to the phrase πάντα τε οὐρανὸν πᾶσάν τε γένεσιν, it seems

was a possibility never contemplated by any Greek thinker: even the atomists, who held that this *moles et machina mundi* would one day be given over to ruin, believed that there are innumerable other *mundi* to outlast it.

The secondary argument thus concluded, Socrates declares that this self-moved entity is nothing other than soul: in fact to speak of it in those terms is to state the essence of soul. For this he simply appeals to language: we use the word ἔμψυχον to describe anything whose source of motion is within itself; that implies that the nature of ψυχή is self-motion.

Lastly we should note that, on the strength of the secondary argument, it is asserted in the final sentence that soul is not only ἀθάνατος but also ἀγένητος. That soul is ungenerated has not been explicitly asserted by Plato before; it may however be deduced from the statement that the human soul has been in possession of knowledge 'for all time' (τὸν ἀεὶ χρόνον, *Meno* 86A), and from its affinity to the eternal Forms (*Phaedo* 79Bff.). Usually he is content with asserting the priority of the human soul to its body, or to its union with the body;[1] and this is all that is formally deduced from the ἀνάμνησις doctrine in the *Phaedo*. In the *Timaeus* the account of the creation of the World-Soul follows that of the creation of the body of the universe, but we are expressly told that the soul is in fact 'earlier and older in becoming and in excellence' (34C). The words γενέσει προτέραν must however be interpreted in accordance with the general scheme of the creation myth, in which an analysis of factors in the universe is presented in the guise of a cosmogony: both soul and body of the universe are in fact everlasting. In *Laws* X (891–899) the Athenian frequently uses γίγνεσθαι and γένεσις[2] in speaking of soul: and this may surprise us, more especially as the doctrine of self-moving soul is there repeated and indeed expanded, and we might therefore have expected its ungenerated nature to be reasserted. The explanation probably is that, since the Athenian's purpose is to confute the atheistic materialists who make body prior in origin to soul, he adopts their temporal category and confines himself to demonstrating the reverse priority.[3]

---

to be another instance of ambiguous πᾶς. It may mean either 'any and every universe and any and every sort of Becoming' or 'the whole universe and the whole of Becoming'. But translation and comment have to adopt one or other rendering of an ambiguous expression. As to the reading, γένεσιν should not be replaced, as in Burnet's text, by Philoponus's γῆν εἰς ἕν.

[1] e.g. *Phaedo* 87A: ὅτι μὲν γὰρ ἦν ἡμῶν ἡ ψυχὴ καὶ πρὶν εἰς τόδε τὸ εἶδος ἐλθεῖν, οὐκ ἀνατίθεμαι μὴ οὐχὶ πάνυ χαριέντως καὶ...πάνυ ἱκανῶς ἀποδεδεῖχθαι.

[2] In the recapitulatory passage of *Laws* XII (967D) the word γονή is used.

[3] In an article on 'Plato's Theism' in *C.Q.* XXX (1936) I offered a different explanation of the puzzling passages in the *Laws*. I now believe that to have been wrong, though I think the main conclusions of my paper may stand without it.

The whole argument owes something to Alcmaeon, a younger contemporary of Pythagoras, as is commonly recognised; but the all-important distinction between what is self-moved and what is moved by something else was not, so far as we know, drawn by Alcmaeon, and there is no reason to doubt that it is Plato's own distinction, or rather that he was the first to make any philosophical use of a distinction obvious to common sense and reflected, as Socrates notes (245 E), in common parlance. Prof. Taylor however writes:[1] 'It would be rash to say that its introduction [viz. the introduction of the present argument] shows that we are dealing with a post-Socratic development of Plato's own thought, since in principle the argument is that of Alcmaeon of Crotona, that the soul is immortal because it "is like immortal things, and is like them in the point that it is always in motion" (Arist. de anima 405 A 30).' Here the vagueness of the safe-guarding words 'in principle' tends to obscure the importance of Plato's development of Alcmaeon's dictum. What Alcmaeon may be taken to have suggested to Plato is his first step, the premiss τὸ ἀεικίνητον ἀθάνατον, in other words his approach to the question of soul's immortality by way of the category of κίνησις.

It has also been rightly observed[2] that there is a close connexion between the *Phaedrus* proof of immortality and the final argument of the *Phaedo*. Reduced to its essentials, that argument is that soul necessarily and always participates in the Form of life and therefore cannot admit death. Stripped of the terminology of the Ideal theory, this amounts to saying that the notion of life is bound up with the notion of soul, and what it really yields is not (as Socrates maintains) the conclusion that soul is immortal but the tautological proposition that so long as soul exists it is alive. What the *Phaedrus* does is to remould an argument about the relations of words and concepts into one based on observed physical fact, the fact namely of κίνησις. Life, it argues, is bound up with soul because the observed processes or movements which constitute life can only be accounted for by the postulate of a self-moving soul, and the eternity of that self-moving soul is the necessary presupposition of all physical existence. Although it would be too much to say that the *Phaedrus* provides an empirical metamorphosis of the *Phaedo*'s metaphysical or 'rationalist' argument, yet it is rooted, as the other is not, in empirical fact, and that is why Aristotle, whose thought has far more kinship with empiricism than Plato's normally has, is so largely indebted to our present argument for his doctrine of an eternal—albeit unmoved—First Mover.

[1] *Plato, the Man and his Work*, p. 306.
[2] Frutiger, p. 138 n. 1; Skemp, pp. 5–10; J. B. Bury in *Journal of Philology*, xv (1886).

IX

246A–247C MYTH OF THE SOUL. THE CHARIOTEER AND
TWO HORSES. THE PROCESSION OF SOULS

The nature of the Soul must be described in a myth. We may compare it to a winged charioteer driving a team of winged horses. Now the horses belonging to the souls of gods are all good, but a human soul has one good horse and one evil. So long as its wings are undamaged, the soul travels through the heavens; but some souls lose their wings, fall to earth and take to themselves earthly bodies. There follows a vivid picture of the procession of souls, headed by Zeus, to the rim of heaven, and of the difficulty experienced by the human souls in following the divine. The latter finally pass outside the heaven and stand upon its back, contemplating the sights beyond as they are carried round by its revolution.

As to soul's immortality then we have said enough, but as to its 246A nature there is this that must be said: what manner of thing it is would be a long tale to tell, and most assuredly a god alone could tell it; but what it resembles, that a man might tell in briefer compass: let this therefore be our manner of discourse. Let it be likened to the union of powers in a team of winged steeds and their winged charioteer.[1] Now all the gods' steeds and all their charioteers are good, and of good stock;[2] but with other beings it is not wholly so. With us men, in the B first place, it is a pair[3] of steeds that the charioteer controls; moreover one of them is noble and good, and of good stock, while the other has the opposite character, and his stock is opposite. Hence the task of our charioteer is difficult and troublesome.

[1] That ὑποπτέρου belongs to ἡνιόχου as well as to ζεύγους follows from 251B7, πᾶσα γὰρ ἦν τὸ πάλαι πτερωτή.

[2] The expression ἀγαθοὶ καὶ ἐξ ἀγαθῶν recurs at 274A, where it is used of the gods themselves and can hardly bear the literal meaning which I take it to have here. From the use of πονηρὸς κἀκ πονηρῶν (Ar. *Frogs* 731, *Knights* 337), we may probably infer that the phrase became stereotyped, and often meant no more than 'wholly good'.

[3] It seems to be generally assumed by commentators that ζεύγους in A7 means a *pair* of horses; but the word often means a larger number (see *Apol.* 36D and Burnet's note, and cf. Aesch. *frag.* 346 (Nauck), ζεῦγος τέθριππον). Plato, while definitely affirming triplicity in the souls destined to inhabit human bodies, deliberately leaves vague the number of 'parts' of soul in general, and of the gods' souls. Robin's assertion (p. lxxx) that συνωρίς means 'un attelage dont les chevaux sont couplés mais ne sont pas identiques' is supported by no evidence, and seems incompatible with τέκνων ξυνωρίδα (used of Medea's children) at Eur. *Medea* 1145; it evidently springs from the erroneous assumption about ζεῦγος.

And now we must essay to tell how it is that living beings are called
mortal and immortal. All soul has the care of all that is inanimate, and
traverses the whole universe, though in ever-changing forms. Thus
c when it is perfect and winged it journeys on high and controls the
whole world; but one that has shed its wings sinks down until it can
fasten on something solid, and settling there it takes to itself an earthy
body which seems by reason of the soul's power to move itself. This
composite structure of soul and body is called a living being, and is
further termed 'mortal': 'immortal' is a term applied on no basis of
reasoned argument at all, but our fancy pictures the god whom we have
D never seen, nor fully conceived, as an immortal living being, possessed
of a soul and a body united for all time.[1] Howbeit let these matters,
and our account thereof, be as god pleases; what we must understand
is the reason why the soul's wings fall from it, and are lost. It is on this
wise.

The natural property of a wing is to raise that which is heavy and
carry it aloft to the region where the gods dwell; and more than any
E other bodily part it shares in the divine nature, which is fair, wise and
good, and possessed of all other such excellences. Now by these
excellences especially is the soul's plumage nourished and fostered,
while by their opposites, even by ugliness and evil, it is wasted and
destroyed. And behold,[2] there in the heaven Zeus, mighty leader,
drives his winged team:[3] first of the host of gods and daemons he
proceeds, ordering all things and caring therefor: and the host follows
247 after him, marshalled in eleven companies. For Hestia abides alone in
the gods' dwelling-place; but for the rest, all such as are ranked in the
number of the twelve as ruler gods lead their several companies, each
according to his rank.

Now within the heavens are many spectacles of bliss upon the
highways[4] whereon the blessed gods pass to and fro, each doing his
own work; and with them are all such as will and can follow them: for
jealousy has no place in the choir divine. But at such times as they go

---

[1] ἀθάνατον in c 6 stands for ζῷον (nominative) ἀθάνατον ἔσχεν ἐπωνυμίαν.
The meaning is that the ζῷα to whom we commonly apply the epithet
ἀθάνατα, the anthropomorphic gods of Homer, are the creations of fancy.
Whether there are or are not immortal beings composite of soul and body is for
the present left open.

[2] This abrupt transition to the account of the celestial procession is arresting,
and doubtless intentional.

[3] For this meaning of ἅρμα cf. Eur. H.F. 881, ἅρμασιν ἐνδίδωσι κέντρον.

[4] I take θέαι τε καὶ διέξοδοι as a hendiadys.

to their feasting and banquet, behold they climb the steep ascent even unto the summit of the arch that supports the heavens; and easy is that B ascent for the chariots of the gods, for that they are well-balanced and readily guided; but for the others it is hard, by reason of the heaviness of the steed of wickedness, which pulls down his driver with his weight, except that driver have schooled him well.

And now there awaits the soul the extreme of her toil and struggling. For the souls that are called immortal, so soon as they are at the summit, come forth and stand upon the back of the world: and straightway the revolving heaven carries them round, and they[1] look upon the regions C without.

It will be convenient, before commenting on the general purport of this section, to call attention to the assertions that soul 'cares for' (ἐπιμελεῖσθαι) the inanimate (246B) and that Zeus, heading the procession of souls, orders and 'cares for' all things (246E); for these are noteworthy as being the earliest intimation of the central doctrine of Plato's theology, a doctrine common to the myth of the *Timaeus* and the rational exposition of *Laws* x. In the latter work the priority of soul to body is either indistinguishable from or immediately involves its control of body (892A, 896C); this control is however not in all cases intelligent and providential, for a distinction is drawn between beneficent soul and maleficent (896E), or between ψυχὴ νοῦν προσλαβοῦσα and ψυχὴ ἀνοίᾳ ξυγγενομένη (897B). The speaker is vague as to the precise scope and effects of the latter, but clearly it has the same significance as the 'Necessity' of the *Timaeus*, which is for the most part persuaded and ruled by Reason (48A): it is in fact the principle of cosmic imperfection or evil. It is, however, the 'best' soul that controls the great cosmic movements, 'the whole course and motion of the heavens' (897C) and 'cares for the whole universe' (δῆλον ὡς τὴν ἀρίστην ψυχὴν φατέον ἐπιμελεῖσθαι τοῦ κόσμου παντός, *ibid.*). Whether Plato means a single 'best soul' or the best kind of soul need not be discussed here; in either case ψυχὴ νοῦν προσλαβοῦσα, or the νοῦς βασιλεὺς οὐρανοῦ τε καὶ γῆς[2]—and these are virtually identical, since νοῦς must always come to be 'in a soul' (*Phil.* 30C, *Tim.* 30B)—is Plato's God in the truest sense of that word—the sense in which it is used in all theistic systems, though the word θεός is used by him of other divine beings also, including the visible universe.

---

[1] αἱ δέ refers to the same souls as αὐτάς, and is not in antithesis to αἱ μέν two lines above. This αἱ μέν is not answered until we reach αἱ δὲ ἄλλαι ψυχαί at 248A 1, for Socrates breaks off into a long description of the ὑπερουράνιος τόπος and the θεῶν βίος.   [2] *Phil.* 28C.

Here in the *Phaedrus* we have only a passing allusion to the theology to be afterwards developed; we have no hint of any irrational or maleficent world-soul. The words ψυχὴ πᾶσα παντὸς ἐπιμελεῖται τοῦ ἀψύχου, πάντα δὲ οὐρανὸν περιπολεῖ do not indeed definitely preclude such a conception, but neither do they suggest it; while the ἐπιμέλεια exercised by Zeus is plainly a beneficent rational providence.

The words with which Socrates introduces his myth of the soul make it clear that the myth will be in part an allegory, that is to say a description in symbolic terms which can be readily translated into what they stand for.[1] It is of course obvious that the charioteer with his two horses symbolises the tripartite soul familiar to us from *Rep.* IV, the soul composite of a reflective or calculative part (λογιστικόν), a 'spirited' or passionate (θυμοειδές), and an appetitive (ἐπιθυμητικόν). But there is much in the present section and in the pages which follow that cannot be so translated, and that Plato does not intend to be translated; for the most part the myth is the vision of a poet whose images are not disguised doctrine but spring from a non-rational intuition: the reader must therefore allow his rational and critical faculty to be suspended as he reads, seeking to feel with the poet rather than 'understand' him and turn his poetry into prose.[2]

This warning is especially needed in respect of the present section, with its majestic picture of the procession of souls. We are not to look here for astronomical doctrine allegorically expressed; it is true that there is an astral or astronomical element, but it is impossible to analyse into religious (or theological) and scientific components what the myth has fused into a whole. The twelve gods are undoubtedly those familiar to every Athenian from the altar set up in the Agora by

---

[1] It is obvious that Plato's myths are not all of one kind. Probably the most helpful classification is that of Frutiger into *allegorical, genetic* and *parascientific* (p. 180). He recognises indeed that this must not be applied rigidly: 'Each has a dominant character which justifies its being assigned to a definite class, but they often trench on other classes in this or that particular' (p. 181). Of the third class, to which he assigns our present myth, he writes: 'To complete the results of λόγος, to extend them beyond the limits of pure reason, to take the place, by way of δεύτερος πλοῦς, of dialectic when it comes up against some impenetrable mystery —that is the function of those myths which, for want of a better epithet, we have called parascientific' (p. 223). I would agree that our myth belongs to this class, with the reservation (which Frutiger would doubtless accept) that it contains a large measure of allegory.

[2] From the standpoint of the rationalist, when he looks back on the myth, it is all παιδιά, 'playfulness' (265 c). Cf. Cornford, *Plato's Cosmology*, p. 32, on the myth of the *Timaeus*: 'There remains an irreducible element of poetry, which refuses to be translated into the language of scientific prose.' The *Timaeus* however gradually sheds its mythical character, and sets forth undisguised doctrine in physics and physiology: the *Phaedrus* myth is mythical to the end, and yet (as we shall see) is interrupted by occasional 'parentheses' of rational doctrine such as that at 249 B–C.

the younger Pisistratus towards the end of the sixth century,[1] and from the east frieze of the Parthenon.[2] Zeus and Hestia are mentioned here, and later (252C–253B) we hear of Ares, Hera and Apollo. But save for the mention of their going to feast (247A 8; cf. *Iliad* I, 423) there is little or nothing left of Homeric anthropomorphism; the all too human gods have become stars, or rather astral souls, fulfilling each its appointed function in an ordered universe, passing along heaven's highways.[3] The myth, however, permits a confusion between the whole soul and its controlling part, so that Zeus is represented as the driver of his winged car.

The astral element in Plato's religion will become prominent in his latest works, *Timaeus*, *Laws*, and the doubtfully genuine *Epinomis*; but it was already implicit in such casual allusions as that of *Rep.* 508A (τῶν ἐν οὐρανῷ θεῶν), and for that matter every Greek thought of the heavenly bodies as divine, though they did not figure in official cults, as the *Epinomis* (988A) recommends that they should. The semi-metamorphosis of Homer's gods into star-souls is therefore natural enough. What of the distinction of Hestia from the other eleven? Its purpose, I should say, is simply to bring more vividly before the mind's eye the picture of the starry heaven revolving round a fixed central body, the earth. How early the goddess of the central hearth came to be thought of as residing at, or as being, the centre of the universe it is impossible to say; but every contemporary reader of our passage, whether or not he knew anything of Pythagoreanism, would at once seize the point of Hestia abiding alone in the house of the gods while the others went on their journey.[4]

It has been too readily assumed, both in ancient and modern times, that the relation of Hestia to the rest necessarily implies some astronomical scheme or planetary system into which the number eleven (or twelve) can be fitted. To my mind there is no such necessity: the mention of Hestia is not significant of anything beyond what I have suggested above. However that be, the only two systems which, so far as I know, have been proposed are both impossible.

The first identifies Hestia not with a central earth, but with the central fire of a Pythagorean cosmology well known to us from Aristotle (*de caelo* 293A 18ff.) and attributed by Stobaeus (*Ecl.* I, 22) and Aetius to

[1] Thuc. VI, 54.
[2] On which, however, Hestia was replaced by Dionysus (Weinreich in Roscher's *Lexicon der gr. und röm. Mythologie s.v.* 'Zwölfgötter', p. 823; Guthrie, *The Greeks and their Gods*, p. 111).
[3] διέξοδοι, a word commonly used for the orbits of heavenly bodies.
[4] The earliest literary allusion to the 'centrality' of Hestia (who is not a goddess in Homer himself) is in *Homeric Hymn* (v) *to Aphrodite*, l. 30: καί τε μέσῳ οἴκῳ κατ' ἄρ' ἕζετο, πῖαρ ἑλοῦσα. For Hestia as the earth, cf. Eur. *frag.* 944N: καὶ Γαῖα μῆτερ· Ἑστίαν δέ σ' οἱ σοφοὶ | βροτῶν καλοῦσιν ἡμένην ἐν αἰθέρι and Soph. *frag.* 558N.

Philolaus; but more than a century ago it was pointed out by H. Martin[1] that the total number of bodies in this system was not eleven, but ten; moreover it is improbable, as H. von Arnim remarks,[2] that earth, moon and sun (and, one might add, the counter-earth postulated in this system) should be represented as leaders of hosts of star-souls.

The other view is that given by Robin in his note on 247 A. This goes back at least to the commentary of Chalcidius (fourth century A.D.) on the *Timaeus*,[3] though Robin does not mention him. The number 12 is made up of the sphere of the fixed stars, the seven known planets (including sun and moon), three regions or zones of aether, air and water, and the earth. The three zones intermediate between moon and earth evidently come from *Epinomis* 984 B ff., where however nothing is said of any ἄρχοντες of the daemons inhabiting them, though this is essential to Chalcidius's interpretation.

To this, as to the former theory, it seems an insuperable objection that the planets of Greek astronomy did not have hosts of satellites.

As against these planetary interpretations, some scholars have seen here an allusion to the twelve signs of the Zodiac, or rather to the twelve deities guarding[4] or inhabiting them. It is possible—though I am incompetent to judge of this—that the connexion between groups of twelve gods, which are found in many other countries besides Greece, and the signs is very ancient; in any case it seems established that the famous astronomer and geographer Eudoxus, whom Plato may have known as early as the date of the *Phaedrus*, identified these deities with the twelve Olympians; and there is perhaps a trace of this in the proposal at *Laws* 828 C to make each month sacred to one of the twelve.[5] The suggestion is bound up with a theory that Plato was influenced by Chaldaean astrological beliefs, chiefly through the medium of Eudoxus. So far as any astrological ideas can be detected in the *Phaedrus* itself, they seem confined to the passage 252 C–253 B, which however seems to me explicable without them.[6]

[1] *Etudes sur le Timée* II, p. 114. I owe this reference to Prof. J. B. Skemp (*The Theory of Motion in Plato's Later Dialogues*, p. 72) who follows Martin in rejecting the identification. [2] *Platons Jugenddialoge*, p. 184.

[3] p. 227f. Wrobel: 'Volucris uero currus imperatoris dei aplanes intellegenda est, quia et prima est ordine et agilior ceteris omnibus motibus, sicut ostensum est. Undecim uero partes exercitus dinumerat hactenus: primam aplanem, deinde septem planetum, nonam aetheris sedem, quam incolunt aetherii daemones, decimam aëriam, undecimam umectae substantiae, duodecimam terram, quae inmobilis ex conuersione mundi manet.'

[4] cf. Manilius, *Astron.* II, 434: 'noscere tutelas adiectaque numina signis.'

[5] But it is difficult, as von Arnim (*loc. cit.*) notes, to fit into this interpretation the remark about Hestia.

[6] On this whole question see J. Bidez, 'Platon, Eudoxe et l'Orient', in *Bulletin Acad. Belgique* XIX (1933), pp. 195 ff. and 273 ff.; A. J. Festugière, 'Platon et l'Orient', in *Rev. de Philologie* XXI (1947), pp. 5 ff.; and E. R. Dodds in *J.H.S.* LXV (1945), p. 24f. It was Prof. Dodds's paper that directed me to that of Bidez.

If then we may set aside the astronomical puzzle as unreal, the chief problem that remains concerns the tripartite nature of the discarnate souls, both those which are destined to be united to human, and perhaps animal, bodies, and those which remain in the dwelling-place of the gods. The problem of the tripartite soul is amongst the thorniest of all Platonic problems, and in spite of a vast amount of discussion in recent years it cannot be said to be solved.[1] I shall not attempt to reargue the whole question in detail, since the only ground for doing so would be a hope of establishing either a consistent psychological doctrine, held by Plato from first to last, or a development ending in something firm and precise; and I entertain no such hope; rather do I agree with Wilamowitz's conclusion that Plato never attained to a full reconciliation of the various views expressed in the dialogues.[2]

The bare bones of the problem may be briefly set out: in the *Phaedo* we find simplicity of soul and its restriction to νοῦς: in *Rep.* IV tripartition, though with some expression of doubt (435 D); in *Rep.* X a suggestion (tentatively enough expressed) that the soul in its 'true nature' may be incomposite (611 D–612 A); here in the *Phaedrus* tripartition of the human soul, before and after its incarnation, and composite souls of gods; in the *Timaeus* (69 Cff.) tripartition again of the human soul, with local habitats for the three parts and restriction of immortality to reason, but again some expression of doubt (72 D); in *Laws* X attribution to the world-soul (and by inference to the individual soul in its 'true nature') of much besides reason, viz. 'wish, reflection, forethought, counsel, opinion true and false, joy, grief, confidence, fear, hate, love, and all the motions akin to these'.[3]

Now the *Laws* is the latest dialogue, and the *Timaeus* one of the latest; and since the appearance of Cornford's edition of the *Timaeus* I do not deem it necessary to argue that the *Timaeus* records Plato's own beliefs or speculations. But there is complete disagreement in the psychology of the two passages just referred to: the *Timaeus* excludes from the ἀρχὴ ψυχῆς ἀθάνατος (69 C, called τὸ θεῖον at 69 D), which is provided by the Demiurge himself as distinct from the subordinate gods who provide the ψυχῆς θνητὸν γένος (69 E), 'dread and necessary affections: first pleasure, the strongest lure of evil; next pains that take flight from good; temerity moreover and fear, a pair of unwise counsellors, passion hard to entreat, and hope too easily led astray; these they combined with irrational sense and desire that shrinks from

---

[1] An excellent discussion will be found in Frutiger, pp. 76–96, taking account of all views of importance down to 1930.

[2] *Platon* I, p. 475: 'Er hat es tatsächlich zu keiner vollen logischen Einheit in dem gebracht, was er über die Menschenseele lehrt und glaubt.'

[3] 897 A, Bury's translation. Possibly the ψυχή whose 'motions' are here enumerated is rather ψυχὴ πᾶσα (the totality of soul, including both the world-soul and individual souls) than the world-soul itself: but *peu importe*.

no venture, and so of necessity compounded the mortal element'.[1] All this implies that emotions and desires are evil and no part of the 'true' soul. Although it is not explicitly said that the divine, immortal part of soul is reason, yet it is located in the head which is τῶν ἐν ἡμῖν πάντων δεσποτοῦν (44D), while the part located in the breast is τοῦ λόγου κατήκοον (70A). Clearly the immortal part is the 'simple' soul of the *Phaedo*; no less clearly the παθήματα excluded here are included among the motions of unembodied soul in the *Laws*.

What does this point to? Is there any good ground for accepting either of these views as more final than the other? I do not think so; rather, Plato wavers to the end between the religious, Orphic-Pythagorean, conception of a divine soul essentially (in its 'true nature') divorced from all physical functions, all 'lower' activities, and a more secular and scientific conception of soul as essentially a source of motion both to itself and to τὰ ἄλλα, of ψυχὴ πᾶσα as παντὸς τοῦ ἀψύχου ἐπιμελουμένη (246B). The 'motions' or functions of soul, in the latter view, cannot be divorced from the body that it 'cares for': it can only move the body in virtue of itself possessing 'motions' over and above the reason which contemplates the eternal Forms; as Plato's follower was to observe, διάνοια αὐτὴ οὐδὲν κινεῖ.[2]

It is significant that the two dialogues in which the moving function of soul is prominent—*Phaedrus* and *Laws*—are the only two in which passions (emotions) and desires are clearly attributed to discarnate soul. The *Laws* in effect, though not explicitly, regards discarnate soul as tripartite, and, if for that reason alone, we ought to take the explicit statement of the *Phaedrus* to that effect as seriously meant.[3]

In the souls of the gods both horses are 'good and of good stock'. One hesitates whether or not to 'translate' this statement; but if we are to do so, I think the implication is that, whereas the tripartition of *Rep.* IV was deduced from the fact of moral conflict, we may still postulate three[4] parts of soul when there is no question of such conflict: even 'pure' soul is θυμοειδής and ἐπιθυμητικός as well as λογιστικός. It may further be observed with Frutiger (p. 82) that the doctrine seems necessary to account for the fall of the soul (246C).

Scholars have speculated as to the source of the chariot-imagery. I can see little resemblance between Plato's chariot and that in which

---

[1] *Timaeus* 69D, Cornford's translation. [2] Arist. *E.N.* 1139A 36.

[3] Here I disagree with Taylor, *Plato*, p. 307, and Wilamowitz, *Platon* I, p. 467: 'Das komplizierte Bild des Seelenwagens mit den zwei verschieden gemuteten Rossen ist allein für das Verhalten der Seele im Menschenleibe erfunden; da ist es von glücklichster Wirkung, und um des willen hat Platon es in den Kauf genommen, dass die Rosse Wille (*sic*) und Begierde vor den Wagen der Seele, schon ehe sie das erstemal eingekörpert ist, gespannt sind, ja dass auch die Götterseele so kompliziert ist.'

[4] Or perhaps more than three: see note on 246A, p. 69 above.

Parmenides[1] made his journey to an unnamed goddess, passing the gates of Night and Day, and guided by the daughters of the sun: equally doubtful is any allusion to the chariot of Empedocles, of which we hear in a single obscure line;[2] neither of these poets suggests any comparison to the soul.[3] But surely the representation of the ruling part of soul as a charioteer is so obvious and natural, especially in view of the common metaphorical use of ἡνιοχεύειν and its cognates,[4] that we need look no further than to the *Republic* itself for the simile. That the horses (but not of course the chariot, which has no symbolic value) should be winged is normal enough: we remember Pegasus, and the winged horses of Pelops.[5] I know of no parallel to the winged charioteer, but in view of his symbolic meaning his wings are of course necessary: it would be impossible to exclude from the controlling part of the soul that power of 'raising that which is heavy and carrying it aloft to the region where the gods dwell' spoken of at 246 D.

[1] Diels-Kranz, *Vors.* 28 B 1.   [2] *ibid.* 31 B 3, line 5.
[3] More possible is a reminiscence of the two immortal horses of Achilles (*Iliad* XVI, 148–54), though there is nothing to correspond to the trace-horse of that passage, ὃς καὶ θνητὸς ἐὼν ἕπεθ' ἵπποις ἀθανάτοισι.
[4] An early and apposite example is Anacreon IV, 1, 5: οὐκ εἰδὼς ὅτι τῆς ἐμῆς | ψυχῆς ἡνιοχεύεις.   [5] Pindar *Ol.* I, 87.

X

In the region above the heavens is that true Being which is apprehended by reason alone. This is the food that sustains the gods; this is the vision which they contemplate until the revolution is completed, after which they return home and give refreshment to the steeds of their chariots.

Other souls share in the vision in different degrees, according to the difficulty experienced by their drivers in controlling their horses; many get their wings broken, and none have the full vision; so they fall back and eat the food of semblance (τροφὴ δοξαστή).

The fallen souls are first incarnated not in the bodies of lower animals, but of men. There are nine types of human life assigned to them at their first birth, ranging from that of the philosopher, who has had the fullest vision of true Being, to that of the tyrant, who has seen least.

247 C   Of that place beyond the heavens none of our earthly poets has yet sung, and none shall sing worthily. But this is the manner of it, for assuredly we must be bold to speak what is true, above all when our discourse is upon truth. It is there that true Being dwells, without colour or shape, that cannot be touched; reason alone, the soul's pilot, can behold it, and all true knowledge is knowledge thereof. Now even

D   as the mind of a god is nourished by reason and knowledge, so also is it with every soul that has a care to receive her proper food;[1] wherefore when at last she has beheld Being she is well content, and contemplating truth she is nourished and prospers, until the heaven's revolution brings her back full circle. And while she is borne round she discerns justice, its very self, and likewise temperance, and knowledge, not the knowledge that is neighbour to Becoming and varies with the various

E   objects to which we commonly ascribe being, but the veritable knowledge of Being that veritably is. And when she has contemplated likewise and feasted upon all else that has true being, she descends again within the heavens and comes back home. And having so come, her

---

[1] Although the sentence beginning at D 1 is so expressed that the grammatical subject of ἀγαπᾷ and the following verbs is mind both divine and non-divine, yet logically the inclusion of the latter is parenthetical: that is to say, it is the felicity of the divine souls that is described down to E 6, the reference to other souls being momentarily dropped, and only resumed at 248A 1.

charioteer sets his steeds at their manger, and puts ambrosia before them and draught of nectar to drink withal.

Such is the life of gods: of the other souls that which best follows 248 a god and becomes most like thereunto raises her charioteer's head into the outer region, and is carried round with the gods in the revolution, but being confounded by her steeds she has much ado to discern the things that are; another now rises, and now sinks, and by reason of her unruly steeds sees in part, but in part sees not. As for the rest, though all are eager to reach the heights and seek to follow, they are not able: sucked down as they travel they trample and tread upon one another, this one striving to outstrip that. Thus confusion B ensues, and conflict and grievous sweat: whereupon, with their charioteers powerless,[1] many are lamed, and many have their wings all broken; and for all their toiling they are baulked, every one, of the full vision of Being, and departing therefrom, they feed upon the food of semblance.

Now the reason wherefore the souls are fain and eager to behold the Plain of Truth, and discover it, lies herein: to wit, that the pasturage that is proper to their noblest part comes from that Meadow, and the C plumage by which they are borne aloft is nourished thereby.

Hear now the ordinance of Necessity. Whatsoever soul has followed in the train of a god, and discerned something of truth, shall be kept from sorrow until a new revolution shall begin; and if she can do this always, she shall remain always free from hurt.[2] But when she is not able so to follow, and sees none of it, but meeting with some mischance[3] comes to be burdened with a load of forgetfulness and wrongdoing, and because of that burden sheds her wings and falls to the earth, then thus runs the law: in her first birth she shall not be planted in any brute D beast, but the soul that hath seen the most of Being shall enter into the human babe that shall grow into a seeker after wisdom or beauty, a follower of the Muses and a lover; the next, having seen less, shall

[1] Just as ἀρετή often means successful performance of function, so κακία here means, not 'vice', but imperfect functioning.
[2] The words ἀπήμονα and ἀβλαβῆ doubtless imply exemption from the fall into a body, as Hermeias says. The sentence is probably meant to provide for the existence of δαίμονες intermediate between gods and men (cf. στρατιὰ θεῶν τε καὶ δαιμόνων, 246E).
[3] At the nature of the mischance (συντυχία) Plato has left us to guess: even in a myth he will not affect to reveal the full secret of pre-natal sin, though he hints that something must be postulated over and above the defective vision of true Being.

dwell in a king that abides by law, or a warrior and ruler; the third in a statesman, a man of business or a trader; the fourth in an athlete, or E physical trainer or physician; the fifth shall have the life of a prophet or a mystery-priest; to the sixth that of a poet or other imitative artist shall be fittingly given; the seventh shall live in an artisan or farmer, the eighth in a sophist or demagogue,[1] the ninth in a tyrant.

The account of the gods proceeding to the circumference of the heavenly sphere, of their being carried round on the outside of it until the revolution has brought them back to their starting place, and of their subsequent return home to the interior of heaven, is mythical rather than allegorical. Allegory is indeed present in the description of the ὑπερουράνιος τόπος with its content of colourless, shapeless and intangible Being; but we are not to infer that the gods' contemplation of that Being is only occasional, and limited on each occasion to the definite time occupied by the revolution. The journey from their home and the return to it are as mythical as the refreshment provided for their horses, the nectar and ambrosia which plainly do not symbolise the 'noetic τροφή' of 247D 1 or anything else. The gods' movements are merely consequent upon the conception of a supra-celestial region, for since star-gods no less than the traditional gods of Homer dwell in heaven they have to be brought to and from that region, and it is natural enough that the duration of their stay there should be what the myth makes it. But it is idle to inquire with Robin[2] whether the περίοδος occupies twenty-four hours or the whole time of a τέλεος ἐνιαυτός—the *magnus annus* completed when all the heavenly bodies have returned to the same relative positions (*Timaeus* 39D). There is not the slightest ground for finding the *magnus annus* here; on the other hand a period of twenty-four hours is plainly ridiculous. The question, however, is futile because it wrongly assumes that myth is careful to be rational and precise. The myth-maker can use astronomical imagery at will, but he is not tied to any astronomical facts or theories: the revolution is not conceived as occupying any *definite* time, although it provides a framework of recurrent periods which is useful, inasmuch as it will enable Plato to adapt his eschatology to a temporal succession of lives, in the body and out of it, resembling—perhaps reproducing—that of Orphic belief.

No earlier myth has told of a ὑπερουράνιος τόπος, but this is not the first occasion on which true Being, the οὐσία ὄντως οὖσα, has

---

[1] δημοκοπικός (*T*) is preferable to δημοτικός (*B*), and is accepted by Burnet and Robin. The word means 'mob-flatterer', but 'demagogue' conveys the sense sufficiently well, since for Plato the leader of the δῆμος is always its κόλαξ. In *Soph.* 268B the word δημολογικός is used.   [2] p. lxxxv.

been given a local habitation. In the passage of *Rep.* VI which introduces the famous comparison of the Form of Good to the sun we have a νοητὸς τόπος contrasted with a ὁρατός (508C): but a spatial metaphor is hardly felt there, any more than in our own use of such words as 'province' or 'sphere' for the purpose of differentiating one man's duties or interests from another's. A truer approximation to the ὑπερουράνιος τόπος occurs in the simile of the Cave in *Rep.* VII, where we are plainly told that the prisoners' ascent into the light of day symbolises τὴν εἰς τὸν νοητὸν τόπον τῆς ψυχῆς ἄνοδον (517B); in fact the νοητὸς τόπος of the first simile has in the second developed into a real spatial symbol. In the myth of the *Phaedo*, which no doubt precedes the *Republic*, the simile of the Cave is, so to say, anticipated in another form: the world of sense-experience lies in a hollow of the earth (which has many such hollows), and the world of truth and reality on the earth's surface.

In these myths and similes Plato's imagination has probably been to some extent conditioned by traditional pictures of Elysium or the Islands of the Blest; he has imagined the other world as near to this earth of ours, if not upon it. Now, however, in the *Phaedrus*, the wings of his fancy take a higher flight; the world of true Being is not merely above the earth, but above the very heaven, *extra flammantia moenia mundi*. This may be thought to be no more than a natural development, as natural as for one of our own poets to sing 'My soul, there is a country far beyond the stars'; but I think the significance is deeper. Plato's new conception of Soul as self-mover has forced on his mind the problem of its status relatively to the eternal, unchanging (unmoved) Forms. In the *Sophist* (248Aff.) he will argue through the mouth of the Eleatic Stranger, and in opposition to these εἰδῶν φίλοι who insisted on the *exclusive* reality of the εἴδη, that τὸ παντελῶς ὄν comprises both ἀκίνητα and κινούμενα: and since there is there no hint of one of these constituents being inferior to the other, we may infer that they are conceived of as having equal status. In the *Timaeus* (30Cff.) however, the myth, taken at its face value, assigns a higher status to the Forms, since the νοητὸν ζῷον is the model to which the Demiurge looks in fashioning both the soul and body of the universe; if the Forms are then in some sense prior to the world-soul, they must *a fortiori* be prior to individual souls. Here in the *Phaedrus* the same priority appears to be attached to them, by giving them a location higher than that of the heavenly dwelling-place of souls; though it is moral Forms, Justice and Temperance (247D) and Beauty (250C) that Plato is chiefly[1] thinking of rather than the Forms of ζῷα, as in the *Timaeus*.

---

[1] Yet the words τἄλλα ὡσαύτως τὰ ὄντα ὄντως θεασαμένη (247E) allow for other types.

But in both dialogues it is very difficult to be sure whether the assertions and implications of myth ought to be taken at their face value. It may be permissible to suggest that the problem of the relative status of Forms and souls is dealt with only in mythical passages, and passed by in dialectical discussions like that of the *Sophist*, for the very reason that Plato could not, or did not wish to, offer any rational solution of it. The question is perhaps rather for a commentator on the *Timaeus*. It may, however, be noted that a little later (249 c) he almost goes out of his way to underline the priority of the Forms by speaking of them as 'those things a god's nearness whereunto makes him truly god' (ἐκείνοις...πρὸς οἷσπερ θεὸς ὢν θεῖός ἐστιν).

In his description of the fall of the soul Plato is of course drawing on Orphic doctrine and imagery. That the human soul is a fallen δαίμων is one of the main tenets of Orphism, most familiar to us through the fragments of Empedocles's religious poem *Purifications*.[1] But there are here elements of what M. Diès has called[2] 'transposition' or adaptation, as distinct from mere borrowing: thus the 'oracle of Necessity', ἀνάγκης χρῆμα (Empedocles 115), is probably echoed in the θεσμὸς 'Αδραστείας, but the contents of the two are only partly identical; the 'plain of truth' or 'meadow' recalls, but wholly changes, the "Ατης λειμών of Empedocles 121.[3] Later (250 B–C) we shall find a similar 'transposition' of the mystery-rites of Eleusis.

A notable expression is the 'food of semblance' (τροφὴ δοξαστή, 248 B), on which the fallen soul feeds. This is of course the antithesis of νοῦς καὶ ἐπιστήμη by which the discarnate souls are sustained (247 D), and is no doubt intended to recall to the reader familiar with the simile of the Divided Line (*Rep.* VI) the double contrast between 'opinable' and intelligible objects as well as between the παθήματα ψυχῆς, the conditions of soul when cognising those objects respectively; τροφὴ δοξαστή is half-unreal food and food appropriate to the condition of δόξα. The phrase is arresting, but eminently happy in reminding us of the element of allegory in the myth.

With the mention of the 'ordinance of Necessity' the myth passes fully into an Orphic milieu, and for that reason we are entitled, indeed we are compelled, to affix a definite duration to the περίοδος of 248 C 4, despite our refusal to do so earlier. After what has been said above this need cause us no embarrassment; the period of revolution has in fact become the Orphic period of 1000 years (the actual figure

---

[1] Hence Diels-Kranz print the whole passage 248 B 5–249 B 5 in their Empedocles chapter as *Anklang*.

[2] In a valuable chapter of *Autour de Platon*: see especially pp. 432–49. For Orphic elements in the Platonic myths see the parallel lists in Frutiger, pp. 254–60.

[3] In *Gorgias* 524 A the λειμών is the place of judgment of souls.

is given in the next section, περιόδῳ τῇ χιλιετεῖ, 249Α 7) which elapsed between one incarnation and the next.[1]

Finally we come to the 'order of merit' of lives, the highest of which falls to the lot of those who have had the fullest vision of the Forms, the lowest to those who have seen least.[2] The series seems to be one of decreasing worth to society. The first life needs no comment, save that the φιλόκαλος, μουσικός and ἐρωτικός are not persons other than the φιλόσοφος, but denote aspects of him, the first two being virtual synonyms, while the third will find its best elucidation in the general content of the whole myth.

The second life seems to imply the same point of view as Plato adopts in the later dialogue *Statesman*, where constitutional monarchy is the best, or rather the least unsatisfactory, substitute in default of the ideally wise ruler (297D–E, 302E); the πολεμικός καὶ ἀρχικός conjoined with the βασιλεὺς ἔννομος in this second class is best understood as a subordinate sharing his military and civil duties and responsibilities, the adjective ἔννομος applying to him also.[3]

Plainly this life demands high qualities of character. Rather less is demanded from, and contributed by, the third life, in which the πολιτικός may be understood as roughly corresponding to our administrative civil servant, while the οἰκονομικός is the head of a household and the χρηματιστικός a man of business. All these callings demand integrity, but just because they are not the lives of men in a commanding position, with power over the lives and fortunes of all their fellows, their integrity counts for less socially. Hence if there are to be persons of less moral worth than those of the first two classes, these are callings which they may follow without doing much harm, and in which they can do some good.

The next four are lives which, in their social aspect (and it is this that Plato has in mind throughout), are worth little, even if not positively

---

[1] The 1000-year Orphic period is implied in Empedocles's statement (*frag.* 115, 20) that the fallen soul must wander apart from the gods for thrice ten thousand seasons (τρίς μιν μυρίας ὥρας ἀπὸ μακάρων ἀλαλῆσθαι). 30,000 seasons = 10,000 years (see Taylor, *Plato*, p. 308), and this corresponds to the ἔτη μύρια made up of ten περίοδοι χιλιετεῖς in 249Α. It has usually been thought that there is a discrepancy between this and the myth of *Rep.* x, inasmuch as the latter makes the 1000 years include the earthly lifetime reckoned at 100, whereas the *Phaedrus* does not (see Adam on *Rep.* 615Α). But Frutiger (p. 255) argues that the περίοδος χιλιετής of 249Α extends from the beginning, not the end, of an earthly life. This may be right, but if there is a discrepancy it is of little importance.

[2] It is clear from 249Β 5 that all human souls have seen something; hence ὅταν...μὴ ἴδῃ (248C 5) must not be pressed to mean utter failure, and ἀτελεῖς (248Β 4) should be understood as 'without full success'.

[3] To this interpretation I do not consider it a valid objection that in the succeeding lives there is real discrimination, e.g. between πολιτικός, οἰκονομικός and χρηματιστικός.

harmful as are the eighth and ninth. The athlete, the physical trainer and the physician are all concerned with the body; we cannot of course forget that according to the *Republic* (410–412) γυμναστική has a beneficial effect upon the soul as well, but even there it is argued that, unless duly tempered by μουσική, its effect is bad.[1]

The μαντικὸς βίος ἢ τελεστικός, which comes fifth, is no doubt that of the shadier sort of religious 'expert' to whom Socrates refers with such contempt at *Rep.* 364 Bff.; Plato is not thinking here of the 'divine madness' found in a Pythia or a Sibyl, and the μάντις here is an οἰωνιστικός.

Similarly, when he assigns to the sixth place the life of 'a poet or other imitative artist', Plato cannot have in mind the inspired poetry of 245 A which 'glorifies the countless mighty deeds of ancient times for the instruction of posterity'. It has been pointed out by Prof. J. Tate[2] that μίμησις and its cognates, when used by Plato in discussing poetry, have sometimes a good sense, sometimes a bad; but it can hardly be contested that the bad sense predominates, and in the present phrase Plato must be thinking of that sort of poetical μίμησις which is condemned in the *Republic*; it need not, and indeed cannot, imply that every sort of ποιητικὸς βίος is so low in the scale of values; if it seems to do so, that is doubtless because uninspired poetry is far commoner than inspired. The seventh life is perhaps the most surprising of all. Why should the artisan and the farmer be of less value to the community than the physical trainer, the doctor, or the man of business? The explanation, so far as the artisan is concerned, is no doubt that Plato shared the common contempt of the Greek aristocrat for manual labour;[3] this did not normally, at least in Athens, extend to farming, but farmers are grouped with artisans to form the third class of the *Republic* which, though an economic necessity, is politically repressed.[4]

The penultimate life is that of the sophist or the demagogue, for whose close relation we may refer to *Sophist* 268 B–C; there is nothing surprising in their position in the list. Last comes the life of the tyrant, as every reader of *Rep.* IX would expect.

[1] οἱ μὲν γυμναστικῇ ἀκράτῳ χρησάμενοι ἀγριώτεροι τοῦ δέοντος ἀποβαίνουσιν (*Rep.* 410D).　　[2] *C.Q.* XXII (1928), pp. 16ff.

[3] Cf. *Rep.* 495 E, with Adam's informative note.

[4] The third class actually includes all 'producers': but by commonly referring to it as the class of δημιουργοί καὶ γεωργοί Plato shows that it is labourers of whom he is chiefly thinking. At *Laws* 846D the practice of manual crafts is forbidden to citizens.

XI

248E–249D REINCARNATION AND FINAL LIBERATION OF
THE SOUL. THE PHILOSOPHER'S PRIVILEGE

*In general the soul cannot regrow its wings and return to its heavenly home
in less than 10,000 years; but for the philosopher this is shortened to 3000.
After every thousand years souls begin a new incarnate life, determined
partly by lot, partly by their own choice; between each life and the next there
is a period of reward or punishment.*

*Incarnations may be in an animal body, but the first is always in that of
a man. Man's power to think conceptually is due to his reminiscence of the
Forms which his soul beheld in the divine procession; and the philosopher's
earlier liberation is due to his constant devotion to the Forms and his living
in conformity thereto. Detached from men's ordinary pursuits, he is
accounted insane, though in fact he is possessed by a god.*

Now in all these incarnations he who lives righteously has a better 248 E
lot for his portion, and he who lives unrighteously a worse.[1] For
a soul does not return to the place whence she came for ten thousand
years, since in no lesser time can she regain her wings, save only his 249
soul who has sought after wisdom unfeignedly, or has conjoined his
passion for a loved one with that seeking.[2] Such a soul, if with three
revolutions of a thousand years she has thrice chosen this philosophic
life, regains thereby her wings, and speeds away after three thousand
years; but the rest, when they have accomplished their first life, are
brought to judgment, and after the judgment some are taken to be
punished in places of chastisement beneath the earth, while others are
borne aloft by Justice to a certain region of the heavens,[3] there to live

[1] These words refer, not to the final destiny of the souls, but to the period of
reward or punishment between two incarnations. They are caught up again in the
sentence beginning at 249 A 5, and the intervening lines, referring to the soul's
ultimate 'home-coming' and to the special privilege in respect thereto enjoyed
by philosophers, are in effect a parenthesis. The γάρ of E 5 conceals, as often, an
ellipse: '(I do not speak as yet of his ultimate μοῖρα) for. . . .'

[2] These are not two different persons, any more than the φιλόκαλος, μουσικός
and ἐρωτικός were different from the φιλόσοφος at 248D 2. But that this is the
case we shall not fully understand until later in the myth.

[3] This vague phrase is probably intended to suggest a different habitat for the
soul which is not yet rewinged (liberated from the κύκλος γενέσεως) from the
final heavenly abode. Guthrie (*Orpheus*, pp. 184f.) points out that the distinction,
necessary on Orphic principles, between Elysium and a yet higher sphere is not
always maintained in Orphic passages of extant literature.

B in such manner as is merited by their past life in the flesh. And after a thousand years these and those alike come to the allotment and choice of their second life, each choosing according to her will; then does the soul of a man enter into the life of a beast, and the beast's soul that was aforetime in a man goes back to a man again. For only the soul that has beheld truth may enter into this our human form: seeing that man must needs understand the language of Forms, passing from a plurality C of perceptions to a unity gathered together by reasoning;[1] and such understanding is a recollection of those things which our souls beheld aforetime as they journeyed with their god, looking down upon the things which now we suppose to be, and gazing up to that which truly is.

Therefore is it meet and right that the soul of the philosopher alone[2] should recover her wings: for she, so far as may be, is ever near in memory to those things a god's nearness whereunto makes him truly god.[3] Wherefore if a man makes right use of such means of remembrance,[4]

---

[1] I accept Heindorf's insertion of τό before κατ' εἶδος, since I do not think συνιέναι κατ' εἶδος λεγόμενον is possible Greek for 'to understand by way of what is called a Form'; that would need συνιέναι κατὰ τὸ εἶδος λεγ. or συνιέναι κατ' εἶδος λεγ. τι. My translation follows the interpretation of von Arnim (op. cit. p. 198): 'Zum Wesen der menschlichen Seele gehört es τὸ κατ' εἶδος λεγ. zu verstehen, d.h. Wörter, welche Allgemeinbegriffe bezeichnen.' In the same line I accept Badham's ἰόντ' for ἰόν. Not only is there force in Thompson's comment that 'to speak of the εἶδος itself as ἰόν, proceeding or advancing to a "unity", itself being that "unity" which is the result of the process, is a licence of bad writing in which it is difficult to believe that Plato would indulge', but also the received text seems bad Platonism, inasmuch as it can hardly fail to imply that the εἶδος is merely the common element in the sensible particulars. If Plato ever thought that, he certainly does not think so now, since it is flatly contradictory of the ἀνάμνησις doctrine (cf. J. Stenzel, Studien zur Entwicklung der plat. Dialektik, p. 107, and von Arnim, op. cit. p. 200). It is the man, not the εἶδος, who proceeds from a plurality to a unity which may rightly be described as λογισμῷ συναιρούμενον, since ἀνάμνησις involves or is accompanied by a generalising process, although the object recollected is not a mere universal. For this use of ἰέναι cf. Rep. 476B: οἱ...ἐπ' αὐτὸ τὸ καλὸν δυνατοὶ ἰέναι. No doubt ἰόντα ἐφ' ἕν would be expected rather than ἰόντα εἰς ἕν, but cf. ἀνακύψασα εἰς τὸ ὂν ὄντως in c 3 below.

[2] The word 'alone' is strictly inconsistent with 248E 5–7, where it is implied that all souls ultimately regain their wings. But in the present sentence Plato is thinking only of events within a 10,000-year period, and giving the ground for his assertion that the philosopher alone can shorten the period of πτέρωσις.

[3] I retain θεῖος, but in English one can hardly speak of a god as 'godlike'.

[4] Thompson says 'the εἴδη, it would seem, are not themselves ὄντα but only "memoranda" suggestive of ὄντα'. I think this is wrong. τοῖς τοιούτοις ὑπο-μνήμασιν are not the εἴδη denoted by ἐκείνοις in the previous line: the words mean such reminders of the Forms by their imperfect sensible copies as the ἀνάμνησις doctrine asserts: see Phaedo 73 cff. The philosopher employs these aright (ὀρθῶς χρώμενος) when he conforms his conduct to what he is reminded of. So at Rep.

and ever approaches to the full vision of the perfect mysteries,[1] he and he alone becomes truly perfect. Standing aside from the busy doings of mankind, and drawing nigh to the divine, he is rebuked by the D multitude as being out of his wits, for they know not that he is possessed by a deity.

The escape of the lover of wisdom from the 'wheel of birth' after 3000 years is probably another 'transposition' of Orphic doctrine, of which an echo is preserved in Pindar's second Olympian ode.[2] We have here a noteworthy variation on the doctrine of the *Phaedo*, according to which the philosopher escapes after a single lifetime (80D–81A).[3] A difference from the *Gorgias* and *Republic* myths is the absence of eternal punishment[4] which may have been asserted in the earlier dialogues only out of deference to Homer;[5] in the *Phaedrus* all souls regain their wings after 10,000 years; but to the questions how long they remain winged, and whether the attempt to follow the procession of gods is repeated immediately, the myth has no answer, nor should we seek to supply one.

There is not a word in our dialogue to suggest that individual souls are ultimately absorbed into a world-soul; on the contrary everything points to the retention of individual existence. The same is true of the *Republic*, where the words ἀεὶ ἂν εἶεν αἱ αὐταί (611A) preclude absorption, of the *Phaedo* (114C), and of the *Timaeus* (42C–D). No doubt belief in individual immortality should involve belief in the continuity of memory,[6] and Plato's doctrine of ἀνάμνησις does not involve any *personal* memory, memory, that is, of personal experiences in a former life; indeed the non-existence of such personal memory is recognised symbolically in the myth of *Rep.* x where the souls come to

540A the philosopher-rulers use the Form of Good as a pattern (παράδειγμα), and order their city and themselves accordingly (Ἰδόντας τὸ ἀγαθὸν αὐτό, παραδείγματι χρωμένους ἐκείνῳ, καὶ πόλιν καὶ ἰδιώτας καὶ ἑαυτοὺς κοσμεῖν τὸν ἐπίλοιπον βίον).

[1] The words τελέους ἀεὶ τελετὰς τελούμενος are untranslatable, since τελούμενος means both 'being initiated' (*sc.* into a mystery, or revelation of sacred objects) and 'being made perfect or complete' (i.e. realising to the full the moral and spiritual potentialities of one's nature). The Greek words for *mystery, initiate,* and *perfect* all derive from the same root, seen in its simplest form in τέλος, 'end', 'goal', 'perfection'. In saying τέλεος ὄντως μόνος γίγνεται Plato hints that true perfection is not to be won by participation in the ordinary mysteries.

[2] ll. 68ff.

[3] This is perhaps sufficiently explained by closer adherence in the *Phaedrus* to the details of Orphic eschatology. The *Phaedo* passage is not—or at least not ostensibly—mythical. The *Republic* myth says nothing of the final liberation, but this may be simply due to a limitation of purview.

[4] *Gorgias* 525C, *Rep.* 615Cff.   [5] cf. Guthrie, *Orpheus*, p. 168.

[6] So it is recorded of Pythagoras that 'in life he could recall everything, and when he died he still kept the same memory' (*D.L.* VIII, 4).

the Plain of Lethe and drink the water of Unmindfulness (621 A). We must, I think, be content to believe either that Plato overlooked this difficulty or else—and this seems more likely—that he felt (wrongly, as it seems to us) that the impersonal memory of the ἀνάμνησις doctrine sufficiently met it.[1]

After its first life in the body the soul comes to the place of judgment and is rewarded or punished according to the good or evil of its incarnate life, as in the other three eschatological myths. Then follow the 'allotment and choosing' (κλήρωσις τε καὶ αἵρεσις), which are dwelt on at length in the Myth of Er, but here only thus briefly alluded to;[2] the meaning is of course that our lives are partly predestined, partly self-chosen.

In the next sentence there is an equally brief allusion to another point expanded in *Rep.* x, the transmigration of human souls into animal bodies. Did Plato seriously believe in this?[3] There are undoubtedly difficulties in the way of accepting an affirmative answer to this question, difficulties which have been set out perhaps most forcibly by Prof. Taylor in commenting on a passage at the end of the *Timaeus* (90 Eff.) where a summary account of the evolution of the lower animals is given. Perhaps the greatest difficulty is that the animals do not—at all events in Plato's view—possess reason; that he plainly admits at *Rep.* 441 A–B; yet possibly this same passage may help us to surmount the difficulty. Children, we are told, are either wholly devoid of τὸ λογιστικόν or only come to possess it late in childhood. Yet the child's soul is surely conceived as the same as that of the adult into which he develops; if then the human soul has had, within the limits of its life in one and the same human body, a period of non-rationality, why should it not be possible for it to lose that rationality again, and yet still retain its identity, when it comes to inhabit the body of an animal?

Secondly, there is, as Taylor points out, the silence of *Laws* x on transmigration into animal bodies, in a passage (904A–905A) where we might well expect some mention of it. The gist of the doctrine there is that virtue and vice are recompensed by a sort of moral law of gravitation, by which the soul goes in the after-life to the company of such other souls as it has fitted itself to associate with. Thus although

---

[1] cf. A. D. Ritchie, *Essays in Philosophy*, p. 134: 'Plato's doctrine of "recollection"...definitely excludes the perpetuity of memory in the ordinary sense.'

[2] Von Arnim (*P.'s Jugenddialoge*, p. 172) rightly argues that the allusion would hardly be intelligible without a knowledge of *Rep.* x. This is one of his most convincing arguments for dating the *Phaedrus* later than the *Republic*.

[3] The later Neoplatonists rejected the literal interpretation; cf. Proclus, *in Tim.* III, 329 D–E (Diehl), Whittaker, *Neoplatonists*, pp. 291–3. Plotinus (III, 4, 2) appears to accept it; but see Inge, *The Philosophy of Plotinus* II, p. 33, who thinks that he 'does not take the doctrine of reincarnation very seriously as scientific truth'.

reincarnation in a human body is here doubtless implied, the other sort seems implicitly denied. 'The absolute silence', says Taylor,[1] 'about any migration into animal forms, which might so easily have been got in as one way of sinking into the company of "worse ψυχαί", seems to show that such a migration was alien to Plato's own imagination.'

There is great force in this argument, but I do not think we are entitled to say more than that Plato did not believe in transmigration when he wrote *Laws* x. That was very near the end of his life, and it is only to be expected that this belief, and perhaps others which figure in the myths, had been by then long exposed to criticism within the school; it may well be that Aristotle had already[2] expressed mistrust of the notion that 'any soul can enter any body' (*de anima* 407B 22).

But the *Phaedrus* was probably written before Aristotle joined the Academy, and the occurrence of this feature in the *Phaedo* and *Republic* as well as in our dialogue should preclude us, save for incontrovertible reasons, from doubting Plato's seriousness. It is apposite to quote the well-known passage which closes the myth of the *Phaedo* (114D): 'To maintain that these things are just as I have said would ill befit a man of common sense, but that either this or something like it is the truth about our souls and their dwelling-places seems to me (seeing that the soul has been proved to be immortal) to be fitting, and I think it a risk worth taking for the man who thinks as we do.'

I do not believe that Plato could have written thus at the end of a myth which involves reincarnation and transmigration if he had not believed in them both. It is true that reference to the latter is confined, in that myth, to the words πάλιν ἐκπέμπονται εἰς τὰς τῶν ζῴων γενέσεις:[3] but that surely is because the doctrine had been fully explained at 81 E–82 B, a passage to which I shall refer in a moment.

In the great eschatological myths there are (as we have already recognised in the case of the *Phaedrus*) elements of allegory and imaginative poetry; there is also the element of speculation or conjecture, but such conjecture is not purely fanciful or arbitrary: it is designed to furnish answers to real and important questions: and one such question is that of the relation between the human and the animal soul. For Plato 'all soul' is a single sort of entity, over against another single sort, body, and the function of soul is to 'care for' (ἐπιμελεῖσ-θαι) body. But just as body is found in different shapes, so soul πάντα οὐρανὸν περιπολεῖ ἄλλοτ' ἐν ἄλλοις εἴδεσι γιγνομένη (256B). It may have one εἶδος in a star, another in a human body, a third in an animal body: the star, the man, the animal are 'all besouled', ἔμψυχα

---

[1] Commentary on *Timaeus*, p. 641.
[2] That he had occupied himself with psychology in Plato's lifetime we know from the fragments of his *Eudemus* (*circ.* 354 B.C.).
[3] 113A.

ζῷα, and soul is essentially the same in them all. And yet there is the patent difference that animals have not reason, cannot think in concepts, while men can. Was it not then a reasonable conjecture that man is nearer to the gods, so that the first incarnation will be in a human body, while animals are further from them, so that their existence involves a further 'descent' of the soul? And if a descent, why not a corresponding reascent? That is mythical belief, no doubt, but an εἰκὼς μῦθος none the less.

It is often said (e.g. by Taylor, *op. cit.* p. 640) that transmigration into animal bodies is only asserted by Plato in mythical passages. This is not strictly true, for in *Phaedo* 81 E ff. it is asserted by Socrates in an argument with Cebes which is at least ostensibly dialectical. Nevertheless, I do not think this passage gives any good ground for supposing that Plato, even when he wrote the *Phaedo*, meant to establish the belief on a purely rational basis; for in the context Socrates is advancing Orphic beliefs rather in a spirit of persuasion than of reasoned argument; the *Phaedo* indeed, taken as a whole, proceeds gradually from εἰκότα to ἀποδείξεις, as is commonly recognised—to close however with a large-scale myth.[1]

Before leaving this point I must return to the passage at the end of the *Timaeus* (90 E ff.) already referred to. Taylor says that 'the brief account of the lower species and of transmigration is manifestly little more than friendly burlesque' (*sc.* of early Pythagorean views). Although I do not agree with this interpretation—which is of course bound up with the author's notion that the dialogue does not represent Plato's own views at all—I think it must be admitted that the passage is highly fanciful, even to the point of becoming grotesque: though I am not sure that it is more grotesque than some other parts of the *Timaeus*. It reads, to my mind, like the rather perfunctory discharge of a task about which Plato did not care much, but which he felt imposed upon him by his general scheme, and in particular by the words he had attributed to the Demiurge at 42 C; in any case, the grotesqueness lies not in the application of the transmigration principle *per se*, but in the attempt to describe a *physical* metamorphosis, e.g. of a man's body into that of a bird, which is quite another matter. What is relevant to our present problem is not this passage at the end of the dialogue, but the earlier announcement of the principle of transmigration at 42 C, a principle which is part of the laws of Destiny revealed by the Demiurge to the created gods. There the *mise en scène* lifts the principle to the level of serious mythical belief, at which the four great

[1] I would not deny that the dialogues contain passages on the borderline between myth and dialectic, persuasion and argument. In attempting to interpret Plato we are compelled to distinguish his elements—the rationalist, the poet, the moralist or what not, but we must not forget the dangers of a rigid schematisation.

myths of the soul—in *Gorgias, Phaedo, Republic* and *Phaedrus*—are all set.

Plato is careful to insist that the soul of an animal can pass into the body of a man only if the reverse transmigration has preceded (249 B 4). This has of course already been said, or implied, at 248 D 1, but the reason for it is now given,[1] namely that only souls which have seen true Being in the supra-celestial procession can possess that power of conceptual thought which distinguishes man. If it were possible to imagine a soul starting its existence in an animal, its capacity of thinking when it passed into a man's body could not be accounted for.

It is declared in the next sentence that the process of conceptual thinking is just the recollection of those constituents of true Being of which the myth has been telling us. We must not make the mistake of regarding this assertion as itself wholly mythical; it is indeed partly mythical in expression: the use of such words as συμπορευθεῖσα and ἀνακύψασα are evidence enough of that; but in substance it is a strictly philosophical assertion. For the doctrine of ἀνάμνησις, inextricably bound up as it is with Plato's belief both in the Forms and in the soul's immortality, must, on a fair examination of the evidence,[2] be accepted as a wholly serious tenet at least of Plato's middle period, though its absence from the later dialogues may perhaps mean its later abandonment.

---

[1] The force of γάρ in B 5 (οὐ γὰρ ἥ γε μήποτε ἰδοῦσα κτλ.) is that the sentence which it introduces gives the reason for the words ὅς ποτε ἄνθρωπος ἦν which precede.

[2] See especially *Phaedo* 92 D, where Simmias says ὁ δὲ περὶ τῆς ἀναμνήσεως καὶ μαθήσεως λόγος δι' ὑποθέσεως ἀξίας ἀποδέξασθαι εἴρηται: and see the excellent discussion by Frutiger, *op. cit.* pp. 67–76. I fully agree with his conclusion: 'L'exposé du *Ménon* a un caractère mythique indéniable. Celui du *Phédon* n'est pas un simple complément du premier, comme on le croit d'ordinaire, car il traite la question sur un autre plan, celui de la dialectique.'

XII

By the sight of a beautiful object the soul is reminded of the true Beauty, and seeks to wing its flight upward thereto. This love of Beauty is the fourth and highest type of divine madness. But recollection is not always easy: some souls saw little of the vision, and some forget what they saw, being corrupted by evil associations.

Yet the Form of Beauty may be more readily recollected than the other Forms, since its image is discerned by sight, the keenest of our senses.

249 D   Mark therefore the sum and substance of all our discourse touching the fourth sort of madness: to wit, that this is the best of all forms of divine possession, both in itself and in its sources,[1] both for him that has it and for him that shares therein; and when he that loves beauty is E touched by such madness he is called a lover. Such an one, as soon as he beholds the beauty of this world, is reminded of true beauty, and his wings begin to grow; then is he fain to lift his wings and fly upward; yet he has not the power, but inasmuch as he gazes upward like a bird, and cares nothing for the world beneath, men charge it upon him that he is demented.[2]

Now, as we have said, every human soul has, by reason of her nature, had contemplation of true Being: else would she never have 250 entered into this human creature; but to be put in mind thereof by things here is not easy for every soul; some, when they had the vision, had it but for a moment; some when they had fallen to earth consorted unhappily with such as led them to deeds of unrighteousness, wherefore they forgot the holy objects of their vision. Few indeed are left that can still remember much: but when these discern some likeness of the things yonder, they are amazed, and no longer masters of themselves, and know not what is come upon them by reason of their perception B being dim.

[1] The phrase ἀρίστη τε καὶ ἐξ ἀρίστων (E 1–2) may perhaps have lost its literal sense and become no more than a strong superlative; cf. ἀγαθοῦ τε καὶ ἐξ ἀγαθῶν (274A) and note on 246A 8 above.

[2] The editors are doubtless right in regarding the words ἣν ὅταν...διακείμενος as parenthetical. The parenthesis is however awkward to preserve in translation, and I have therefore postponed it so as to make an indΙ pendent sentence. In consequence of this the γάρ of E 4 cannot be translated.

Now in the earthly likenesses of justice and temperance and all other prized possessions of the soul there dwells no lustre; nay, so dull are the organs wherewith men approach their images that hardly can a few behold that which is imaged; but with beauty it is otherwise.[1] Beauty it was ours to see in all its brightness in those days when, amidst that happy company, we beheld with our eyes that blessed vision, ourselves[2] in the train of Zeus, others following some other god; then were we all initiated into that mystery which is rightly accounted blessed beyond all others; whole and unblemished were we that did celebrate it, c untouched by the evils that awaited us in days to come; whole and unblemished likewise, free from all alloy, steadfast and blissful were the spectacles on which we gazed in the moment of final revelation; pure was the light that shone around us, and pure were we, without taint of that prison-house which now we are encompassed withal, and call a body, fast bound therein as an oyster in its shell.

There let it rest then, our tribute to a memory that has stirred us to linger awhile on those former joys for which we yearn. Now beauty, D as we said, shone bright amidst these visions, and in this world below we apprehend it through the clearest of our senses, clear and resplendent. For sight is the keenest mode of perception vouchsafed us through the body; wisdom, indeed, we cannot see thereby—how passionate had been our desire for her, if she had granted us so clear an image of herself to gaze upon—nor yet any other of those beloved objects, save only beauty; for beauty alone this has been ordained, to be most manifest to sense and most lovely of them all.

The first long sentence (249 D 4–E 4) of this section brings us back to the conception of 'divine madness'. It will be remembered that the whole account of the soul's nature, its immortality and its after-life, was introduced for the sake of proving that the madness of the lover is the supreme gift of the gods.[3] Now that we have learnt of the soul's vision of the Forms, and of its power of recalling them to memory, the proof can be given; in brief it is this, that love is the restoration of the soul's wings, in other words the regaining of its divine purity (246D),

[1] This last clause is not in the Greek, but I have added it to make the run of the argument clearer, in view of the quasi-digression which extends from B 5 to c 8.
[2] Plato alludes to himself rather than to Socrates. As Hermeias says, λέγει... ὡς τὸν οἰκεῖον θεὸν ἐπιγνοὺς ὁ Πλάτων, and this is borne out by 252E, where the Zeus-like nature is φιλόσοφος τε καὶ ἡγεμονικός. The οἰκεῖος θεός of Socrates, if he had one, was rather Apollo (*Apol.* 23 B, *Phaedo* 85 B).
[3] ἀποδεικτέον...ὡς ἐπ' εὐτυχίᾳ τῇ μεγίστῃ παρὰ θεῶν ἡ τοιαύτη μανία δίδοται (245 B).

through the contemplation of the Form of beauty. All the rest of the μυθικὸς ὕμνος is an expansion of this conception of love, together with an account of that σκαιὸς ἔρως (as it comes to be called, 266A) which results immediately from the indiscipline of the horse of evil, and ultimately from the imperfect vision, or the inability to recall the vision, of beauty itself.

In the two earlier speeches love had been considered only from the standpoint of the ἐρώμενος. That was natural enough, for in both of them the speaker was concerned to set forth the advantage or detriment ensuing to the recipient. But now we are told that love is a supreme blessing 'both for him that has' the madness 'and for him that shares therein' (τῷ τε ἔχοντι καὶ τῷ κοινωνοῦντι αὐτῆς, 249E). These are the lover and the beloved respectively. Since the whole of Socrates's second discourse is addressed, like the other two, to the παῖς καλός (243E 9, 256E 3), the benefit ensuing τῷ ἔχοντι is, strictly speaking, an irrelevant consideration; but in point of fact the cadre of the speech is half-forgotten by Socrates (and Plato), as it probably will have been by the reader, and it would be cavil to reckon this as an artistic defect; in any case the good of the lover and of the beloved are one and indivisible, as we shall soon see.

An important point made here is that inability to recall the Forms may be due, or partly due, to another cause besides the imperfection of the soul's vision 'yonder': namely to forgetfulness consequent upon evil associations (ὁμιλιῶν, 250A 3) in this world. This is another point that has been expanded in the *Republic*, where Plato has drawn a memorable picture of the πολλοὶ ὄλεθροι καὶ μεγάλοι (491B) which threaten the few elect in an alien society. There, as here, it is only the few that can survive: ὀλίγαι δὴ λείπονται here (250A) reminds us of the remnant which divine providence may rescue there.[1]

Plato now proceeds to note the exceptional position of beauty amongst the Forms in regard to ἀνάμνησις. A difficulty is caused here by the reference to 'dull organs' (δι' ἀμυδρῶν ὀργάνων) through which we discern the likenesses (ὁμοιώματα) of the other moral Forms. What are these ὄργανα? They must be in some sense comparable or co-ordinate with the 'clearest of our senses' through which, as we are told a little later (250D 2), we discern the sensible copies of beauty; and for that reason it is impossible to accept Robin's suggestion[2] that laws and rules of conduct are meant. Hermeias is, I think, on the right lines in commenting: δι' ὀργάνων καὶ συλλογισμῶν καὶ προτάσεων μανθάνομεν ὅτι ἡ δικαιοσύνη καὶ ἡ σωφροσύνη αἱρετόν, and in proceeding to observe that it required a long and elaborate argument

---

[1] εὖ γὰρ χρὴ εἰδέναι, ὅτι περ ἂν σωθῇ τε καὶ γένηται οἷον δεῖ ἐν τοιαύτῃ καταστάσει πολιτειῶν, θεοῦ μοῖραν αὐτὸ σῶσαι λέγων οὐ κακῶς ἐρεῖς (*Rep.* 492E).

[2] p. xcvi.

for Plato to discover the copy of justice in the ideal state of the *Republic*. The 'dull organs' are in fact the inadequate reasoning powers of man; a few, like Plato himself, possessed of exceptionally acute analytic and constructive reason, can build a society in which justice, temperance and so forth might be, albeit imperfectly, embodied; but at best, and even for a Plato, the way is dark and the 'tools' are hardly adequate to their task. No doubt there are faint and fitful gleams of the moral Forms even in existing societies and individuals; otherwise the ὄργανα could not essay their task at all; but unreformed society did not, in Plato's judgment, exhibit anything deserving to be called εἰκόνες τῶν ὅσα τίμια ψυχαῖς.

With the mention of the ideal beauty at 250B 5 Socrates—or Plato—suffers himself to be carried away into a quasi-digression of great eloquence and power, for which he half apologises at the end of 250C. The result is that the point he is making about the exceptional position of beauty as compared with the other moral Forms is postponed, or rather the exposition is momentarily interrupted and only caught up again at the beginning of 250D. Yet the slight inconvenience to the reader is more than compensated by the content of the digression, with its mystery-symbolism taken probably from Eleusis,[1] and as certain to stir the emotions of its first readers as it does our own.

---

[1] As Hermeias suggests. But the last words, ἀσήμαντοι...δεδεσμευμένοι, allude to the Orphic σῶμα-σῆμα doctrine (the body as the prison of the soul). For a recent account of the Eleusinian mysteries see Guthrie, *The Greeks and their Gods*, pp. 281 ff.

XIII

Socrates continues with a vivid account of the regrowing of the soul's wings achieved through the perception of physical beauty and the consequent recollection of Beauty itself, the Form seen in the supra-celestial vision. The pangs of love unsatisfied are followed by a deep joy and satisfaction, for Love is the healer of suffering. The lover's state is one of reverent devotion and utter absorption in the beloved. What men call Eros the gods call by another name, Pteros, the winged one, because of his power to renew the plumage of the soul.

250 E   Now he whose vision of the mystery is long past, or whose purity has been sullied, cannot pass swiftly hence to see Beauty's self yonder, when he beholds that which is called beautiful here; wherefore he looks upon it with no reverence, and surrendering to pleasure he essays to go after the fashion of a four-footed beast, and to beget offspring of the flesh; or consorting with wantonness he has no fear nor shame in 251 running after unnatural pleasure. But when one who is fresh from the mystery, and saw much of the vision, beholds a godlike face or bodily form that truly expresses beauty, first there comes upon him a shuddering and a measure of that awe which the vision inspired, and then reverence as at the sight of a god: and but for fear of being deemed a very madman he would offer sacrifice to his beloved, as to a holy image of deity. Next, with the passing of the shudder, a strange B sweating and fever seizes him: for by reason of the stream of beauty entering in through his eyes there comes a warmth, whereby his soul's plumage is fostered; and with that warmth the roots of the wings are melted, which for long had been so hardened and closed up that nothing could grow; then as the nourishment is poured in the stump of the wing swells and hastens to grow from the root over the whole substance of the soul: for aforetime the whole soul was furnished with C wings. Meanwhile she throbs with ferment in every part, and even as a teething child feels an aching and pain in its gums when a tooth has just come through, so does the soul of him who is beginning to grow his wings feel a ferment and painful irritation. Wherefore as she gazes upon the boy's beauty, she admits a flood of particles streaming there-

from—that is why we speak of a 'flood of passion'[1]—whereby she is warmed and fostered; then has she respite from her anguish, and is filled with joy. But when she has been parted from him and become D parched, the openings of those outlets at which the wings are sprouting dry up likewise and are closed, so that the wing's germ is barred off; and behind its bars, together with the flood aforesaid, it throbs like a fevered pulse, and pricks at its proper outlet; and thereat the whole soul round about is stung and goaded into anguish; howbeit she remembers the beauty of her beloved, and rejoices again. So between joy and anguish she is distraught at being in such strange case, perplexed and frenzied; with madness upon her she can neither sleep by night nor E keep still by day, but runs hither and thither, yearning for him in whom beauty dwells, if haply she may behold him. At last she does behold him, and lets the flood pour in upon her, releasing the imprisoned waters; then has she refreshment and respite from her stings and sufferings, and at that moment tastes a pleasure that is sweet beyond compare. Nor will she willingly give it up: above all others does she 252 esteem her beloved in his beauty: mother, brother, friends, she forgets them all: naught does she reck of losing worldly possessions through neglect: all the rules of conduct, all the graces of life, of which aforetime she was proud, she now disdains, welcoming a slave's estate and any couch where she may be suffered to lie down close beside her darling; for besides her reverence for the possessor of beauty she has found in him the only physician for her grievous suffering. B

Hearken, fair boy to whom I speak: this is the experience that men term love (ἔρως), but when you hear what the gods call it, you will probably smile at its strangeness. There are a couple of verses on love quoted by certain Homeric scholars from the unpublished works, the second of which is remarkably bold and a trifle astray in its quantities: they run as follows:

> Eros, cleaver of air, in mortals' speech is he named;
> But, since he must grow wings, Pteros the celestials call him.[2]

You may believe that or not, as you please; at all events the cause and C the nature of the lover's experience are in fact what I have said.

---

[1] The suggestion is that ἵμερος is derived from ἱέναι + μέρη + ῥοή.

[2] For such double names cf. *Iliad* I, 404; XIV, 291; XX, 74. The name given by the gods is normally the more significant. It is uncertain whether the two lines are simply invented by Plato or modified from existing lines fathered upon Homer, perhaps by some Orphic writer. See Thompson's note.

This powerful analysis of the nature of a sublimated παιδεραστία may be left for the most part without comment. What strikes us first is the initial stage, the shuddering awe (251 A) which the *holiness* of beauty inspires; it would seem that Plato finds the origin of spiritual love in that same 'sense of the holy' in which some modern thinkers have found the origin of religion.[1] It may perhaps be thought of as the more positive aspect of σωφροσύνη: not a passionless self-suppression but a passionate self-surrender, which is nevertheless a profound satisfying of self. But though love starts in worship or reverence, it presses on to a union closer than these can give; and here again the religious parallel holds good: man seeks communion with God, the mystics seek absolute union with Him. In his description of this further stage Plato emphasises the point that in loving we find healing of spiritual pain or sickness;[2] this is an instance of the general principle that any satisfaction involves previous dissatisfaction, a principle apparent in Heraclitus and made use of by Plato in his analysis of pleasure in *Rep.* IX and *Philebus* (though he does seek to prove that some pleasures involve no antecedent pain).

Before full satisfaction is attained there is a stage of acute distress mixed with joy, and by reason of this tension the lover is maddened or distraught (251 D). We must, however, not identify this transitional stage with the 'divine madness' with which love in general has been identified; the madness of our present passage leaves the lover when full spiritual union with the beloved is achieved.

A word must be added on the contemptuous reference to heterosexual love at 250 E. If we press this passage we shall have to believe that Plato regarded this as deserving of equal condemnation with the unnatural pursuit of pleasure (i.e. a purely carnal homosexual relationship) of which he speaks in the same breath. I do not think he really means this. No doubt both alike are in his eyes incomparable in worth with the ideal homosexual relation which he is describing; it may well be, moreover, that Plato personally disliked the heterosexual relation; but that he advocated abstention therefrom for all men is in itself unthinkable, and incompatible with the dignity with which he invests marriage in his ideal state (see *Rep.* 458 E with Adam's note), as also with the privilege claimed for conspicuous valour on active service at *Rep.* 468 c.

---

[1] Indeed the words θύοι ἂν ὡς ἀγάλματι καὶ θεῷ τοῖς παιδικοῖς almost identify the erotic with the religious impulse.

[2] Love as the kindly healer has already appeared in the *Symposium* (189 D, speech of Aristophanes).

XIV

252C–253C   THE VARIOUS TYPES OF LOVER

The nature of the lover, his choice of and demeanour towards the beloved,
will vary according as he has followed in the train of this god or of that, and
all his effort will be towards shaping him into the likeness of the god whose
image he sees in the person of the beloved. A follower of Zeus, the 'great
leader' (246E), looks for one who shall be a philosopher and a leader of men;
and the inspiration which he draws from Zeus he pours out again into the
soul of the other.

Now if he whom Love has caught be amongst the followers of Zeus, he 252 c
is able to bear the burden of the winged one[1] with some constancy; but
they that attend upon Ares, and did range the heavens in his train, when
they are caught by Love and fancy that their beloved is doing them
some injury, will shed blood and not scruple to offer both themselves
and their loved ones in sacrifice. And so does each lover live, after the
manner of the god in whose company he once was, honouring him and D
copying him so far as may be, so long as he remains uncorrupt and is
still living in his first earthly period; and in like manner does he
comport himself towards his beloved and all his other associates.
And so each selects a fair one for his love after his disposition, and
even as if the beloved himself were a god he fashions for himself as it
were an image, and adorns it to be the object of his veneration and
worship.

Thus the followers of Zeus seek a beloved who is Zeus-like in soul;[2] E
wherefore they look for one who is by nature disposed to the love of
wisdom and the leading of men,[3] and when they have found him and
come to love him they do all in their power to foster that disposition.

---

[1] For Love as a burden, cf. *Anth. Pal.* XII, 48 (Meleager): κεῖμαι· λὰξ ἐπίβαινε κατ'
αὐχένος, ἄγριε δαῖμον· | οἶδά σε, ναὶ μὰ θεούς, καὶ βαρὺν ὄντα φέρειν.

[2] It is not unlikely that the word δῖον conceals an allusion to Plato's friend
Dion of Syracuse: Wilamowitz (*op. cit.* I, p. 537) regards this as certain. The
warmth of Plato's admiration for Dion comes out in *Epistle* VII, especially at
327A. An epigram (*Anth. Pal.* VII, 99: *D.L.* III, 30) on Dion's death is attributed
to Plato; its authenticity has been doubted, but is assumed by Wilamowitz and
has recently been well defended by C. M. Bowra, in *Amer. Journ. of Phil.* LIX
(1938), pp. 394–404.

[3] ἡγεμονικός because Zeus is the μέγας ἡγεμών (246E); φιλόσοφος because wisdom
is the natural possession of the supreme god: cf. Μῆτις as first wife of Zeus in
Hesiod, *Theog.* 886.

And if they have not aforetime trodden this path, they now set out upon it, learning the way from any source that may offer or finding it for themselves; and as they follow up the trace within themselves of 253 the nature of their own god their task is made easier, inasmuch as they are constrained to fix their gaze upon him;[1] and reaching out after him in memory they are possessed by him, and from him they take their ways and manners of life, in so far as a man can partake of a god. But all this, mark you, they attribute to the beloved, and the draughts which they draw from Zeus they pour out, like Bacchants, into the soul of the beloved,[2] thus creating in him the closest possible likeness to the B god they worship.

Those who were in the train of Hera look for a royal nature,[3] and when they have found him they do unto him all things in like fashion. And so it is with the followers of Apollo and each other god: every lover is fain that his beloved should be of a nature like to his own god;[4] and when he has won him, he leads him on to walk in the ways of their god, and after his likeness, patterning himself thereupon and giving counsel and discipline to the boy. There is no jealousy[5] nor petty spitefulness in his dealings, but his every act is aimed at bringing the C beloved to be every whit like unto himself and unto the god of their worship.

So therefore glorious and blissful is the endeavour of true lovers in that mystery-rite, if they accomplish that which they endeavour after

[1] I take ἀνευρίσκειν to be governed not by εὐποροῦσι (as does Robin, who prints a comma after ἰχνεύοντες δέ) but by ἰχνεύοντες, the infinitive being pleonastically added because ἰχνεύοντες is felt as equivalent to ζητοῦντες. The phrase ἰχνεύοντες παρ' ἑαυτῶν ἀνευρίσκειν τὴν τοῦ σφετέρου θεοῦ φύσιν seeks to express the notion that the vestige of Zeus's nature within the soul of his votary affords a starting-point for his discovery and imitation of that nature in its fullness.

[2] I accept Madvig's χἂν for κἄν, and remove the comma after βάκχαι. I take it that what the Bacchants redispense is not their miraculous draughts of milk and honey, but their 'enthusiasm' itself. The point is that in both sorts of divine madness the immediate subject of possession 'infects' another or others. Similarly with poets at *Ion* 533 E: οὕτω δὲ καὶ ἡ Μοῦσα ἐνθέους μὲν ποιεῖ αὐτή, διὰ δὲ τῶν ἐνθέων τούτων ἄλλων ἐνθουσιαζόντων ὁρμαθὸς ἐξαρτᾶται.

[3] Hera is the queen of heaven, but not traditionally possessed of the wisdom of her consort; hence her followers are βασιλικοί, but not φιλόσοφοι. It will be remembered that the life of a βασιλεὺς ἔννομος was ranked second in the scale of values at 248 D.

[4] Dr Bury points out to me that a comparison with A 1 and B 1 makes it highly probable that κατὰ τὸν θεὸν τὸν σφέτερον go together (not τὸν σφέτερον παῖδα); and this makes ἰόντες impossible. I suggest πάντες in its place.

[5] Contrast φθονερὸν δὴ ἀνάγκη εἶναι κτλ. (239 A 7 ff., of the lover in Socrates's first speech).

the fashion of which I speak, when mutual affection arises through the madness inspired by love. But the beloved must needs be captured: and the manner of that capture I will now tell.

The main upshot of this section seems to be that a man may be a true lover in the sense that has been, or is being, explained, without being a philosopher. A distinction was drawn earlier (250B) between 'us', who are followers of Zeus, the mighty leader, and those who follow other gods; and Plato seems strongly inclined to confine the ideal ἔρως—the means of regrowing the soul's wings—to a pair jointly pursuing the philosophic life—the life which he has most fully delineated in *Rep.* VI–VII. It is in our present section that he shows signs of resisting this inclination, feeling, I believe, that room must be found for those whom Greek, and more particularly Dorian, sentiment held up as examples of sublimated ἔρως—those pairs of lovers in the camp and on the battlefield of whom Spartan history is full. In the *Symposium* (178E) Phaedrus had suggested the desirability of a whole community or a whole army of such pairs; and not long before the time when the present dialogue was being written Thebes had constituted her famous Sacred Band, which first fought at Leuctra in 371 B.C. These facts will sufficiently account for what might otherwise be surprising, namely the prominence here given to the followers of Ares. In contrast to the 'constancy' of those who follow Zeus, these are quick to resent a slight, even to the point of shedding their own blood and that of their loved ones, in what nowadays would be called an 'affair of honour'. We can hardly doubt that Plato sees in such pairs an inferior type of love to the former, though he does admire them.

Of the followers of the other two deities mentioned, Hera and Apollo, so little is said that we should be chary of attributing a definite character to them. I am inclined to think that Plato has no very definite types in mind here as he had in the case of Zeus and that of Ares; in other words, he is admitting the possibility of ideal love between yet other pairs besides the pairs of philosophers and warriors, but leaving it at that. These further types would doubtless exhibit the ideal only defectively, as the second type does.

The lover's task of moulding the beloved into the likeness of their common god requires the discovery by the lover within himself of traces of that god's nature; for although these traces are within him *ex hypothesi* (because his soul had followed the god when discarnate) yet he might be blind to them, were it not that he is constrained by the very fact of 'possession' to keep his gaze fixed upon the god (253 A 2). In other words, ἐνθουσιασμός necessarily involves a concentration of the soul upon the possessing deity, and thereby facilitates the ὁμοίωσις θεῷ.

Further, since this ὁμοίωσις θεῷ is concurrent with, and indeed hardly to be distinguished from, the love of ἐραστής for παιδικά, it is ascribed by the former to the latter, and enhances his love for him; and in consequence the divine grace bestowed upon the lover is poured by him in turn into the soul of the beloved, so that the latter too becomes assimilated to their common deity.

The words 'reaching out after him in memory' (253 A 2) must be taken in connexion with the reference to ἀνάμνησις at 249 c, especially with the words πρὸς γὰρ ἐκείνοις ἀεί ἐστιν μνήμη κατὰ δύναμιν, πρὸς οἷσπερ θεὸς ὢν θεῖός ἐστιν. Plato seems here to come very near to identifying remembrance of the Forms with remembrance of the gods who led the procession of souls; and it would seem that the two memories correspond respectively to the metaphysical and religious aspects of his philosophy; though not strictly identical, the two are inseparable, and the words of 249 c imply that the memory of the Forms is the more ultimate of the two.

As was mentioned above (p. 74) this section has been thought to disclose astrological doctrine reaching Plato from the Orient. The possibility cannot be ruled out, but the diverse characteristics which account for the different types of ἐρασταί and παιδικά appear to be of genuine Greek origin; and the combination of these characteristics with the Pythagoreo-Platonic ὁμοίωσις θεῷ would seem sufficient to account for all that is said here.

XV

*Reverting to the imagery of the charioteer and two horses, one good and the
other evil, Socrates describes the conflict within the soul of the lover,
a conflict in which the evil horse can only with great effort be subjugated.
Next, passing to the beloved, he tells of the gradual awakening of 'counter-
love' (ἀντέρως) in his soul, and of the special felicity of a pair who are
proof against the temptations of carnal lust through leading the life of
philosophy: and also of the lesser happiness of a pair who, content with
a lower life, lapse at times from the ideal of true love.*

In the beginning of our story we divided each soul into three parts, 253 c
two being like steeds and the third like a charioteer. Well and good.
Now of the steeds, so we declare, one is good and the other is not; but D
we have not described the excellence of the one nor the badness of the
other, and that is what must now be done. He that is on the more
honourable side is upright and clean-limbed, carrying his neck high,
with something of a hooked nose: in colour he is white, with black
eyes: a lover of glory, but with temperance and modesty: one that
consorts with genuine renown,[1] and needs no whip, being driven by
the word of command alone. The other is crooked of frame, a massive E
jumble of a creature,[2] with thick short neck, snub nose, black skin, and
grey eyes; hot-blooded, consorting with wantonness and vainglory;
shaggy of ear, deaf, and hard to control with whip and goad.

Now when the driver beholds the person of the beloved, and causes
a sensation of warmth to suffuse the whole soul,[3] he begins to experience

---

[1] ἀληθινῆς δόξης cannot mean 'true opinion': taken as above it is contrasted
with ἀλαζόνεια (E 3).

[2] I delete the comma after πολύς which I take predicatively with συμπεφορη-
μένος.

[3] τὸ ἐρωτικὸν ὄμμα is a difficult expression: the literal meaning is probably
'the form (or face) which stirs him to love'. If αἰσθήσει is right (and it is attested
by Hermeias, though doubted by some modern editors) it can hardly mean
'at (or by) the perception', which would require the definite article. I think
αἰσθήσει διαθερμαίνειν is a bold phrase for αἴσθησιν θερμότητος ἐμποιεῖν, 'to cause a
sensation of heat'. A further difficulty is the ascription of this action to the
ἡνίοχος rather than to the ἐρωτικὸν ὄμμα itself. The explanation seems to be that it
is the rational part of the soul that the sight of the beloved *immediately* affects,
the affection being then communicated by it to the other two parts.

254 a tickling or pricking of desire;[1] and the obedient steed, constrained now as always by modesty, refrains from leaping upon the beloved; but his fellow, heeding no more the driver's goad or whip, leaps and dashes on, sorely troubling his companion and his driver, and forcing them to approach the loved one and remind him of the delights of love's

B commerce. For a while they struggle, indignant that he should force them to a monstrous and forbidden act; but at last, finding no end to their evil plight, they yield and agree to do his bidding. And so he draws them on, and now they are quite close and behold the spectacle of the beloved flashing upon them. At that sight the driver's memory goes back to that form of Beauty, and he sees her once again enthroned by the side of Temperance upon her holy seat; then in awe and reverence he falls upon his back, and therewith is compelled to pull the

C reins so violently that he brings both steeds down on their haunches, the good one willing and unresistant, but the wanton sore against his will. Now that they are a little way off, the good horse in shame and horror drenches the whole soul with sweat, while the other, contriving to recover his wind after the pain of the bit and his fall, bursts into angry abuse, railing at the charioteer and his yoke-fellow as cowardly

D treacherous deserters. Once again he tries to force them to advance, and when they beg him to delay awhile he grudgingly consents. But when the time appointed is come, and they feign to have forgotten, he reminds them of it, struggling and neighing and pulling until he compels them a second time to approach the beloved and renew their offer; and when they have come close, with head down and tail stretched out he takes the bit between his teeth and shamelessly plunges

E on. But the driver, with resentment even stronger than before, like a racer recoiling from the starting-rope, jerks back the bit in the mouth of the wanton horse with an even stronger pull, bespatters his railing tongue and his jaws with blood, and forcing him down on legs and haunches delivers him over to anguish.

And so it happens time and again, until the evil steed casts off his wantonness; humbled in the end, he obeys the counsel of his driver, and when he sees the fair beloved is like to die of fear. Wherefore at long last the soul of the lover follows after the beloved with reverence and awe.

---

[1] πόθου κέντρων is awkward, as Dr Bury points out to me, since κέντρων must be taken in a different sense from that which it has in E 4 above and 254A 3 below. Nevertheless it is unlikely to be a gloss, and the word has been used of the prickings of desire at 251E (and cf. κεντουμένη, 251D 5).

Thus the loved one receives all manner of service, as peer of the 255 gods, from a lover that is no pretender but loves in all sincerity; of his own nature, too, he is kindly disposed to him who pays such service. Now it may be that in time past he has been misled, by his school-fellows or others, who told him that it is shameful to have commerce with a lover, and by reason of this he may repel his advances; neverthe-less as time goes on ripening age and the ordinance of destiny together lead him to welcome the other's society; for assuredly fate does not B suffer one evil man to be friend to another, nor yet one good man to lack the friendship of another.

And now that he has come to welcome his lover and to take pleasure in his company and converse, it comes home to him what a depth of kindliness he has found, and he is filled with amazement, for he per-ceives that all his other friends and kinsmen have nothing to offer in comparison with this friend in whom there dwells a god. So as he continues in this converse and society, and comes close to his lover in the gymnasium and elsewhere, that flowing stream which Zeus, as the c lover of Ganymede, called the 'flood of passion', pours in upon the lover; and part of it is absorbed within him, but when he can contain no more the rest flows away outside him; and as a breath of wind or an echo, rebounding from a smooth hard surface, goes back to its place of origin, even so the stream of beauty turns back and re-enters the eyes of the fair beloved; and so by the natural channel it reaches his soul and gives it fresh vigour,[1] watering the roots of the wings and quickening them to growth: whereby the soul of the beloved, in its D turn, is filled with love. So he loves, yet knows not what he loves: he does not understand, he cannot tell what has come upon him; like one that has caught a disease of the eye from another, he cannot account for it, not realising that his lover is as it were a mirror in which he beholds himself. And when the other is beside him, he shares his respite from anguish; when he is absent, he likewise shares his longing and being longed for; since he possesses that counter-love which is the image of love, though he supposes it to be friendship rather than love, and calls E it by that name. He feels a desire, like the lover's yet not so strong, to behold, to touch, to kiss him, to share his couch: and now ere long the desire, as one might guess, leads to the act.

---

[1] ἀναπτερῶσαν is awkward, as it seems prematurely to anticipate ὥρμησε πτεροφυεῖν. If it is kept it must, I think, be taken as more or less equivalent to ἀναψύξασαν. Heindorf's ἀναπληρῶσαν, adopted by Robin, seems to me unlikely. A possible conjecture is ἀναπετάσασαν, with removal of comma.

So when they lie side by side, the wanton horse of the lover's soul would have a word with the charioteer, claiming a little guerdon for 256 all his trouble. The like steed in the soul of the beloved has no word to say, but swelling with desire for he knows not what embraces and kisses the lover, in grateful acknowledgment of all his kindness. And when they lie by one another, he is minded not to refuse to do his part in gratifying his lover's entreaties; yet his yoke-fellow in turn,[1] being moved by reverence and heedfulness, joins with the driver in resisting. And so, if the victory be won by the higher elements of mind guiding them into the ordered rule of the philosophic life, their days on earth B will be blessed with happiness and concord; for the power of evil in the soul has been subjected, and the power of goodness liberated: they have won self-mastery and inward peace. And when life is over, with burden shed and wings recovered they stand victorious in the first of the three rounds in that truly Olympic struggle;[2] nor can any nobler prize be secured whether by the wisdom that is of man or by the madness that is of god.

C But if they turn to a way of life more ignoble and unphilosophic, yet covetous of honour, then mayhap in a careless hour, or when the wine is flowing, the wanton horses in their two souls will catch them off their guard, bring the pair together, and choosing that part which the multitude account blissful achieve their full desire. And this once done, they continue therein, albeit but rarely, seeing that their minds are not wholly set thereupon. Such a pair as this also are dear friends, but not so dear as that other pair, one to another, both in the time of D their love and when love is past; for they feel that they have exchanged the most binding pledges, which it were a sin to break by becoming enemies. When death comes they quit the body wingless indeed, yet eager to be winged, and therefore they carry off no mean reward for their lovers' madness: for it is ordained that all such as have taken the first steps on the celestial highway shall no more return to the dark pathways beneath the earth, but shall walk together in a life of shining E bliss, and be furnished in due time with like plumage the one to the other, because of their love.

---

[1] αὖ in A 6 marks the parallelism with the good horse of the ἐραστής.

[2] The reference is partly to 249 A (τρὶς ἐφεξῆς), partly to the requirement of three throws in an Olympic wrestling-match; cf. ἓν μὲν τόδ' ἤδη τῶν τριῶν παλαισμάτων (Aesch. Eum. 589).

The description of the two horses, with which this section opens, conforms to the psychological analysis of *Rep.* IX (580–581) rather than to that of *Rep.* IV. In Book IV desire was restricted to the lowest part of soul, the highest being conceived as having the function of deliberation and rational control, and the intermediate part as its natural ally, supporting its decisions through the force of feeling or emotion, as distinct from desire. But in Book IX it was recognised that each of the three parts has its own desire, so that the real distinction becomes that of the objects respectively desired, namely wisdom, honour (together with power and repute), and money as the means to the satisfaction of sensual appetites.

The good horse is here, conformably to this scheme, called a τιμῆς ἐραστής and ἀληθινῆς δόξης ἑταῖρος: but these features once mentioned do not appear to be made use of in the account of psychical conflict which follows. The fact is that in the case before us the desire of the good horse cannot be discriminated from that of the charioteer: they both want precisely the same kind of satisfaction from the beloved; but Plato's concern at present (253 D–254 E) is not to describe that satisfaction: he has done that in part in the previous section and he will return to it in the latter part (255 A–256 B) of this one: his present concern is complementary to this, namely to describe the subjugation of sheer lust. In this subjugation the charioteer and the good horse are so much one in purpose and function that their distinction can hardly be maintained if we seek to go behind the imagery. The most that we can say is that continence is conceived as in one aspect intellectual, its source being knowledge or recollection of ideal beauty,[1] and in another as emotional.[2]

The description of the evil horse, and the account of its behaviour, call for no special comment. Both in *Rep.* IV and *Rep.* IX the part of soul for which it stands is wholly concerned with sensual satisfaction, though in Book IX more stress perhaps is laid on its concern with obtaining the means to such satisfaction, namely wealth.[3] In our passage Plato brings out with great force the headstrong, ruthless character of carnal desire, its ἀναίδεια, its ὕβρις, its κακηγόρος γλῶττα. When finally humbled, the evil steed 'is like to die of fear' (254 E). The phrase φόβῳ διόλλυται is arresting; it seems to imply a more complete suppression of the lowest part of soul than that of *Rep.* IV,

---

[1] ἰδόντος δὲ τοῦ ἡνιόχου ἡ μνήμη πρὸς τὴν τοῦ κάλλους φύσιν ἠνέχθη, καὶ πάλιν εἶδεν αὐτὴν μετὰ σωφροσύνης ἐν ἁγνῷ βάθρῳ βεβῶσαν (254 B).

[2] ὁ μὲν εὐπειθὴς τῷ ἡνιόχῳ τῶν ἵππων, ἀεί τε καὶ τότε αἰδοῖ βιαζόμενος, ἑαυτὸν κατέχει κτλ. (254 A); ὁ μὲν ὑπ᾽ αἰσχύνης τε καὶ θάμβους ἱδρῶτι πᾶσαν ἔβρεξε τὴν ψυχήν (254 C).

[3] ἐπιθυμητικὸν γὰρ αὐτὸ κεκλήκαμεν διὰ σφοδρότητα τῶν περὶ τὴν ἐδωδὴν ἐπιθυμιῶν καὶ πόσιν καὶ ἀφροδίσια καὶ ὅσα ἄλλα τούτοις ἀκόλουθα, καὶ φιλοχρήματον δή, ὅτι διὰ χρημάτων μάλιστα ἀποτελοῦνται αἱ τοιαῦται ἐπιθυμίαι (580 E).

where it has a legitimate function and needs to be controlled rather than suppressed; it must not go too far, and seek to dominate the soul.[1] Even in *Rep.* IX, where it has become a 'many-headed beast', it can still be brought into harmony with the higher parts (589 B). Plato has in our dialogue cut himself off from the conception of a real harmony or equilibrium in the soul by labelling the left-hand steed as evil from the start. But we should not, I think, press this point unduly; we must remember that his real purpose is not to propound a psychological doctrine for its own sake, but to contrast the θεῖος ἔρως with the σκαιός (266 A); he makes what the *Republic* calls τὸ ἐπιθυμητικόν intrinsically evil—not merely evil when in excess—chiefly because he can thereby bring the σκαιὸς ἔρως most vividly before us. Moreover the fact that since he wrote *Rep.* IV he has come to recognise that desire belongs to every part of soul makes it possible for him to redistribute it in such a way that evil desire can be located in one part and good spread out over the other two.

Thus we may believe that by the words φόβῳ διόλλυται he means at bottom no more than that evil desire, in the relevant form of carnal lust, is rendered temporarily—not of course permanently—inoperative.

The purpose of this whole section being to describe how the beloved is captured (253 C 6), it is natural that Socrates should pass at 255 A from the soul of the ἐρῶν, the captor, to that of the ἐρώμενος. We should note that the first stages are devoid of passion: it is the converse and companionship (λόγον καὶ ὁμιλίαν) of the other that the boy values, and the 'kindliness' (εὔνοια) that 'amazes' him.[2] The awakening of passion follows in due course, and the account of it is most striking: the stream of beauty which, as we have been told earlier (251 C–D), enters into the soul of the lover and initiates the process of regrowing its wings is not all used up in this way; some of it is drawn back 'like a wind or an echo' into the eyes, and through the eyes into the soul of the ἐρώμενος, and does the same for him; thus a counter-love (ἀντέρως) is born, whose nature is not apparent to its possessor, because he does not realise that his lover has become a mirror in which his own beauty is reflected.[3]

This account of 'counter-love' is based on the principle that the sublimated love of the ἐρώμενος, no less than that of the ἐρῶν, must originate in the sight of physical beauty, and on the complementary fact that the physical beauty resides wholly in the person of the

[1] 442 A.
[2] Even at a later stage it is ὡς σφόδρ' εὔνουν that he welcomes his lover (256 A).
[3] It is possible that in using the word ἀντέρως Plato is thinking of Aesch. *Ag.* 544: τῶν ἀντερώντων ἱμέρῳ πεπληγμένοι. The whole account, and particularly the words καλεῖ δὲ αὐτὸν καὶ οἴεται οὐκ ἔρωτα ἄλλα φιλίαν εἶναι (255 E), suggest that the ἐρώμενος was not ordinarily thought of or spoken of as ἐρῶν: he was regarded as a recipient of another's love, not a giver of his own.

ἐρώμενος. There follows a description of conflict within the soul of the ἀντερῶν, similar to but much briefer than that given in the case of the ἐρῶν, and of the supreme felicity attained by a pair who remain continent. The strong but controlled eloquence of this passage (256A 7–B 7), which throbs with deep sincerity, is, I would say, as impressive as anything in the dialogue.

The last part of the section (256C–D), with its promise of a limited felicity to those who fall short of the ideal of sublimated love, may well surprise us by its apparent condonation of conduct which has earlier (250E) been scornfully condemned, and of which at the end of his life Plato writes[1] in terms of unequivocal reprobation. But it is important to observe that what is described here is not the deliberate act of a pair to whom the nobler sort of passion makes no appeal; neither of lover nor of beloved can it be said in the words of 250E that ὕβρει προσομιλῶν οὐ δέδοικεν οὐδ' αἰσχύνεται παρὰ φύσιν ἡδονὴν διώκων. It is in an unguarded hour that they yield to an admittedly strong temptation, and what they do is 'that on which their minds are not wholly set'.[2]

---

[1] Laws VII, 837C, 841D–E.

[2] Wilamowitz (Platon I, pp. 468f.) has some interesting comment on this matter. Who, he asks, will not set it to Plato's credit that he makes the heavenly judges less severe than he himself, as lawgiver, can afford to be? But it is not true to say that 'Plato doubtless assumes that the pair in question have, apart from these lapses, led a philosophic life which deserved the full reward'; on the contrary, it is only ἐὰν διαίτῃ φορτικωτέρᾳ τε καὶ ἀφιλοσόφῳ, φιλοτίμῳ δὲ χρήσωνται that the lapses will occur. The δίαιτα φιλότιμος is that of the 'timocratic' man of Rep. VIII, of whom it is said that τὴν ἐν ἑαυτῷ ἀρχὴν παρέδωκε τῷ μέσῳ τε καὶ φιλονίκῳ καὶ θυμοειδεῖ, καὶ ἐγένετο ὑψηλόφρων τε καὶ φιλότιμος ἀνήρ (550B). He represents the first stage of deterioration from the philosopher. Such a life, though good within its limits—it may be recalled that according to Aristotle (E.N. 1095B 26) its fundamental motive is ἀρετή rather that τιμή—cannot safeguard a man against moral temptation: the only adequate φρουρά (256C 3) of the soul is philosophy, that is to say an all-absorbing devotion to a progressively better understood moral ideal.

XVI

256E–257B THE SPEECH CONCLUDED. A PRAYER FOR
LYSIAS AND PHAEDRUS

In a short peroration Socrates first contrasts the ideal love that he has described with the false theory of Lysias's speaker, and then addresses the God of Love directly with a prayer that Lysias may be turned to philosophy, and that his admirer Phaedrus may cease to hesitate between two ways of life.

256 E   These then, my boy, are the blessings great and glorious which will come to you from the friendship of a lover. He who is not a lover can offer a mere acquaintance flavoured with worldly wisdom, dispensing a niggardly measure of worldly goods; in the soul to which he is attached he will engender an ignoble quality extolled by the multitude

257   as virtue, and condemn it to float for nine thousand years[1] hither and thither, around the earth and beneath it, bereft of understanding.

Thus then, dear God of Love, I have offered the fairest recantation and fullest atonement that my powers could compass; some of its language, in particular, was perforce poetical, to please Phaedrus. Grant me thy pardon for what went before, and thy favour for what ensued: be merciful and gracious, and take not from me the lover's talent wherewith thou hast blest me, neither let it wither by reason of thy displeasure, but grant me still to increase in the esteem of the fair.

B   And if anything that Phaedrus and I said earlier sounded discordant to thy ear, set it down to Lysias, the only begetter of that discourse; and staying him from discourses after this fashion turn him towards the love of wisdom, even as his brother Polemarchus has been turned. Then will his loving disciple here present no longer halt between two opinions, as now he does, but live for Love in singleness of purpose with the aid of philosophical discourse.

We are reminded at the beginning of this section of what we may well have forgotten, namely that the whole of Socrates's second

---

[1] The period of 9000 years is the sum of the periods between successive earthly lives during which souls are rewarded or punished. περὶ γῆν (*around*, not *upon* the earth) must be taken as equivalent to, or perhaps rather as a slight variation of, εἰς τοὐρανοῦ τινα τόπον (249 A): both are contrasted with ὑπὸ γῆς: cf. Frutiger, *op. cit.* p. 256.

discourse, including the account of the soul's nature and immortality as well as the doctrine of love as divine madness, has been addressed to a boy, as were the two previous speeches. Plato thus provides himself with an opportunity to extol his own interpretation of ἔρως in contrast with that put into the mouth of Lysias's speaker, whose morality is contemptuously called worldly wisdom (σωφροσύνη θνητή), a sort of level-headedness which hardly rises above the lowest utilitarian considerations.

The second paragraph, addressed to the God of Love himself, reminds the reader that the discourse has been a palinode, a recantation of Socrates's own first conception of love, although, as we have seen, there was no real change of attitude on Socrates's part. The quasi-apology for poetical language is a typical piece of Socratic irony: he affects to be one who naturally expresses himself in the plainest prose: the poetry was a concession to Phaedrus, who likes that sort of thing. But in the next sentence Socrates's regular[1] claim to possess the ἐρωτικὴ τέχνη is serious enough, though of course it is not the art as commonly conceived.

The reference to Lysias as 'only begetter of the discourse' reinforces the point which we have already noted,[2] namely that Socrates's first speech was made from the standpoint of Lysias's speaker, not from his own. The phrase τοῦ λόγου πατήρ had been applied to Phaedrus himself at *Symp.* 177D, as the person who had suggested the subject of the series of discourses in that dialogue.

It might be thought that the prayer that Lysias may be turned away from such discourses as the one to which Socrates and Phaedrus have been listening, to follow philosophy, provides strong testimony to the authenticity of that discourse. But in point of fact the prayer tells neither one way nor the other. From the point of view of 'Socrates' the Lysian authorship is unquestionable: it is a datum for the interlocutors in the dialogue, whatever be the historical fact; and if the speech is, as I believe, a pastiche, Plato is here doing no more than keeping up the fiction of a transcript.

At the same time it is permissible to wonder whether Plato has some purpose, external to the dramatic situation, in this passage. I am inclined to think that he wishes to contrast the Lysias who did not *in fact* turn to philosophy (despite the prayer of 'Socrates') both with Polemarchus[3] who in fact did, and also with Phaedrus. For the reference to Phaedrus at the end of the section implies, I suspect, a hope in due time fulfilled: a period of hesitation between the ideals of Socrates and of Lysias—

---

[1] cf. *Symp.* 177D, 212B; *Lysis* 204B.   [2] p. 37 above.

[3] Polemarchus, in whose house the whole conversation of the *Republic* takes place, seems to have been intimate with Socrates as his brother Lysias was not. He met his end at the hands of the Thirty in 404–403 B.C.

a halting between two opinions—was terminated by a right decision. Of course this is conjecture: we know virtually nothing of Phaedrus outside the pages of Plato; but when Socrates near the end of our dialogue gives what is in effect a description of his own activity as a teacher, and Phaedrus emphatically echoes his prayer that 'you and I may become like that',[1] we can hardly resist the inference that he did, in fact, become like Socrates, at least in some degree.

---

[1] παντάπασι μὲν οὖν ἔγωγε βούλομαί τε καὶ εὔχομαι ἃ λέγεις (278 B).

XVII

*Phaedrus expresses his admiration for Socrates's discourse, and doubts
whether Lysias will venture a rejoinder, more especially as he has recently
been abused by a certain politician for being a ' speech-writer' (λογογράφος).
Socrates replies that the term cannot have been meant offensively, since the
most distinguished politicians practise speech-writing themselves, and
expect to gain immortal fame therefrom. It cannot be writing or speaking
in general that is shameful, but only doing it badly. It is therefore our
business to inquire what constitutes good and bad writing and speaking,
a task which Phaedrus envisages with delight.*

Ph. If that be for our good, Socrates, I join in your prayer for it. 257 B
And I have this long while been filled with admiration for your speech C
as a far finer achievement than the one you made before. It makes me
afraid that I shall find Lysias cutting a poor figure, if he proves to be
willing to compete with another speech of his own. The fact is that
only the other day, my dear good sir, one of our politicians was railing
at him and reproaching him on this very score, constantly dubbing
him a 'speech-writer'; so possibly we shall find him desisting from
further composition to preserve his reputation.

Soc. What a ridiculous line to take, young man! And how utterly
you misjudge our friend, if you suppose him to be such a timid creature! D
Am I to believe you really do think that the person you speak of
meant his raillery as a reproach?

Ph. He gave me that impression, Socrates; and of course you know
as well as I do that the men of greatest influence and dignity in political
life are reluctant to write speeches and bequeath to posterity compositions of their own, for fear of the verdict of later ages, which might
pronounce them Sophists.[1]

Soc. Phaedrus, you are unaware that the expression 'Pleasant Bend'
comes from the long bend in the Nile:[2] and besides the matter of the E

---

[1] The implication is that most prose works hitherto had come from the pens of
Sophists; and a glance at the relevant *testimonia* in Diels-Kranz, *Vors.* II, makes
this easy to believe.

[2] There is no justification for bracketing the words ὅτι…ἐκλήθη with Heindorf
and Robin; indeed γλυκὺς ἀγκὼν λέληθέν σε would be intolerably abrupt and
obscure by itself. The proverb γλυκὺς ἀγκών was variously explained in antiquity

Bend you are unaware that the proudest of politicians have the strongest desire to write speeches and bequeath compositions; why, whenever they write a speech, they are so pleased to have admirers that they put in a special clause at the beginning with the names of the persons who admire the speech in question.

Ph. What do you mean? I don't understand.

258 *Soc.* You don't understand that when a politician begins a composition[1] the first thing he writes is the name of his admirer.

Ph. Is it?

Soc. Yes, he says maybe 'Resolved by the Council' or 'by the People' or by both: and then 'Proposed by so-and-so'—a pompous piece of self-advertisement on the part of the author; after which he proceeds with what he has to say, showing off his own wisdom to his admirers, sometimes in a very lengthy composition. This sort of thing amounts, don't you think, to composing a speech?

B *Ph.* Yes, I think it does.

Soc. Then if the speech holds its ground, the author quits the scene rejoicing; but if it is blotted out, and he loses his status as a recognised speech-writer, he goes into mourning, and his friends with him.

Ph. Quite so.

Soc. Which clearly implies that their attitude to the profession is not one of disdain, but of admiration.

Ph. To be sure.

Soc. Tell me then: when an orator, or a king, succeeds in acquiring c the power of a Lycurgus, a Solon or a Darius,[2] and so winning immortality among his people as a speech-writer, doesn't he deem himself a peer of the gods while still living, and do not people of later ages hold the same opinion of him when they contemplate his writings?

Ph. Yes, indeed.

Soc. Then do you suppose that anyone of that type, whoever he might be, and whatever his animosity towards Lysias, could reproach him simply on the ground that he writes?

(see Thompson's note), but the gist of Plato's explanation, and of his intention in quoting it, is clearly that given by Hermeias: a bend in the river, which considerably lengthened the voyage between two points, had come to be called the Pleasant Bend, κατ' ἀντίφρασιν: which shows that people sometimes mean just the opposite of what they say. That, suggests Socrates, is the case with Phaedrus's abusive politician.

[1] I follow Bergk and Robin in reading ἐν ἀρχῇ ἀνδρὸς πολιτικοῦ συγγράμματος.

[2] cf. with Thompson *Ep.* VII, 332B, where it is said of Darius that ἔδειξε παράδειγμα οἷον χρὴ τὸν νομοθέτην καὶ βασιλέα τὸν ἀγαθὸν γίγνεσθαι.

Ph. What you say certainly makes that improbable; for apparently he would be reproaching what he wanted to do himself.

Soc. Then the conclusion is obvious, that there is nothing shameful D in the mere writing of speeches.

Ph. Of course.

Soc. But in speaking and writing shamefully and badly, instead of as one should, that is where the shame comes in, I take it.

Ph. Clearly.

Soc. Then what is the nature of good writing and bad? Is it incumbent on us, Phaedrus, to examine Lysias on this point, and all such as have written or mean to write anything at all, whether in the field of public affairs or private, whether in the verse of the poet or the plain speech of prose?

Ph. Is it incumbent! Why, life itself would hardly be worth living E save for pleasures like this: certainly not for those pleasures that involve previous pain, as do almost all concerned with the body, which for that reason are rightly called slavish.[1]

The main purpose of this section is to pave the way for an examination of rhetoric in its most general sense, a sense indeed which goes considerably beyond that commonly recognised, namely any form of address, spoken or written, on any subject, in which a man seeks to commend his proposals or opinions to his audience. The statesman drafting a law is, argues Socrates, engaged in essentially the same business as the epideictic orator to whom Phaedrus had been listening; the one is 'showing off' (ἐπιδεικνύμενος, 258 A 7) his wisdom to his fellow-citizens in Council or Assembly just as the other to his circle of admirers; the successful political speaker becomes through his 'compositions' (συγγράμματα), namely his measures permanently inscribed in the statute-book, an 'immortal speech-writer'.

Hence in what follows Plato will be examining not merely the merits and demerits of that display oratory of which we have had a specimen in the first discourse, nor yet of the forensic oratory for which Lysias was equally, if not more, renowned, but of persuasive speech and persuasive writing in general. Rhetoric is at bottom persuasion, and persuasion is generically the same whatever be the mode of its expression,

[1] Phaedrus's words recall the doctrine of *Rep.* 584B–C, and of *Philebus* 51Bff. There is no evidence that it was pre-Platonic, though the fact that pain frequently *follows* pleasure is mentioned by Antiphon, περὶ ὁμονοίας, *frag.* 49 (Diels-Kranz). It has the air of being dragged in here as a deliberate allusion to the *Republic* passage, and I think we must admit that its attribution to Phaedrus is a dramatic fault.

oral or written, poetry or prose. We do not indeed find this stated in so many words in the present section, but the repeated use of πείθειν at 260A–D is sufficient evidence, if any be needed. When Socrates comes to define 'rhetoric as a whole' at 261A, he calls it 'a kind of influencing of the mind by means of words' (ψυχαγωγία τις διὰ λόγων).

With the lowering of emotional tone, unmistakable notes of humour are to be heard. The politician who sneered at Lysias as a λογογράφος must, if he ever existed, have been referring to his profession as a speech-writer for clients in the courts; the word had no other sense in contemporary Attic; and when Phaedrus suggests that the sneer might deter Lysias from composing a rejoinder to Socrates's great discourse, he is playing on the etymology of λογογραφεῖν, pretending that it embraced the writing of show-pieces such as the ἐρωτικὸς λόγος already recited. Socrates affects to take this suggestion seriously, but keeps up the humour by suggesting that the politician meant no offence by so describing Lysias; and in what follows the two suggestions are developed together to reach the quite serious conclusion that all writing and speaking of λόγοι is generically the same, and also that *per se* it is not an activity which it is offensive to impute to anybody. Such development is characteristic of Plato's subtle artistry, which delights those readers who do not miss it.[1]

---

[1] Further touches of humour or sarcasm appear at 257E, οἱ μέγιστον φρονοῦντες τῶν πολιτικῶν μάλιστα ἐρῶσι λογογραφίας: 258B, γεγηθὼς ἀπέρχεται ἐκ του θεάτρου ὁ ποιητής: 258C, ἀθάνατος λογογράφος...ἰσόθεον ἡγεῖται αὐτὸς αὑτὸν ἔτι ζῶν.

XVIII

A brief interlude now follows, in which the midday scene is recalled to our minds, with the cicadas chirping in the hot sunshine. These creatures, Socrates says, are watching to see whether their music lulls us to drowse in idleness or whether we resist their spell. He proceeds to narrate a little myth about their origin, suggesting that we can secure through their help the favour of the Muses of Philosophy, who will aid us in the inquiry upon which we are about to embark.

Soc. Well, I suppose we can spare the time; and I think too that the 258 E cicadas overhead, singing after their wont in the hot sun and conversing with one another, don't fail to observe us as well. So if they were to see 259 us two behaving like ordinary folk at midday, not conversing but dozing lazy-minded under their spell, they would very properly have the laugh of us, taking us for a pair of slaves that had invaded their retreat like sheep, to have their midday sleep beside the spring. If however they see us conversing and steering clear of their bewitching siren-song, they might feel respect for us and grant us that boon which B heaven permits them to confer upon mortals.

Ph. Oh, what is that? I don't think I have heard of it.

Soc. Surely it is unbecoming in a devotee of the Muses not to have heard of a thing like that! The story is that once upon a time these creatures were men—men of an age before there were any Muses: and that when the latter came into the world, and music made its appearance, some of the people of those days were so thrilled with pleasure that they went on singing, and quite forgot to eat and drink until they C actually died without noticing it. From them in due course sprang the race of cicadas, to which the Muses have granted the boon of needing no sustenance right from their birth, but of singing from the very first, without food or drink, until the day of their death: after which they go and report to the Muses how they severally are paid honour amongst mankind, and by whom. So for those whom they report as having honoured Terpsichore in the dance they win that Muse's favour; for D those that have worshipped in the rites of love the favour of Erato; and so with all the others, according to the nature of the worship paid to each. To the eldest, Calliope, and to her next sister Urania, they tell of those who live a life of philosophy and so do honour to the music of those twain whose theme is the heavens and all the story of gods and men, and whose song is the noblest of them all.[1]

Thus there is every reason for us not to yield to slumber in the noontide, but to pursue our talk.

Ph. Of course we must pursue it.

From the last paragraphs of the previous section it was plain that a new chapter is about to open; indeed this was almost formally announced at 258 D 7–E 5. With his usual art, therefore, Plato has inserted a short interlude at this point. It has, I suggest, three distinguishable purposes: first, to provide a temporary relaxation of the reader's mind by means of a charming little myth;[2] secondly to appeal, under cover of a warning by Socrates to Phaedrus and himself against lazy-mindedness, for a renewal (or continuance) of the reader's attention; and thirdly, to indicate the importance and difficulty of the task ahead by appealing for divine support.[3]

We shall probably be right in regarding this third purpose as the most important. Instead of the conventional direct appeal to a Muse or Muses Socrates invokes the cicadas to report favourably upon himself and Phaedrus, and thereby make them dearer (προσφιλεστέρους) to two of them; these are Calliope and Urania, who are conceived not as specially interested in the theme of the coming discussion of rhetoric, but as being the Muses of philosophy in general. The selection of Calliope for this role is probably a bit of Pythagoreanism,[4] while Urania is by her very name fitted to be patroness of the cosmological part of philosophy. By describing the two together as περί τε οὐρανὸν καὶ λόγους οὖσαι θείους τε καὶ ἀνθρωπίνους Socrates is in effect bringing together the two aspects of philosophy, the study of the heavens, with the 'visible gods' (*Tim.* 41 A) who dwell therein, and the study of man's part in the universe; yet λόγοι θεῖοι will, for the reader who comes fresh from the myth of Socrates's second speech, include the study of those other θεῖα, πρὸς οἷσπερ θεὸς ὢν θεῖός ἐστιν (249 C) —the eternal immutable Forms.

[1] In the words ἴᾱσι καλλίστην φωνήν Robin, following Hermeias, detects 'sans doute' an allusion to the Pythagorean harmony of the spheres. This seems to me fanciful.

[2] Frutiger (*op. cit.* p. 233) holds that the myth of the cicadas and that of Theuth, which comes later in our dialogue, are the only two entirely original myths in Plato.

[3] For a more solemn appeal prefacing a greater subject compare Timaeus's words at *Tim.* 27E: ἡμᾶς δὲ τοὺς περὶ τοῦ παντὸς λόγους ποιεῖσθαί πη μέλλοντας.... ἀνάγκη θεούς τε καὶ θεὰς ἐπικαλουμένους εὔχεσθαι πάντα κατὰ νοῦν ἐκείνοις μὲν μάλιστα, ἑπομένως δὲ ἡμῖν εἰπεῖν.

[4] Maximus Tyrius VII, 2, 63 (quoted by Thompson), says that Pythagoras called Philosophy the Muse whom Homer called Calliope. Compare also Empedocles, *frag.* 131 (Diels-Kranz): εὐχομένῳ νῦν αὖτε παρίστασο, Καλλιόπεια, | ἀμφὶ θεῶν μακάρων ἀγαθὸν λόγον ἐμφαίνοντι.

XIX

As a first step in the new inquiry Socrates suggests that any good speech presupposes that the speaker knows the truth about his subject; but Phaedrus demurs: the theory familiar to him is that all the speaker need know is what will seem true, in particular about moral questions, to his audience. By a homely illustration Socrates convinces him that this theory is likely to yield disastrous results. Next, a personified Rhetoric claims that knowledge of the truth, however desirable, is of no use to a speaker without the art of eloquence; but Socrates knows of certain arguments, which he hears advancing, to the effect that rhetoric is no art, but a mere knack. These arguments must have their say, in order that Phaedrus may be convinced that he will never be a successful orator unless he becomes a philosopher.

Soc. Well, the subject we proposed for inquiry just now was the nature 259 E of good and bad speaking and writing: so we are to inquire into that.

Ph. Plainly.

Soc. Then does not a good and successful discourse presuppose a knowledge in the mind of the speaker of the truth about his subject?

Ph. As to that, dear Socrates, what I have heard is that the intending orator is under no necessity of understanding what is truly just, but 260 only what is likely to be thought just by the body of men who are to give judgment; nor need he know what is truly good or noble, but what will be thought so; since it is on the latter, not the former, that persuasion depends.

Soc. 'Not to be lightly rejected',[1] Phaedrus, is any word of the wise; perhaps they are right: one has to see. And in particular[2] this present assertion must not be dismissed.

Ph. I agree.

Soc. Well, here is my suggestion for discussion.

Ph. Yes?

Soc. Suppose I tried to persuade you to acquire a horse to use in B battle against the enemy, and suppose that neither of us knew what a horse was, but I knew this much about you, that Phaedrus believes a horse to be that tame animal which possesses the largest ears.

---

[1] A quotation from *Iliad* II, 361.
[2] For this force of καὶ δὴ καί see Denniston, *Greek Particles*, pp. 255–6.

Ph. A ridiculous thing to suppose, Socrates.

Soc. Wait a moment: suppose I continued to urge upon you in all seriousness, with a studied encomium of a donkey, that it was what I called it, a horse: that it was highly important for you to possess the creature, both at home and in the field: that it was just the animal to
c ride on into battle, and that it was handy, into the bargain, for carrying your equipment and so forth.

Ph. To go to that length would be utterly ridiculous.

Soc. Well, isn't it better to be a ridiculous friend than a clever enemy?[1]

Ph. I suppose it is.

Soc. Then when a master of oratory, who is ignorant of good and evil, employs his power of persuasion on a community as ignorant as himself, not by extolling a miserable donkey as being really a horse, but by extolling evil as being really good: and when by studying the beliefs of the masses he persuades them to do evil instead of good, what
D kind of crop do you think his oratory is likely to reap from the seed thus sown?

Ph. A pretty poor one.

Soc. Well now, my good friend, have we been too scurrilous in our abuse of the art of speech? Might it not retort: 'Why do you extraordinary people talk such nonsense? I never insist on ignorance of the truth on the part of one who would learn to speak; on the contrary, if my advice goes for anything, it is that he should only resort to me after he has come into possession of truth; what I do however pride myself on is that without my aid knowledge of what is true will get a man no nearer to mastering the art of persuasion.'

E   *Ph.* And will not such a retort be just?

Soc. Yes, if the arguments advanced against oratory sustain its claim to be an art. In point of fact, I fancy I can hear certain arguments advancing, and protesting that the claim is false, that it is no art, but a knack that has nothing to do with art: inasmuch as there is, as the Spartans put it, no 'soothfast' art of speech, nor assuredly will there ever be one, without a grasp of truth.[2]

---

[1] The meaning is that the obviously ridiculous mistakes of a well-intentioned speaker are likely to do less harm than the mistakes of an ill-intentioned one who is clever enough to disguise his ignorance and so escape ridicule.

[2] The point urged here is that knowledge of truth must be part and parcel of the art of rhetoric, if it is really to be an art: knowledge cannot be something preliminary or extraneous which the orator can presume in his audience to start with, as had just been suggested by the apologist of rhetoric.

Ph. We must have these arguments, Socrates. Come, bring them 261 up before us, and examine their purport.

Soc. Come hither then, you worthy creatures, and impress upon Phaedrus, who is so blessed in his offspring,[1] that unless he gets on with his philosophy he will never get on as a speaker on any subject; and let Phaedrus be your respondent.

Ph. I await their questions.

At the opening of this section Socrates goes at once to the heart of the matter, the indifference of rhetoric to truth. What Phaedrus says he has heard—that there is no need for the intending orator to know what is really just and good, but only what the people who are to judge a case will think so—corresponds closely to the conception of his art ascribed to Gorgias in the dialogue which bears his name, and we may take it as representing a position commonly taken up by the theorists of rhetoric.[2] The teachers of eloquence, rejecting the demands of the philosophers for exact truth as visionary, and differentiating themselves from Sophists as unconcerned with morals,[3] aimed at imparting (in the words of Aristotle's definition)[4] 'the power to see the possible ways of persuading people about any given subject'.

That Isocrates is here covertly attacked, that he is in Plato's mind as one of the σοφοί of 260A, seems very improbable. Once he had given up his employment as a λογογράφος and set up as teacher and publicist, Isocrates did his best to spread the truth as he saw it in morals and politics. To be sure, he rejected the Socratic or Platonic demand for infallible knowledge in this sphere: the most we can hope for is right opinion (δόξα):[5] and this is a constant matter of opposition between him and Plato. But Isocrates was far from being an example of the toadying orator (κόλαξ) of the *Gorgias*; this can be seen from many of his 'orations', perhaps as well as anywhere in the letter to Nicocles, in which he contrasts himself as the serious and sincere adviser of an

---

[1] The allusion is to Phaedrus as begetter of discourses: cf. 242A–B.

[2] Or at least of forensic rhetoric, which the words τῷ πλήθει οἵπερ δικάσουσιν (260A) most naturally suggest; it seems less applicable to deliberative rhetoric. Thompson thinks that the σοφοί of 260A are 'all the τεχνογράφοι from Corax and Tisias downwards'.

[3] cf. *Meno* 95C: καὶ Γοργίου μάλιστα...ταῦτα ἄγαμαι, ὅτι οὐκ ἄν ποτε αὐτοῦ τοῦτο ἀκούσαις ὑπισχνουμένου, ἀλλὰ καὶ τῶν ἄλλων καταγελᾷ, ὅταν ἀκούσῃ ὑπισχνουμένων· ἀλλὰ λέγειν οἴεται δεῖν ποιεῖν δεινούς.

[4] *Rhet.* 1355B 26.

[5] When he declares that to become a good speaker is ψυχῆς ἀνδρικῆς καὶ δοξαστικῆς ἔργον (*Contra Soph.* § 17) he is certainly not thinking of his art as indifferent to truth. The meaning of δοξαστικῆς may be inferred by comparison with *Panath.* § 9, where he claims the ability δοξάσαι περὶ ἑκάστου τὴν ἀλήθειαν μᾶλλον... τῶν εἰδέναι φασκόντων.

intelligent prince with orators who seek to amuse unintelligent crowds with novelties and thrilling stories.[1]

Whether or no the theory mentioned by Phaedrus at 260A was intended to apply only to forensic oratory, Socrates in the sequel treats it as applying to deliberative, in a passage (260C) which enables us to see that behind the immediate subject of discussion Plato has in his mind what is seldom long absent from it, namely contemporary public morality, good and evil, justice and injustice in the πόλις. But that line of thought is not here pursued, and Rhetoric is now allowed to state a case for herself.

It is a plausible enough case: to know the truth is certainly desirable; it should be a preliminary to learning rhetoric; but to make anyone else believe that truth which you possess is impossible without Rhetoric; and therein her great service lies. (Here again we are reminded of the *Gorgias*, where the famous teacher admits the desirability of his pupils knowing what is right and wrong before they come to him.)

Socrates agrees to this statement; and in point of fact the words put into the mouth of a personified Rhetoric here express just what Plato himself believes and elaborates later on: rhetoric should be an art, or scientific method, of recommending what is true. The question is, how should it set about doing this? In what does its method consist? The reason why the defence of rhetoric at 260D is only plausible is that it has in fact no method, no τέχνη deserving of the name.[2]

The plea delivered by Rhetoric is met by certain personified arguments (λόγοι), which declare that she is no art but an ἄτεχνος τριβή: but this device of a literary ἀγών is soon dropped, having served its momentary purpose of sharpening our attention. The phrase ἄτεχνος τριβή is a virtual quotation from *Gorgias* 463B,[3] and we are no doubt intended to think of what Socrates there said on the point; but the arguments which he now 'hears advancing' are not in fact the arguments of the *Gorgias*. Plato is not now concerned to show that current rhetoric is χάριτός τινος καὶ ἡδονῆς ἀπεργασίας ἐμπειρία (462C), and so a mere matter of knack and κολακεία, but to establish (in the first instance) that from the rhetorician's own point of view, namely success in persuading, no matter what is to be persuaded, knowledge of truth is indispensable. The very notion of τέχνη, he is about to argue, implies that ἐπιστήμη which the contemporary pretenders to a ῥητορικὴ τέχνη affect to regard as both unattainable and unnecessary.

---

[1] *Ad Nicoclem* §§ 45–51; see Introduction p. 6 *supra*. In § 49 ψυχαγωγεῖν has the depreciatory sense of 'allure'. The date of the work is 374 B.C. or a little later (Jebb, *Attic Orators* II, p. 83), and hence very close to that of the *Phaedrus*.

[2] The emphatic position of τέχνη in 260D 9 is intended to direct our attention to this weakness in Rhetoric's defence.

[3] οὐκ ἔστι τέχνη ἀλλ' ἐμπειρία τε καὶ τριβή. cf. 501A, ἄλογος...τριβὴ καὶ ἐμπειρία.

XX

261A–264E KNOWLEDGE OF RESEMBLANCES AND DIFFERENCES

Rhetoric, Socrates proceeds, as a method of influencing men's minds (ψυχαγωγία) *commonly involves disputation* (ἀντιλογία, *the presentation of opposed arguments), as may be seen not only in the fields of forensic and deliberative oratory, but also in the arguments of Zeno the Eleatic. And since disputation involves the ability to represent, or misrepresent, one thing as like another, the successful speaker must know the truth as to how things resemble and differ from one another.*

An examination of Lysias's speech reveals its deficiency in this respect, and also its lack of orderly arrangement.

Soc. Must not the art of rhetoric, taken as a whole, be a kind of 261 A influencing of the mind[1] by means of words, not only in courts of law and other public gatherings, but in private places also? And must it not be the same art that is concerned with great issues and small, its right employment commanding no more respect when dealing with B important matters than with unimportant?[2] Is that what you have been told about it?

Ph. No indeed, not exactly that: it is principally, I should say, to lawsuits that an art of speaking and writing is applied—and of course to public harangues also. I know of no wider application.

Soc. What? Are you acquainted only with the 'Arts' or manuals of oratory by Nestor and Odysseus, which they composed in their leisure hours at Troy? Have you never heard of the work of Palamedes?

Ph. No, upon my word, nor of Nestor either; unless you are casting C Gorgias for the role of Nestor, with Odysseus played by Thrasymachus, or maybe Theodorus.[3]

[1] The word ψυχαγωγεῖν, as we have seen, is used by Isocrates, *ad Nic.* II, § 49, where it has the depreciatory sense of 'allure'. It is quite possible that the use of the corresponding noun was suggested to Plato by this passage, though his use of it is not depreciatory but neutral.

[2] cf. *Soph.* 227A where the speaker points out that dialectic holds all arts in equal respect: πασῶν τεχνῶν τὸ συγγενὲς καὶ τὸ μὴ συγγενὲς κατανοεῖν πειρωμένη τιμᾷ πρὸς τοῦτο ἐξ ἴσου πάσας.

[3] Gorgias is cast for the part of Nestor both on account of his eloquence and because he lived to a great age (though the date of his death is not known). Thrasymachus of Chalcedon, who came to reside at Athens and of whom more will be heard at 267C, is evidently at the height of his fame as a teacher of rhetoric

Soc. Perhaps I am. But anyway we may let them be, and do you tell me, what is it that the contending parties in lawcourts do? Do they not in fact contend with words, or how else should we put it?

Ph. That is just what they do.

Soc. About what is just and unjust?

Ph. Yes.

Soc. And he who possesses the art of doing this can make the same
D thing appear to the same people now just, now unjust, at will?

Ph. To be sure.

Soc. And in public harangues, no doubt, he can make the same things seem to the community now good, and now the reverse of good?

Ph. Just so.

Soc. Then can we fail to see that the Palamedes of Elea[1] has an art of speaking, such that he can make the same things appear to his audience like and unlike, or one and many, or again at rest and in motion?

Ph. Indeed he can.

Soc. So contending with words is a practice found not only in
E lawsuits and public harangues but, it seems, wherever men speak we find this single art, if indeed it is an art, which enables people to make out everything to be like everything else, within the limits of possible comparison,[2] and to expose the corresponding attempts of others who disguise what they are doing.

Ph. How so, pray?

Soc. I think that will become clear if we put the following question. Are we misled when the difference between two things is wide, or narrow?

at the dramatic date of our dialogue (*circ.* 410 B.C.). Only a single fragment of his works is extant, but he is familiar to us as a character in the *Republic*. Little of interest is recorded of his contemporary Theodorus of Byzantium, who is described at 266E as 'the master of rhetorical artifice'. There is probably some point lost to us in comparing these two to Odysseus, but, as E. S. Thompson (on *Meno* 80C) points out, 'Such εἰκασίαι were a fashionable amusement at Greek social gatherings'; cf. also Alcibiades's εἰκόνες of Socrates in *Symp.* 215 A ff.

[1] i.e. Zeno, whose method of argument was to show that an opponent's thesis led to two contradictory consequences. For the contradictory pairs here mentioned cf. *Parm.* 127E 6, 129B 5 and 129E 1; and see F. M. Cornford, *Plato and Parmenides*, pp. 57–9.

[2] The Greek is elliptical and difficult; the literal meaning of πᾶν παντὶ ὁμοιοῦν τῶν δυνατῶν καὶ οἷς δυνατόν is presumably 'to compare everything with everything else amongst the number of those things which can be compared to something else and to which something else can be compared'. If so, the twofold limitation involves a completely illogical antithesis, but this can be tolerated as a verbal artifice.

Ph. When it is narrow. 262

Soc. Well then, if you shift your ground little by little, you are more likely to pass undetected from so-and-so to its opposite than if you do so at one bound.

Ph. Of course.

Soc. It follows that anyone who intends to mislead another, without being misled himself, must discern precisely the degree of resemblance and dissimilarity between this and that.

Ph. Yes, that is essential.

Soc. Then if he does not know the truth about a given thing, how is he going to discern the degree of resemblance between that unknown thing and other things?

Ph. It will be impossible. B

Soc. Well now, when people hold beliefs contrary to fact, and are misled, it is plain that the error has crept into their minds through the suggestion of some similarity or other.

Ph. That certainly does happen.

Soc. But can anyone possibly master the art of using similarities for the purpose of bringing people round, and leading them away from the truth about this or that to the opposite of the truth, or again can anyone possibly avoid this happening to himself, unless he has knowledge of what the thing in question really is?

Ph. No, never.

Soc. It would seem to follow, my friend, that the art of speech c displayed by one who has gone chasing after beliefs, instead of knowing the truth, will be a comical sort of art, in fact no art at all.

Ph. I dare say.

Soc. Then would you like to observe some instances of what I call the presence and absence of art in that speech of Lysias which you are carrying, and in those which I have delivered?

Ph. Yes, by all means: at present our discussion is somewhat abstract, for want of adequate illustrations.

Soc. Why, as to that it seems a stroke of luck that in the two speeches[1] we have a sort of illustration of the way in which one who D

---

[1] The dual τὼ λόγω must be interpreted in the light of c 5–6, and cannot mean anything but the speech of Lysias and that of Socrates. But which speech of Socrates? The first, or the second, or both together regarded as a single speech? That the *second* speech should be meant is incompatible with the reference to misleading the audience; that the *first* is meant (Robin's view) is suggested indeed by that reference, but nevertheless seems improbable since we could hardly

knows the truth can mislead his audience by playing an oratorical joke on them. I myself, Phaedrus, put that down to the local deities, or perhaps those mouthpieces of the Muses that are chirping over our heads have vouchsafed us their inspiration; for of course I don't lay claim to any oratorical skill myself.

Ph. I dare say that is so: but please explain your point.

Soc. Well, come along: read the beginning of Lysias's speech.

E   *Ph.* 'You know how I am situated, and I have told you that I think it to our advantage that the thing should be done. Now I claim that I should not be refused what I ask simply because I am not your lover. Lovers repent when—'

Soc. Stop. Our business is to indicate where the speaker is at fault, and shows absence of art, isn't it?

263   *Ph.* Yes.

Soc. Well now, is not the following assertion obviously true, that there are some words[1] about which we all agree, and others about which we are at variance?

Ph. I think I grasp your meaning, but you might make it still plainer.

Soc. When someone utters the word 'iron' or 'silver', we all have the same object before our minds, haven't we?

Ph. Certainly.

Soc. But what about the words 'just' and 'good'? Don't we diverge, and dispute not only with one another but with our own selves?

Ph. Yes indeed.

B   *Soc.* So in some cases we agree, and in others we don't.

Ph. Quite so.

Soc. Now in which of the cases are we more apt to be misled, and in which is rhetoric more effective?

---

dispense with some indication (e.g. the insertion of κατ' ἀρχάς or the like before εἴπομεν in c 6) that the far longer, more important and more recent second speech is left outside the proposed review. I therefore conclude that τὼ λόγω means Lysias's speech and *both* Socrates's speeches regarded as one. This conclusion is confirmed by the fact that, although later on, when it becomes necessary to the argument to distinguish Socrates's two speeches, τὼ λόγω at 266A 3 undoubtedly means these two speeches, yet at 265 c 5 the words ἀπὸ τοῦ ψέγειν πρὸς τὸ ἐπαινεῖν ἔσχεν ὁ λόγος μεταβῆναι embrace both the speeches in the singular, and the same is probably the case with ὁ λόγος in 265 D 7 and ἀρχόμενος τοῦ λόγου in 263 D 3. Thompson does not consider the difficulties or the possible alternatives, but the view I have taken seems implied in his note: 'Socrates proposes to illustrate his principle by reference to the discourse of Lysias and to his own two discourses.'

[1] I accept Richards's ὀνομάτων for τοιούτων in A 3.

Ph. Plainly in the case where we fluctuate.

Soc. Then the intending student of the art of rhetoric ought, in the first place, to make a systematic division of words, and get hold of some mark distinguishing the two kinds of words, those namely in the use of which the multitude are bound to fluctuate, and those in which they are not.

Ph. To grasp that, Socrates, would certainly be an excellent piece c of discernment.[1]

Soc. And secondly, I take it, when he comes across a particular word he must realise what it is, and be swift to perceive which of the two kinds the thing he proposes to discuss really belongs to.

Ph. To be sure.

Soc. Well then, shall we reckon love as one of the disputed terms, or as one of the other sort?

Ph. As a disputed term, surely. Otherwise can you suppose it would have been possible for you to say of it what you said just now, namely that it is harmful both to the beloved and the lover, and then to turn round and say that it is really the greatest of goods?

Soc. An excellent point. But now tell me this, for thanks to my D inspired condition I can't quite remember: did I define love at the beginning of my speech?[2]

Ph. Yes indeed, and immensely thorough you were about it.

Soc. Upon my word, you rate the Nymphs of Achelous and Pan, son of Hermes, much higher as artists in oratory than Lysias, son of Cephalus. Or am I quite wrong? Did Lysias at the beginning of his discourse on love compel us to conceive of it as a certain definite entity, with a meaning he had himself decided upon? And did he E proceed to bring all his subsequent remarks, from first to last, into line with that meaning? Shall we read his first words once again?

Ph. If you like; but what you are looking for isn't there.

Soc. Read it out, so that I can listen to the author himself.

Ph. 'You know how I am situated, and I have told you that I think it to our advantage that the thing should be done. Now I claim that I should not be refused what I ask simply because I am not your lover. 264

---

[1] I follow C. Ritter (*Neue Untersuch. über Platon*, p. 312) in taking καλὸν εἶδος as practically equivalent to καλόν τι (πρᾶγμα).

[2] I take τοῦ λόγου to mean Socrates's two speeches regarded as one (see note on 262 D). He had in fact defined love in both speeches, but more formally at the beginning of the first (237 C–238 C).

Lovers, when their craving is at an end, repent of such benefits as they have conferred.'

Soc. No: he doesn't seem to get anywhere near what we are looking for: he goes about it like a man swimming on his back, in reverse, and starts from the end instead of the beginning; his opening words are what the lover would naturally say to his boy only when he had finished. Or am I quite wrong, dear Phaedrus?

B   *Ph.* I grant you, Socrates, that the substance of his address is really a peroration.

Soc. And to pass to other points: doesn't his matter strike you as thrown out at haphazard? Do you find any cogent reason for his next remark, or indeed any of his remarks, occupying the place it does? I myself, in my ignorance, thought that the writer, with a fine abandon, put down just what came into his head. Can you find any cogent principle of composition which he observed in setting down his observations in this particular order?

Ph. You flatter me in supposing that I am competent to see into his
C mind with all that accuracy.

Soc. Well, there is one point at least which I think you will admit, namely that any discourse ought to be constructed like a living creature, with its own body, as it were; it must not lack either head or feet; it must have a middle and extremities so composed as to suit each other and the whole work.

Ph. Of course.

Soc. Then ask yourself whether that is or is not the case with your friend's speech. You will find that it is just like the epitaph said to have been carved on the tomb of Midas the Phrygian.

D   *Ph.* What is that, and what's wrong with it?

Soc. It runs like this:

> A maid of bronze I stand on Midas' tomb,
> So long as waters flow and trees grow tall,
> Abiding here on his lamented grave,
> I tell the traveller Midas here is laid.[1]

E I expect you notice that it makes no difference what order the lines come in.

Ph. Socrates, you are making a joke of our speech!

---

[1] The epigram is given also (with two extra lines) in Diog. Laert. 1, 90, where it is 'said by some' to be the work of Cleobulus of Lindus.

At the end of the previous section the arguments which Socrates had 'heard advancing' were bidden to convince Phaedrus that 'unless he gets on with his philosophy he will never get on as a speaker on any subject' (261 A). The personification of these arguments is not kept up, but the whole section may best be regarded as leading up to the demand which is to be made later on (265 D–266 B), that rhetoric should be based on philosophy, that is to say on the method of dialectic. Socrates begins with a widening of the sphere of rhetoric which resembles his earlier suggestion for widening the reference of λογογράφος (257 D ff.). But whereas his object then was to extend the purview of the discussion by regarding all persuasive speech or writing as generically one, his present object is of a different sort: rhetoric is made to include the 'art' of Zeno (the 'Eleatic Palamedes') as well as the art of the forensic and deliberative orator simply in order to establish the point that its important feature is skill in disputation (ἀντιλέγειν), and in disputation of a particular sort, namely that directed to confounding good and evil, truth and falsehood. If Zeno aimed at making people believe that a given hypothesis leads to contradictory conclusions—that the same things are one and many, at rest and in motion—the public speaker or the advocate aims at making people think the same act both right and wrong, or rather at making them think it right to-day and wrong to-morrow, as suits his book or the party for whom he speaks.[1] Such an aim involves indifference to truth in the sense that the speaker has no desire to make the truth prevail; his normal object is in fact to deceive, but since deception can best be achieved by piecemeal methods, that is to say by accumulating slight falsehoods or misrepresentations until black has passed through various shades of grey into white, the speaker must be able to discern 'the precise degree of resemblance and dissimilarity between this and that' (262 A); and the same discernment is called for if he is to avoid becoming the victim of such deception himself.

What should be especially noticed in this argument is that knowledge of truth has come to be conceived as knowledge of how things resemble and differ from one another; we are in fact coming to see that the way to truth is the method of dialectic, with its two parts, Collection and Division.[2]

At this point (262 C) the discussion passes from these general

---

[1] By co-ordinating Zeno with the ἀντίδικοι and δημηγόροι Plato gives the impression that he does not admire him, though the soubriquet of Palamedes recognises his ingenuity. He regards Zeno as the father of eristic, rather than of dialectic. See Cornford, *Plato's Theory of Knowledge*, p. 169, and Diès, *Parménide*, pp. 14–16.

[2] For dialectic as revealing ὁμοιότης and ἀνομοιότης see *Statesman* 285 B, and cf. *Soph.* 253 D: τὸ κατὰ γένη διαιρεῖσθαι καὶ μήτε ταὐτὸν ⟨ὂν⟩ εἶδος ἕτερον ἡγήσασθαι μήτε ἕτερον ὂν ταὐτὸν μῶν οὐ τῆς διαλεκτικῆς φήσομεν ἐπιστήμης εἶναι;

considerations to the speeches delivered by Lysias and by Socrates himself; it is suggested that they may afford illustrations of the presence or absence of 'art', that is to say of the kind of art just desiderated, which involves knowing the truth. Socrates begins in a vein of irony, by suggesting that both speakers were in possession of the truth and contrived to mislead their audience by way of jest; but it later becomes evident that Lysias showed no sign of possessing the truth about his subject, since he made use of the 'disputable' (ἀμφισβητήσιμον) term 'love' without defining it at the outset and thereafter conforming to the definition; Socrates, on the other hand, in his speech (that is to say his first speech and his palinode regarded as one discourse) had been careful to do this.[1] Lysias then displayed little or no τέχνη, while, as for Socrates, he of course will claim no τέχνη for himself, but only for the sources of his inspiration, Pan and the Nymphs.

The last part of this section (264A–D) is of relatively small importance: it does not bear on the question of Lysias's knowledge or ignorance, but upon his style and arrangement; these things are of course matters of τέχνη but, as we might put it, of τέχνη in its purely literary, not its philosophical aspect; though indeed from the way in which Socrates speaks at 264A 4–6 it may be inferred that Plato thought of the two aspects as closely connected.

---

[1] He had in fact defined ἔρως in both speeches, and the definitions were of course different; yet in each he had conformed to the desideratum implied in the words of 263E: πρὸς τοῦτο συνταξάμενος πάντα τὸν ὕστερον λόγον διεπεράνατο. Later (266A) Socrates will point out that the two speeches taken together divided ἔρως into a 'sinister' (σκαιός) and a divine type.

XXI

*Turning to his own two speeches, Socrates points out that their contra-
diction in substance sprang from the identification of love with two opposite
kinds of madness, the human and the divine. A consideration of them from
this point of view will show that taken together they exemplify the method
of dialectic, proper to philosophy, in its two branches, Collection (συναγωγή)
and Division (διαίρεσις). Everything else that he had said was, he now
asserts, of little importance in comparison with this method, of which he is
an enthusiastic practitioner.*

Soc. Well, to avoid distressing you, let us say no more of that—though 264 E
indeed I think it provides many examples which it would be profitable
to notice, provided one were chary of imitating them—and let us pass to
the other speeches;[1] for they, I think, presented a certain feature which
everyone desirous of examining oratory would do well to observe.

Ph. To what do you refer? 265

Soc. They were of opposite purport, one maintaining that the lover
should be favoured, the other the non-lover.

Ph. Yes, they did so very manfully.

Soc. I thought you were going to say—and with truth—madly;
but that reminds me of what I was about to ask. We said, did we not,
that love is a sort of madness?

Ph. Yes.

Soc. And that there are two kinds of madness, one resulting from
human ailments, the other from a divine disturbance of our conventions
of conduct.

Ph. Quite so. B

Soc. And in the divine kind we distinguished four types, ascribing
them to four gods: the inspiration of the prophet to Apollo, that of the
mystic to Dionysus,[2] that of the poet to the Muses, and a fourth type

[1] The use of this plural for the two speeches of Socrates (as opposed to τὼ
λόγω in 262 D, which implied that Socrates had made only one speech) is quite
natural, since they are now to be contrasted (ἐναντίω που ἤστην, 265 A). There is
a reversion to the singular at 265 C 6 and D 7, which again is perfectly natural. See
note on 262 D.

[2] This is inexact, inasmuch as Apollo and Dionysus were not in fact mentioned at 244 B–D. τελεστική probably means something less restricted than the
μανία described at 244 D, namely Dionysiac frenzy in general.

which we declared to be the highest, the madness of the lover, to Aphrodite and Eros; moreover we painted, after a fashion, a picture of the lover's experience, in which perhaps we attained some degree of truth, though we may well have sometimes gone astray;[1] the blend resulting in a discourse which had some claim to plausibility, or shall

c we say a mythical hymn of praise, in due religious language, a festal celebration of my master and yours too, Phaedrus, that god of love who watches over the young and fair.

Ph. It certainly gave me great pleasure to listen to it.

Soc. Then let us take one feature of it, the way in which the discourse contrived to pass from censure to encomium.

Ph. Well now, what do you make of that?

Soc. For the most part I think our festal hymn has really been just a festive entertainment;[2] but we did casually allude[3] to a certain pair of

D procedures, and it would be very agreeable if we could seize their significance in a scientific fashion.

Ph. What procedures do you mean?

Soc. The first is that in which we bring a dispersed plurality[4] under a single form, seeing it all together: the purpose being to define so-and-so, and thus to make plain whatever may be chosen as the topic for exposition. For example, take the definition given just now of love:[5] whether it was right or wrong, at all events it was that which enabled our discourse to achieve lucidity and consistency.

---

[1] This is probably no more than a variant form of Plato's regular admission that his myths are at best approximations to the truth.

[2] The Greek has a sort of pun on the two meanings of (προσ)παίζειν, viz. 'to sing in praise of' and 'to play'; the latter meaning alone belongs to the cognate noun παιδιά, which is here associated with the verb.

[3] The 'casual allusion' is probably to be found at 265 A–B, where μανίαν τινα ἐφήσαμεν εἶναι implies Collection and μανίας εἴδη δύο Division. Or the reference may be to the original passages in the first and second speeches of Socrates where the two procedures first come into view, viz. 237 D ff. and 244 A ff.

[4] The phrase εἰς μίαν ἰδέαν συνορῶντα ἄγειν τὰ πολλαχῇ διεσπαρμένα is probably meant to include both the bringing of particulars under a Form or kind and the subsumption of a narrower Form under a wider one (see my note on Collection in *Plato's Examination of Pleasure*, p. 142). Division, on the other hand, is not concerned with particulars: it reaches an *infima species* and must then stop (cf. *Phil.* 16E).

[5] I accept Schanz's τό for τά in D 5 and would remove Burnet's dashes, which seem unhelpful: τὸ περὶ ἔρωτος ὃ ἔστιν ὁρισθέν is perfectly normal Greek for 'the definition which stated what love is'. By 'definition' here we should understand no more than the determination of the genus of ἔρως, viz. μανία (called alternatively in the next paragraph παράνοια and τὸ ἄφρον τῆς διανοίας), which is alleged to be common to both Socrates's speeches: see next note.

Ph. And what is the second procedure you speak of, Socrates?

Soc. The reverse of the other, whereby we are enabled to divide E into forms, following the objective articulation; we are not to attempt to hack off parts like a clumsy butcher, but to take example from our two recent speeches. The single general form which they postulated was irrationality; next, on the analogy of a single natural body with its 266 pairs of like-named members, right arm or leg, as we say, and left, they conceived of madness as a single objective form existing in human beings: wherefore the first speech divided off a part on the left, and continued to make divisions, never desisting until it discovered one particular part bearing the name of 'sinister' love, on which it very properly poured abuse. The other speech conducted us to the forms of madness which lay on the right-hand side, and upon discovering a type of love that shared its name with the other but was divine, displayed it to our view and extolled it as the source of the greatest goods that B can befall us.[1]

[1] There are serious difficulties in this paragraph. Socrates speaks as though the generic concept of madness (τὸ ἄφρον, παράνοια, μανία) had been common to his two speeches, and there had been a formal divisional procedure followed in both of them. Neither of these things is true. In the first speech Socrates starts by bringing ἔρως under the genus ἐπιθυμία but this is superseded (see note on 237C) by ὕβρις, which is declared to be πολυμελὲς καὶ πολυειδές (238A); it is then shown that ἔρως is a species of ὕβρις, but this is done not by successive dichotomies, but by an informal discrimination from an indefinite number of other species, of which only two are named. It is only in the second speech that Socrates starts with a clear concept of 'madness'; but here again there is no scheme of successive divisions, whether dichotomous or other: there is merely the single step of a fourfold division.

It must therefore be admitted that Socrates's account of the dialectical procedure followed in his speeches is far from exact. Nevertheless it may be said to be substantially true: for it is true to the spirit and implication of what has happened: it describes how the two speeches might naturally be schematised when taken together as part of a design which has gradually unfolded itself. A writer with more concern for exact statement than Plato had, would have made Socrates say something to the following effect: 'I can illustrate these two procedures, Collection and Division, by reference to my two speeches; if you think of them together, you will agree that I was in fact, though not explicitly, operating with a generic concept, μανία, under which I contrived to subsume two sorts of ἔρως: though I grant you that my actual procedure was very informal, and in particular that I tended to leap from genus to *infima species*, without any clear indication of intermediate species.'

It should further be remembered that the word μανία did occur in Socrates's first speech, although more or less casually: the lover whose passion was spent was described as μεταβαλὼν ἄλλον ἄρχοντα ἐν αὑτῷ καὶ προστάτην, νοῦν καὶ σωφροσύνην ἀντ' ἔρωτος καὶ μανίας (241A). Moreover, when introducing his palinode Socrates had said οὐκ ἔστ' ἔτυμος λόγος ὃς ἂν παρόντος ἐραστοῦ τῷ μὴ ἐρῶντι μᾶλλον φῇ δεῖν χαρίζεσθαι, διότι δὴ ὁ μὲν μαίνεται, ὁ δὲ σωφρονεῖ (244A). These passages, taken in

Ph. That is perfectly true.

Soc. Believe me, Phaedrus, I am myself a lover of these divisions and collections, that I may gain the power to speak and to think;[1] and whenever I deem another man able to discern an objective unity and plurality,[2] I follow 'in his footsteps where he leadeth as a god'.[3] Furthermore—whether I am right or wrong in doing so, God alone knows—it is those that have this ability whom for the present I call dialecticians.[4]

It is in this section that Plato for the first time formally expounds that philosophical method—the method of dialectic—which from now onwards becomes so prominent in his thought, especially in the *Sophist*, *Statesman* and *Philebus*, and not less so, if we may trust the evidence of a well-known comic fragment,[5] in the research carried on in the Academy. The verve displayed by Socrates in his account, particularly at 266 B where he speaks of himself as an ἐραστής of these Divisions and Collections (a word used again in the same connexion at *Phil.* 16 B), justifies the belief that here we have Plato's first announcement of a new discovery to which he attaches the highest importance.

We have, it is true, had a dialectical method sketched in an earlier dialogue, the *Republic*; but it was not the same as this, despite some

conjunction with our present passage, will justify a belief that the conception of μανία as the genus of ἔρως was present in Plato's mind from the outset of the dialogue.

[1] By these words Plato is careful to keep before our minds the necessity of applying dialectic to rhetoric.

[2] I read πεφυκόθ' with Burnet, taking it as belonging both to ἕν and πολλά, i.e. both the unity and the plurality discerned by the dialectician exist objectively. Robin defends the πεφυκός of *B* and *T*, rendering by 'porter ses regards dans la direction d'une unité et qui soit l'unité naturelle d'une multiplicité'; but this seems very difficult Greek. The variation of prepositions εἰς and ἐπί with ὁρᾶν is perfectly natural: for εἰς cf. *Phil.* 17E 5, οὐκ εἰς ἀριθμὸν οὐδένα...ἀπιδόντα: and for ἐπί *ibid.* 18 A 7, οὐκ ἐπ' ἀπείρου φύσιν δεῖ βλέπειν εὐθὺς ἀλλ' ἐπί τινα ἀριθμόν.

[3] Perhaps an adaptation of *Odyssey* v, 193, ὁ δ' ἔπειτα μετ' ἴχνια βαῖνε θεοῖο.

[4] Socrates's point is that the honourable title of 'dialectician' is to be reserved for such men. Since διαλεκτική carried the implication of serious philosophical inquiry as opposed to ἐριστική (cf. *Phil.* 17 A), this is equivalent to saying that the practitioner of Division and Collection is, in Socrates's judgment, the only true philosopher.

The diffidence expressed in εἰ μὲν ὀρθῶς...θεὸς οἶδε and in μέχρι τοῦδε does not concern the suitability of the name 'dialectician' to the true philosopher, but reflects Plato's realisation that the fruitfulness of his *novum organum* has yet to be tested in practice. That the method of dialectic sometimes led to disappointment or failure is acknowledged at *Phil.* 16 B, where once again Socrates declares himself to be its ἐραστής, but adds πολλάκις δέ με ἤδη διαφυγοῦσα ἔρημον καὶ ἄπορον κατέστησεν, and admits that it is χρῆσθαι παγχάλεπον.

[5] Epicrates, *frag.* 287 (Kock).

points of resemblance.[1] It should be realised that there can be no objection to Plato, or any philosopher, having two or even more διαλεκτικαὶ μέθοδοι, according as he διαλεκτικῶς μετέρχεται this goal or that. The word διαλεκτικός for Plato meant primarily 'pursuant of serious inquiry', as opposed to ἐριστικός, and must have been originally adopted to express his conviction that the conversing (διαλέγεσθαι) of Socrates with those willing to join him in the quest for truth was wholly different in aim and spirit from the contentious wrangling (ἐρίζειν) of men like Euthydemus and Dionysodorus.[2]

In *Rep.* VI and VII the goal of the dialectician's upward path is the cognition of the Form of the Good conceived as the source of all being and all knowledge, an ἀνυπόθετος ἀρχή in which supreme reality and supreme value coincide. This is not the place to attempt to amplify what Plato tells us about the ἰδέα τἀγαθοῦ: what is relevant is to point out that Plato, for whatever reason, never afterwards speaks of it, at all events *eo nomine*;[3] and that being so, we should not expect the dialectical method, when we meet it again, to be identical with that of the *Republic*. The μέθοδος of the *Phaedrus* and later dialogues, though broad in scope and lofty enough in aim, is directed to something less tremendous (if the word may be permitted) than the μέθοδος of the *Republic*. There is not now any notion of deriving all the truths of philosophy and science from a single first principle; and we may not unreasonably conjecture that the ontological and epistemological flights of the *Republic* have been superseded by

---

[1] At 531 D and 537 C it is provided that the various branches of mathematics which constitute the propaedeutic to dialectic should be united in a 'synoptic' view: ὁ γὰρ συνοπτικὸς διαλεκτικός, adds the latter passage. This is reminiscent, or rather anticipatory, of the συνορᾶν of 265 D, but only in a particular reference: there is no suggestion of 'synopsis' as a general scientific procedure; at most we can say that we have here Collection in embryo. Similarly with Division: at 454 A Socrates speaks of the failure to draw distinctions (τὸ μὴ δύνασθαι κατ' εἴδη διαιρούμενοι τὸ λεγόμενον ἐπισκοπεῖν) as a mark of eristic as opposed to dialectic: but it is a far cry from the recommendation of this elementary precaution to the elaborate scheme of continuous logical division in 265 E–266 A. Moreover, to compare the 'way up' and 'way down' (to and from the ἀνυπόθετος ἀρχή, cf. *Rep.* 510B) with Collection and Division respectively, as is sometimes done, seems to me only to darken counsel: there is no real parallel, and in particular there is no question of ἀναιρεῖν τὰς ὑποθέσεις nor indeed of ὑποθέσεις at all, in the *Phaedrus* dialectic.

[2] These are the only out-and-out Eristics we meet in the dialogues, though other characters such as Euthyphro, Polus and Callicles have touches of the same spirit.

[3] Of course Plato must always have postulated a Form of goodness, taken in a purely ethical sense: the moral Ideas were never abandoned, if indeed any Ideas at all were (see *Epistle* VII, 342 A ff.); moreover we know that he gave a lecture which nobody could understand, περὶ τοῦ ἀγαθοῦ, presumably at a later date than that of the *Republic*; but I am speaking of the Plato of the dialogues, and of the Good that is ἐπέκεινα τῆς οὐσίας.

something less magnificent, but perhaps more practicable, even as were its political and social aspirations. What is now contemplated is a piecemeal approach to knowledge, consisting in a mapping out of one field after another by a classification *per genera et species* which will have the effect of at once discriminating and relating these concepts or class-names which express not mere subjective generalisations but the actual structure of reality.

Here, in the *Phaedrus*, there is little in the way of rules for procedure. Collection and Division are indeed clearly enough described, but we are not told anything of ἄτομα εἴδη, or whether dichotomy is to be invariably employed, or whether more than one *fundamentum divisionis* is allowable; for such amplifications we have to look principally to the *Philebus* and *Statesman*.[1]

There can, I think, be little doubt that the plan of the whole dialogue is centred upon the present section; for it is in the formulation of the new μέθοδος that the formal relevance of the three discourses—the speech of Lysias and the two speeches of Socrates—is alone to be discovered. They are relevant to the question of good and bad rhetoric, good and bad ψυχαγωγία, just because they exemplify the presence or the absence of φιλοσοφία, of love of truth and conscious, systematic endeavour to attain it. Nevertheless formal relevance is not the same thing as intrinsic significance or value. No intelligent reader of the *Phaedrus* can fail to see that Plato attaches an importance to the second speech of Socrates, and indirectly also to the other two speeches by way of foils or contrasts thereto, additional to that derived from the part they play in the total economy of the dialogue. It is, however, this *double* significance of the speeches which has always troubled Plato's readers, and made them feel a lack of unity in the work. I believe this feeling, though natural, to be unjustified: what really needs defence or explanation is the length and elaborate detail of the great speech, its magnificence of expression, its imaginative power, the richness and grandeur of its portraiture. To speak of 'defence' in this reference may seem ridiculous; yet we cannot but feel that, relatively to the formal structure of the whole, the great discourse is both too magnificent and too long; the balance of the dialogue is upset and the structural plan at least partially obscured. Nevertheless, regarded as a contribution to what I have called[2] the main purpose of the dialogue, the vindication of the pursuit of philosophy as the true culture of the soul, the whole speech is relevant, and not a line of it otiose. It is because the structure of the dialogue is accommodated to a less

---

[1] *Phil.* 16D–18D; *Statesman* 262A–263B, 268C, 275D–E. There is a passing allusion to τὸ ἄτμητον at 277B below, but it is not elucidated.

[2] Introduction, p. 9.

important purpose, namely the enunciation of a new *method* of philosophy, that the formal defect has come about. Yet even if we are forced to admit a defect, we cannot but rejoice that Plato has chosen to let it stand. Formal perfection can be achieved at too great a price; and if the poet, the enthusiast and the mystic have had it too much their own way from the standpoint of the rationalist and the careful planner, it is surely well that it is so.

It is, I would suggest, just because Plato realises that this has happened that, now that he has come down to earth again after the μυθικὸς ὕμνος, he makes Socrates pour cold water on what he has written, saying that it was all a παιδιά—an entertainment—without value save as exemplifying dialectical method. It is not so much that Plato is being semi-ironical, or allowing Socrates a touch of his familiar self-depreciation, in saying this; the truth is rather that the rationalist in Plato does look upon his other half as 'playful', as overstepping the limits of serious philosophy.

XXII

A consideration of the technical terms and devices of rhetoric which figure in the manuals leads to the conclusion that these are concerned with no more than the antecedents of the art. A number of the chief figures in Greek oratory of the fifth century are passed in rapid review, not without touches of satire.

266 C   *Soc.* But now tell me what we ought to call them if we take instruction from Lysias and yourself.[1] Or is what I have been describing precisely that art of oratory thanks to which Thrasymachus and the rest of them have not only made themselves masterly orators, but can do the same for anyone else who cares to bring offerings[2] to these princes amongst men?

Ph. Doubtless they behave like princes, but assuredly they do not possess the kind of knowledge to which you refer. No, I think you are right in calling the procedure that you have described dialectical; but we still seem to be in the dark about rhetoric.

D   *Soc.* What? Can there really be anything of value that admits of scientific acquisition despite the lack of that procedure? If so, you and I should certainly not disdain it, but should explain what this residuum of rhetoric actually consists in.

Ph. Well, Socrates, of course there is plenty of matter in the rhetorical manuals.

Soc. Thank you for the reminder. The first point, I suppose, is that a speech must begin with a Preamble. You are referring, are you not, to such niceties of the art?

E   *Ph.* Yes.

---

[1] μαθόντας cannot stand for τοὺς μαθόντας and be taken as the object of καλεῖν, as Robin and others take it; nor would any relevant sense be given if it could; hence Madvig's proposal to insert τούς does not help matters. I think the text as it stands is satisfactory, though there is something to be said for Richards's μαθόντα. Having just said what he himself is inclined to call these practitioners, Socrates now asks what Lysias and Phaedrus would advise them (or, with μαθόντα, advise him) to call them. Then, answering his own question, he ironically suggests that the procedures just described are in fact those followed by the recognised contemporary teachers of rhetoric, and implies that the practitioners in question should therefore be called ῥητορικοί. Whereupon Phaedrus, taking or affecting to take Socrates seriously, denies that the teachers of rhetoric know anything of these procedures: dialectic and rhetoric, he thinks, are two separate arts, and the latter now calls for examination.

[2] The reference to 'offerings' (δωροφορεῖν) is merely a variant on the regular Socratico-Platonic gibe against mercenary sophists.

Soc. And next comes Exposition accompanied by Direct Evidence; thirdly Indirect Evidence, fourthly Probabilities; besides which there are the Proof and Supplementary Proof mentioned by the Byzantine master of rhetorical artifice.

Ph. You mean the worthy Theodorus?[1]

Soc. Of course; and we are to have a Refutation and Supplementary 267 Refutation both for prosecution and defence. And can we leave the admirable Evenus[2] of Paros out of the picture, the inventor of Covert Allusion and Indirect Compliment and (according to some accounts) of the Indirect Censure in mnemonic verse? A real master, that. But we won't disturb the rest of Tisias[3] and Gorgias, who realised that probability deserves more respect than truth, who could make trifles seem important and important points trifles by the force of their language, who dressed up novelties as antiques and vice versa, and B found out how to argue concisely or at interminable length about anything and everything. This last accomplishment provoked Prodicus once to mirth when he heard me mention it: he remarked that he and he alone had discovered what sort of speeches the art demands: to wit, neither long ones nor short, but of fitting length.

Ph. Masterly, Prodicus!

Soc. Are we forgetting Hippias? I think Prodicus's view would be supported by the man of Elis.

Ph. No doubt.

Soc. And then Polus:[4] what are we to say of his *Muses' Treasury of Phrases* with its Reduplications and Maxims and Similes, and of C words *à la* Licymnius[5] which that master made him a present of as a contribution to his fine writing?

---

[1] Coupled by Aristotle (*Soph. El.* 183B 32) with Tisias and Thrasymachus as one of the most important contributors to the development of rhetoric.

[2] A sophist and poet, of whom some fragments survive. He is mentioned in *Apol.* 20B and *Phaedo* 60D.

[3] A pupil of Corax, the founder of the Sicilian school of rhetoric, and a teacher of Gorgias.

[4] A pupil of Gorgias, familiar to us from the *Gorgias*, in which he replaces his master as the second interlocutor of Socrates. The most natural interpretation of Hermeias *ad loc.* is (*pace* Thompson) that Μουσεῖα λόγων was Polus's own title for the work referred to. ὡς, if kept, must (exceptionally)=οἶον, 'for example', but I should prefer to excise it. ὀνομάτων Λικυμνίων must be governed by Μουσεῖα, but it does not follow that Polus wrote another work called Μουσεῖα ὀνομάτων, though of course he may have done so.

[5] Licymnius is mentioned by Aristotle (*Rhet.* 1413B 14) as a dithyrambic poet as well as a rhetorician. At 1414B 17 Aristotle speaks with depreciation of his unnecessary technicalities.

Ph. But didn't Protagoras in point of fact[1] produce some such works, Socrates?

Soc. Yes, my young friend: there is his *Correct Diction*,[2] and many other excellent works. But to pass now to the application of pathetic language to the poor and aged, the master in that style seems to me to be the mighty man of Chalcedon,[3] who was also expert at rousing a

D crowd to anger and then soothing them down again with his spells, to quote his own saying; while at casting aspersions and dissipating them, whatever their source, he was unbeatable.

But to resume: on the way to conclude a speech there seems to be general agreement, though some call it Recapitulation and others by some other name.

Ph. You mean the practice of reminding the audience towards the end of a speech of its main points?

Soc. Yes. And now if you have anything further to add about the art of rhetoric—

Ph. Only a few unimportant points.

268 *Soc.* If they are unimportant, we may pass them over. But let us look at what we have got in a clearer light, to see what power the art possesses,[4] and when.

Ph. A very substantial power, Socrates, at all events in large assemblies.

Soc. Yes indeed. But have a look at it, my good sir, and see whether you discern some holes in the fabric, as I do.

Ph. Do show them me.

Soc. Well, look here: Suppose someone went up to your friend Eryximachus,[5] or his father Acumenus, and said 'I know how to apply such treatment to a patient's body as will induce warmth or coolness,

B as I choose: I can make him vomit, if I see fit, or go to stool, and so on and so forth. And on the strength of this knowledge I claim to be

---

[1] For the use of μέντοι in *nonne* questions see Denniston, *Greek Particles*, p. 403. It seems here to give a touch of protest: Polus may be dismissed with little consideration, but Protagoras went in for the same sort of thing, and we cannot belittle him.

[2] Ὀρθοέπεια may have been the title of a work by Protagoras, though we do not hear of it elsewhere. For Protagoras as the father of Greek grammar see *D.L.* IX, 52–4, and Nestle's edition of the *Protagoras*, p. 30.

[3] Thrasymachus: see note on 261 C.

[4] Vollgraff suggests τό for τήν in A 2: cf. 269 C 7. But αὐτῶν in A 7 seems to point to τά here. τήν seems to me impossible.

[5] One of the speakers in the *Symposium*; for Acumenus cf. 227 A above.

a competent physician, and to make a competent physician of anyone to whom I communicate this knowledge.' What do you imagine they would have to say to that?

Ph. They would ask him, of course, whether he also knew which patients ought to be given the various treatments, and when, and for how long.

Soc. Then what if he said 'Oh, no: but I expect my pupils[1] to manage what you refer to by themselves'?　　　　　　　　　　　　c

Ph. I expect they would say 'The man is mad: he thinks he has made himself a doctor by picking up something out of a book, or coming across some common drug or other, without any real knowledge of medicine.'

Soc. Now suppose someone went up to Sophocles or Euripides and said he knew how to compose lengthy dramatic speeches about a trifling matter, and quite short ones about a matter of moment; that he could write pathetic passages when he chose, or again passages of intimidation and menace, and so forth; and that he considered that by D teaching these accomplishments he could turn a pupil into a tragic poet.

Ph. I imagine that they too would laugh at anyone who supposed that you could make a tragedy otherwise than by so arranging such passages as to exhibit a proper relation to one another and to the whole of which they are parts.

Soc. Still I don't think they would abuse him rudely, but rather treat him as a musician would treat a man who fancied himself to be a master of harmony simply because he knew how to produce the highest possible note and the lowest possible on his strings. The musician would not be so rude[2] as to say 'You miserable fellow, you're E off your head': but rather, in the gentler language befitting his profession 'My good sir, it is true that one who proposes to become a master of harmony must know the things you speak of: but it is perfectly possible for one who has got as far as yourself to have not the slightest real knowledge of harmony. You are acquainted with what

---

[1] τὸν...μαθόντα refers of course not to a patient but to a pupil of the soi-disant ἰατρικός. Socrates is concerned, not with the effect of an orator on his audience, but with his claim to teach his 'art' to others, who in their turn will set up as orators. Similarly with the soi-disant tragic poets of the next paragraph: διδάσκων αὐτὰ τραγῳδίας ποίησιν οἴεται παραδιδόναι.

[2] Reading ἀγροίκως for ἀγρίως with Osann; cf. ὑπ' ἀγροικίας in 269B 1. For the confusion of the two words see *Soph.* 217 E and Cornford's note *ad loc.* (*Plato's Theory of Knowledge*, p. 167).

has to be learnt before studying harmony: but of harmony itself you know nothing.'

Ph. Perfectly true.

269   *Soc.* Similarly then Sophocles would tell the man who sought to show off to himself and Euripides that what he knew was not tragic composition but its antecedents; and Acumenus would make the same distinction between medicine and the antecedents of medicine.

Ph. I entirely agree.

Soc. And if 'mellifluous' Adrastus,[1] or shall we say Pericles, were to hear of those admirable artifices that we were referring to just now—the Brachylogies and Imageries and all the rest of them, which we enumerated and deemed it necessary to examine in a clear light—are we to suppose that they would address those who practise and teach this sort of thing, under the name of the art of rhetoric, with the
B severity you and I displayed, and in rude, coarse language? Or would they, in their ampler wisdom, actually reproach us and say 'Phaedrus and Socrates, you ought not to get angry, but to make allowances for such people;[2] it is because they are ignorant of dialectic that they are incapable of properly defining rhetoric, and that in turn leads them to imagine that by possessing themselves of the requisite antecedent
C learning they have discovered the art itself. And so they teach these antecedents to their pupils, and believe that that constitutes a complete instruction in rhetoric; they don't bother about employing the various artifices in such a way that they will be effective, or about organising a work as a whole: that is for the pupils to see to for themselves when they come to make speeches.'[3]

[1] Adrastus, King of Argos, a contemporary of Theseus: see Eur. *Supplices*. It is possible that he stands for some recent or contemporary orator; Antiphon of Rhamnus has been suggested, but the objections to this are strong: see Thompson's note.

[2] It has been suggested, by Raeder and others, that the words οὐ χρὴ χαλεπαίνειν ἀλλὰ συγγιγνώσκειν are a conscious echo of *Euthyd.* 306C, συγγιγνώσκειν μὲν οὖν αὐτοῖς χρὴ τῆς ἐπιθυμίας καὶ μὴ χαλεπαίνειν. As the *Euthydemus* passage occurs in what is perhaps a covert criticism of Isocrates, this would confirm the belief of those who find Isocrates to be the target in the present passage. It seems to me, however, that the antithesis of the two verbs is so natural that it might well recur accidentally; while as to the sentiment, it may well have been characteristic of the real Socrates to deprecate anger when sympathetic understanding was rather called for; cf. *Rep.* 337A, *Meno* 92B, 95B and (for Plato) *Laws* 888A: ἴτω δὴ πρόρρησις τοιάδε τις ἄθυμος τοῖς οὕτω τὴν διάνοιαν διεφθαρμένοις, καὶ λέγωμεν πρᾴως, σβέσαντες τὸν θυμόν, ὡς ἑνὶ διαλεγόμενοι τῶν τοιούτων.

[3] By the end of this speech the opening exhortation to 'make allowances' has distinctly lost its force, since the imaginary speakers recapitulate the shortcomings of these teachers incisively enough. This is doubtless an effect intended by Plato, who is only semi-serious in his self-reproach at the beginning of 269B.

The purpose of this section is to show that the practice, and even more the theory, of rhetoric, as it had developed in the fifth and fourth centuries, fell far short of anything that would entitle it to the name of τέχνη, a solid scientific accomplishment. We need have no hesitation in believing that Plato is thinking of the rhetoric of his own day: there may of course have been a further development of the πάγκαλα τεχνήματα (269 A) to which Socrates could not have alluded without anachronism, but if so they would hardly affect the general tenor of Plato's review and his conclusions.

The actual catalogue of these τεχνήματα, and their assignment to this or that technographer or orator, are of little importance; the object of mentioning them, apart from mild satire, is merely to substantiate the complaint that current theory and practice are concerned with nothing more than the antecedents of a true art of rhetoric; in particular, what is wanting is the knowledge of the right audience and the right occasion for making use of this or that style, this or that device, and the power to combine the different elements of a speech into a balanced and effective whole.

At the date when the *Phaedrus* was composed the most celebrated teacher of rhetoric was undoubtedly Isocrates; it follows that he must have been prominent in Plato's mind when he wrote the present section; but the problem of precisely assessing the proportion of the whole that is meant for the address of Isocrates as against that meant for the general body of rhetoric teachers is insoluble. It is of course part of the wider problem of the general relations between Plato and Isocrates, which has been discussed so often and so exhaustively[1] that I may be excused from attempting yet another examination. Probably all that can be affirmed with certainty is that the educational theories of the two were fundamentally opposed, Plato believing in an exact science applicable to the life of both individual and πόλις, while Isocrates pitched his ideal no higher than an enlightened judgment based on common sense and an estimate of probability; and that this opposition led to gibes and covert attacks on both sides, though more and plainer on the side of Isocrates, who was, to all seeming, both the more sensitive and the more quarrelsome of the two.[2]

The language in which the accomplishments of Tisias and Gorgias are described at 267 A, τά τε αὖ σμικρὰ μεγάλα καὶ τὰ μεγάλα σμικρὰ

---

[1] See especially Raeder, *Platos Phil. Entwick.* pp. 269–79; Thompson, Appendix II; Wilamowitz, *Platon* II, pp. 106–25; Burnet, *Greek Philosophy* I, pp. 215–19; Robin, *Phèdre*, pp. clx–clxxv; Taylor, *Plato*, p. 318; R. L. Howland in *C.Q.* XXXI (1937), pp. 151–9.

[2] The allusion in *Rep.* 500B to τοὺς φιλαπεχθημόνως ἔχοντας was taken by Isocrates (*Antid.* §§ 258–61), whether rightly or wrongly, as meant for himself. I am inclined to think it was so meant, and that the compliment to him at the end of our dialogue is intended as an *amende*, a generous recognition of Isocrates's merits, though implying no retraction of Plato's criticisms

φαίνεσθαι ποιοῦσι διὰ ῥώμην λόγου, καινά τε ἀρχαίως τά τ' ἐναντία καινῶς, bears a resemblance which can hardly be accidental to a passage of Isocrates, *Panegyric* (IV), composed about 380 B.C.: οἱ λόγοι τοιαύτην ἔχουσι τὴν φύσιν ὥσθ' οἷόν τ' εἶναι περὶ τῶν αὐτῶν πολλαχῶς ἐξηγήσασθαι, καὶ τά τε μεγάλα ταπεινὰ ποιῆσαι καὶ τοῖς μικροῖς μέγεθος περιθεῖναι, καὶ τὰ παλαιὰ καινῶς διελθεῖν καὶ περὶ τῶν νεωστὶ γεγενημένων ἀρχαίως εἰπεῖν (§ 8). Whether or no Tisias or Gorgias had described their accomplishments in these terms, it is plain that Plato, who could not make Socrates quote the *Panegyric*, is indicating the small value that he attaches to what Isocrates deemed of considerable importance. But this should probably be taken as no more than a light-hearted dig at his contemporary, and it is offset by the fact that the chief point insisted upon in the present section is one emphasised by Isocrates himself, namely the necessity of σύστασις (268 D, 269 C), of organic structure in which the parts are accommodated to each other and to the whole, and the lack of which finds its clearest expression in the illustration from tragic composition. The relevant passage of Isocrates is *Contra Soph.* (XIII) § 16 where, speaking of the ἰδέαι, the 'forms' or types of oratory, he says τὸ δὲ τούτων (*sc.* τῶν ἰδεῶν) ἐφ' ἑκάστῳ τῶν πραγμάτων ἃς δεῖ προελέσθαι καὶ μῖξαι πρὸς ἀλλήλας καὶ τάξαι κατὰ τρόπον, ἔτι δὲ τῶν καιρῶν μὴ διαμαρτεῖν[1]...ταῦτα δὲ πολλῆς (*sc.* φημὶ) ἐπιμελείας δεῖσθαι καὶ ψυχῆς ἀνδρικῆς καὶ δοξαστικῆς ἔργον εἶναι.

It may be inferred that, though Plato had much to criticise in Isocrates, he had no hesitation in adopting suggestions from him on occasion.

---

[1] This corresponds to ὁπότε ἕκαστα τούτων ποιεῖν (*sc.* δεῖ) (268 B); cf. also προσλαβόντι καιροὺς τοῦ πότε λεκτέον καὶ ἐπισχετέον (272 A).

XXIII

PHILOSOPHY AND RHETORIC. PERICLES'S
DEBT TO ANAXAGORAS

The true art of rhetoric, which these theorists and orators whom we have passed in review do not possess, needs the outlook and the method of philosophy. We can see this from the example of Pericles, a masterly orator who learnt from Anaxagoras to study 'Nature' (φύσις), the fundamental character of things, and apply that study to his own art. The orator must discern 'soul' in its generality and in its various kinds, and must learn how to fit the various types of discourse to the appropriate types of soul that confront him as ψυχαγωγός. When he has learnt this in theory, and mastered it in practice, he may claim to possess the art, or science, of oratory; but not before.

Ph. Well yes, Socrates: I dare say that does more or less describe 269 C what the teachers and writers in question regard as the art of rhetoric; personally I think what you say is true. But now by what means and from what source can one attain the art of the true rhetorician, the real D master of persuasion?

Soc. If you mean how can one become a finished performer, then probably—indeed I might say undoubtedly—it is the same as with anything else: if you have an innate capacity for rhetoric, you will become a famous rhetorician, provided you also acquire knowledge and practice; but if you lack any of these three you will be correspondingly unfinished.[1] As regards the art itself (as distinct from the artist) I fancy that the line of approach adopted by Lysias and Thrasymachus is not the one I have in view.

Ph. Then what is?

Soc. I am inclined to think, my good friend, that it was not E surprising that Pericles became the most finished exponent of rhetoric there has ever been.

Ph. Why so?

---

[1] Both substance and language here are very similar to Isocrates, *contra Soph.* §§ 16–17, and (in a rather less degree) to the later *Antid.* §§ 186–9. It is quite possible that Plato had been reading the former work recently, but there is no suggestion of attack or even disagreement on this point, and in any case, as Robin says (p. clxvi), it is a commonplace which gives no ground for supposing borrowing on either side.

Soc. All the great arts need supplementing by a study of Nature: 270 your artist must cultivate garrulity and high-flown speculation; from that source alone can come the mental elevation and thoroughly finished execution of which you are thinking; and that is what Pericles acquired to supplement his inborn capacity. He came across the right sort of man, I fancy, in Anaxagoras, and by enriching himself with high speculation and coming to recognise the nature of wisdom and folly[1]—on which topics of course Anaxagoras was always discoursing —he drew from that source and applied to the art of rhetoric what was suitable thereto.

Ph. How do you mean?

B   *Soc.* Rhetoric is in the same case as medicine, don't you think?

Ph. How so?

Soc. In both cases there is a nature that we have to determine, the nature of body in the one, and of soul in the other, if we mean to be scientific and not content with mere empirical routine when we apply medicine and diet to induce health and strength, or words and rules of conduct to implant such convictions and virtues as we desire.

Ph. You are probably right, Socrates.

C   *Soc.* Then do you think it possible to understand the nature of the soul satisfactorily without taking it as a whole?

Ph. If we are to believe Hippocrates the Asclepiad, we can't understand even the body without such a procedure.

Soc. No, my friend, and he is right. But we must not just rely on Hippocrates: we must examine the assertion and see whether it accords with the truth.

Ph. Yes.

Soc. Then what is it that Hippocrates and the truth have to say on D this matter of nature? I suggest that the way to reflect about the nature of anything is as follows: first, to decide whether the object in respect of which we desire to have scientific knowledge, and to be able to impart it to others, is simple or complex; secondly, if it is simple, to inquire what natural capacity it has of acting upon another thing, and through what means; or by what other thing, and through what means, it can be acted upon; or, if it is complex, to enumerate its parts and observe in respect of each what we observe in the case of the simple object, to wit what its natural capacity, active or passive, consists in.

----

[1] I retain ἀνοίας with *B* and *T*.

Ph. Perhaps so, Socrates.

Soc. Well, at all events, to pursue an inquiry without doing so would be like a blind man's progress. Surely we mustn't make out E that any sort of scientific inquirer resembles a blind or deaf person. No, it is plain that if we are to address people scientifically, we shall show them precisely what is the real and true nature of that object on which our discourse is brought to bear. And that object, I take it, is the soul.

Ph. To be sure.

Soc. Hence the speaker's whole effort is concentrated on that, for it 271 is there that he is attempting to implant conviction. Isn't that so?

Ph. Yes.

Soc. Then it is plain that Thrasymachus, or anyone else who seriously proffers a scientific rhetoric, will, in the first place, describe the soul very precisely, and let us see whether it is single and uniform in nature or, analogously to the body, complex; for to do that is, we maintain, to show a thing's nature.

Ph. Yes, undoubtedly.

Soc. And secondly he will describe what natural capacity it has to act upon what, and through what means, or by what it can be acted upon.

Ph. Quite so.

Soc. Thirdly, he will classify the types of discourse and the types of B soul,[1] and the various ways in which souls are affected, explaining the reasons in each case, suggesting the type of speech appropriate to each type of soul, and showing what kind of speech can be relied on to create belief in one soul and disbelief in another, and why.

---

[1] At 271 D 2 we have εἴδη (ψυχῆς) instead of γένη, but I think Frutiger (*op. cit.* p. 91 n. 2) is wrong in discriminating the words (which are so often synonymous) as *parts* and *kinds* of soul respectively. I do not believe that Plato has here in mind the tripartite scheme of *Rep.* IV and of the *Phaedrus* myth. The whole context suggests that there are not only three εἴδη or γένη ψυχῆς with three corresponding εἴδη λόγων: the task of the rhetorician would be comparatively simple in that case; nor is it likely that Plato would contemplate a type of oratory addressed exclusively to the 'appetitive' part of the soul. Nor do I think Wilamowitz (*op. cit.* I, p. 473) is right in saying that the present passage 'behandelt als problematisch, ob sie [i.e. die Seele] einheitlich oder zusammengesetzt ist'. The rhetorician is indeed bidden to start by asking himself whether soul is all of one sort or of many sorts, but plainly he is expected to decide upon the latter alternative. There is of course nothing here *inconsistent* with the tripartite doctrine: Plato is simply thinking of an unspecified number of types of discourse to which an unspecified number of types of mind will be respectively appropriate: unspecified, yet determinate (271 D); cf. ἐὰν μή τις τῶν ἀκουσομένων τὰς φύσεις διαριθμήσηται (273 E).

Ph. I certainly think that would be an excellent procedure.

Soc. Yes: in fact I can assure you, my friend, that no other scientific
C method of treating either our present subject or any other will ever be
found, whether in the models of the schools[1] or in speeches actually
delivered. But the present-day authors of manuals of rhetoric, of whom
you have heard, are cunning folk who know all about the soul but keep
their knowledge out of sight. So don't let us admit their claim to write
scientifically until they compose their speeches and writings in the way
we have indicated.

Ph. And what way is that?[2]

Soc. To give the actual words would be troublesome; but I am
quite ready to say how one ought to compose if he means to be as
scientific as possible.

Ph. Then please do.

Soc. Since the function of oratory is in fact to influence men's souls,
D the intending orator must know what types of soul there are. Now
these are of a determinate number, and their variety results in a variety
of individuals. To the types of soul thus discriminated there corresponds
a determinate number of types of discourse. Hence a certain type of
hearer will be easy to persuade by a certain type of speech to take such-
and-such action for such-and-such reason, while another type will be
hard to persuade. All this the orator must fully understand; and next
he must watch it actually occurring, exemplified in men's conduct, and
E must cultivate a keenness of perception in following it, if he is going to
get any advantage out of the previous instruction that he was given in
the school. And when he is competent to say what type of man is
susceptible to what kind of discourse; when, further, he can, on
272 catching sight of so-and-so, tell himself 'That is the man, that
character now actually before me is the one I heard about in school,
and in order to persuade him of so-and-so I have to apply *these*
arguments in *this* fashion'; and when, on top of all this, he has further

[1] I take ἐνδεικνύμενον to refer not to a public epideictic speech ('morceau
d'apparat', as Robin calls it), which would rather require ἐπιδεικνύμενον, but to
models or 'fair copies' issued to pupils in the schools.
[2] Phaedrus asks τίνα τοῦτον; because he feels that Socrates has not as yet
actually described the τρόπος of writing and speaking, but only the necessary
preliminaries. But by saying τὸν τρόπον τοῦτον Socrates implies that the actual
manner of composition is implicit in, or can be deduced from, his statement
of the preliminaries. Nevertheless he is ready, not indeed to give an actual
example, or model speech (αὐτὰ τὰ ῥήματα), but further to elucidate the theory of
oratory which he has already adumbrated.

grasped the right occasions for speaking and for keeping quiet, and has come to recognise the right and the wrong time for the Brachylogy, the Pathetic Passage, the Exacerbation and all the rest of his accomplishments, then and not till then has he well and truly achieved the art. But if in his speaking or teaching or writing he fails in any of these requirements, he may tell you that he has the art of speech, but one B mustn't believe all one is told.

And now maybe our author[1] will say 'Well, what of it, Phaedrus and Socrates? Do you agree with me, or should we accept some other account of the art of speech?'[2]

Ph. Surely we can't accept any other, Socrates; still it does seem a considerable business.

The question sometimes raised, whether Plato is here reversing (or mitigating) the adverse judgment passed on Pericles in the *Gorgias*, is misplaced, for he was there regarded as a bad statesman whereas here it is merely his oratorical excellence, which neither Socrates nor Plato would deny, that is affirmed.[3] But what is by no means obvious is the exact nature of the debt owed by Pericles as orator to Anaxagoras, and in general by the art of rhetoric to μετεωρολογία φύσεως πέρι. I understand Plato's point to be that Anaxagoras convinced Pericles of the importance of discovering the fundamental character of a thing as distinct from its various manifestations. The φύσις with which Anaxagoras was at all events primarily concerned was the fundamental character of the universe; what exactly his theory of matter was is a disputed question, which fortunately does not here concern us: the point is that he, like all the pre-Socratic φυσικοί, postulated a reality behind sense-appearances. What Pericles took from him was not a doctrine, but a method of viewing things, of viewing anything; namely to look to the φύσις, the 'nature' revealed in a whole, rather than to the characters of its parts. This is what is meant by saying that he took over, and applied to the art of oratory, that *element* in Anaxagoras's philosophy which was suitable thereto: ἐντεῦθεν εἵλκυσεν ἐπὶ τὴν τῶν λόγων τέχνην τὸ πρόσφορον αὐτῇ (270 A).

Plato makes his point clearer by an illustration from medicine. To treat a patient scientifically, not by mere rule of thumb, the doctor must know the φύσις σώματος, the nature of body, what 'body' in

---

[1] 'Our author' is the 'anyone who seriously proffers a scientific rhetoric' of 271 A.

[2] I retain ἤ before ἄλλως in B 3, seeing no reason for Burnet's μή.

[3] Nevertheless I do not think that Plato would have written as he does here if he had not in fact revised his opinion of Pericles; but the revision occurs not here but in the *Meno* (93 A ff., 99 B ff.).

general[1] is, as distinct from the particular bodies, with their individual peculiarities, that he has to treat. Similarly the orator and the teacher of rhetoric, being a ψυχαγωγός, must know the φύσις ψυχῆς, as distinct from the particular ψυχαί which confront him. That is what is meant by τῆς τοῦ ὅλου φύσεως at 270c 2. Plato is not saying that the doctor and the orator must know the nature of the universe, but that they must know the general character of the object that their art deals with, the nature of body as a whole, or soul as a whole.[2]

If this interpretation of the whole passage is correct, we are now in a position to understand the general statement of 269E: πᾶσαι ὅσαι μεγάλαι τῶν τεχνῶν προσδέονται ἀδολεσχίας καὶ μετεωρολογίας φύσεως πέρι. It does not mean, as might be thought if taken in isolation, that all important sciences must be based on physics or cosmology, but rather that they must apply to their several provinces the same theoretical treatment—the essence of which is the discovery of the One behind the Many, or the One-in-Many—as physics and cosmology apply to the universe. *All* science is, or ought to be, περὶ φύσεως ἱστορία, and *all* scientists (including rhetoricians, if rhetoric is to be a science) must expose themselves to the common gibes of 'garrulity' or word-spinning (ἀδολεσχία, cf. *Phaedo* 70c and Burnet *ad loc.*), and of 'high-flown speculation' or tall-talk (μετεωρολογία). This latter word I take to be used here not so much in its literal sense of discourse about τὰ μετέωρα (the things in the heavens), but rather in the metaphorical sense of speculation which 'rises above' the objects of sense to 'higher' concepts and principles.

Two difficulties however remain:

(1) Why should Anaxagoras be credited with a concern for the φύσις νοῦ τε καὶ ἀνοίας? So far as we know his teaching, it was the cosmic νοῦς and its διακόσμησις of chaotic matter that he was concerned with, whereas the reference here can hardly be to anything but human wisdom and folly. My belief is that Socrates (Plato) is merely suggesting[3] that Anaxagoras *in his converse with Pericles* would

---

[1] Not indeed 'body' in the *most* general sense, 'the corporeal', but *human* body: as of course the orator's concern is with *human* soul.

[2] Prof. G. M. A. Grube (*Plato's Thought*, p. 213) alone of scholars known to me has seen that τοῦ ὅλου does not mean the universe, as most scholars (e.g. Robin and recently Jaeger, *Paideia* III, p. 192) suppose, misled, as he remarks, by the reference to μετεωρολογία above. But Grube seems to think that the doctor is bidden to study the *particular* body that he is treating as a whole. This is indeed the point made at *Charm.* 156B, but the point here is different. The meaning seems to me to be put beyond doubt by 270E: ἂν τῷ τις τέχνῃ λόγους διδῷ, τὴν οὐσίαν δείξει ἀκριβῶς τῆς φύσεως τούτου πρὸς ὃ τοὺς λόγους προσοίσει· ἔσται δέ που ψυχὴ τοῦτο. For this sense of τὸ ὅλον cf. *Symp.* 205B.

[3] The particle δή (270A 6) being used to give the semblance of certainty to mere conjecture. The alteration of ἀνοίας (*B, T*, Hermeias) to διανοίας is doubtless due to the assumption that τὸν πόλυν λόγον refers to Anaxagoras's public teaching or writings, which did not touch on ἄνοια.

naturally have passed from speculation on the general nature of νοῦς to its manifestations, varying in degree down to vanishing point, in human beings.

(2) To what work of Hippocrates does Socrates refer? I am very doubtful whether any treatise in our Hippocratic corpus will fill the bill; in any case the question is one rather for the student of Greek medicine than for the Platonist. Galen indeed (see Thompson's note) affirmed confidently that the allusion is to περὶ φύσιος ἀνθρώπου: but this belief seems to be based on what is said at 270 D about the possibility of πλείω εἴδη σώματος rather than on the earlier assertion that, according to Hippocrates, we ought not to study a particular (human) body apart from (human) body as a whole; and I strongly suspect that when the question is asked τί ποτε λέγει 'Ιπποκράτης καὶ ὁ ἀληθὴς λόγος, Plato is about to read into Hippocrates what he wants to find there; it is analogous, I suggest, to what Protagoras told his disciples in secret (*Theaet.* 152 c) or the real meaning of what Heraclitus expresses badly (*Symp.* 187 A). If we could point to any Hippocratic treatise in which it is plainly declared that the doctor ought to have a general knowledge of physiology before he treats a patient, our doubts would be at rest; but this does not appear to be possible, though chapter xx of περὶ ἀρχαίης ἰητρικῆς comes somewhere near saying so.[1]

The upshot is that we are back again at dialectic as the right μέθοδος for the orator: he must discern ψυχή as at once a One and a Many; but there is something more now added (270 D ff.): the various types of soul act and are acted upon in various ways, and the orator must discern how this happens. It is clear from 271 B that it is the παθήματα that are important rather than the ποιήματα: the orator must know how this or that soul is affected by this or that type of oratory;[2] the soul's δύναμις τοῦ ποιεῖν is probably mentioned only because Plato does not wish us to think of ψυχή as purely passive; it moves both itself and body in various ways; but that is irrelevant to the present context.

[1] For the most recent discussion, see W. H. S. Jones, *Philosophy and Medicine in Ancient Greece*, pp. 16–20.
[2] This is rightly emphasized by Robin (p. xlviii): 'Le plus important de cette théorie, c'est que la seule rhétorique constituant un enseignement positif est celle qui ne se fond pas seulement sur une classification *parallèle* des âmes et des discours, mais qui en outre envisage spécialement leur *interaction*.'

XXIV

272B–274B THE TRUE METHOD OF RHETORIC.
ITS DIFFICULTY AND ITS JUSTIFICATION

Can we find any easier substitute for this admittedly laborious procedure?
To convince Phaedrus that we cannot, Socrates recalls the contention that
the orator need not concern himself with the truth, but only with plausibility
or (it is now added) probability. After quoting from Tisias's manual an
example of forensic argument based on 'the probable', and showing its
absurdity, Socrates remarks that this is really no new point, and has
already been met.

The way of the true rhetoric is difficult and laborious, but its justification
is that in seeking the truth we are seeking to do the pleasure of the gods.
They are our good and gracious masters, and it is they, not our fellow-
slaves, that we should seek to please.

272 B   *Soc.* You are right, and that makes it necessary thoroughly to
overhaul all our arguments, and see whether there is some easier and
c shorter way of arriving at the art; we don't want to waste effort in
going off[1] on a long rough road, when we might take a short smooth
one. But if you can help us at all through what you have heard from
Lysias or anyone else, do try to recall it.

    Ph. As far as trying goes, I might; but I can suggest nothing on the
spur of the moment.

    Soc. Then would you like me to tell you something I have heard
from those concerned with these matters?

    Ph. Why, yes.

    Soc. Anyhow, Phaedrus, we are told that even the devil's advocate
ought to be heard.

D   *Ph.* Then you can put his case.

    Soc. Well, they tell us that there is no need to make such a solemn
business of it, or fetch such a long compass on an uphill road. As we
remarked at the beginning[2] of this discussion, there is, they maintain,
absolutely no need for the budding orator to concern himself with the
truth about what is just or good conduct, nor indeed about who are
just and good men whether by nature or education. In the lawcourts
nobody cares a rap for the truth about these matters, but only about

    [1] ἀπίῃ has been doubted: possibly διίῃ, 'traverse', should be read.
    [2] 260 A ff.

what is plausible. And that is the same as what is probable, and is what E must occupy the attention of the would-be master of the art of speech. Even actual facts ought sometimes not to be stated, if they don't tally with probability; they should be replaced by what is probable, whether in prosecution or defence; whatever you say, you simply must pursue this probability they talk of, and can say good-bye to the truth for ever. Stick to that all through your speech, and you are equipped with 273 the art complete.

Ph. Your account, Socrates, precisely reproduces what is said by those who claim to be experts in the art of speech. I remember that we did touch briefly on this sort of contention a while ago;[1] and the professionals regard it as a highly important point.

Soc. Very well then, take Tisias himself; you have thumbed him[2] carefully, so let Tisias tell us this: does he maintain that the probable is anything other than that which commends itself to the multitude? B

Ph. How could it be anything else?

Soc. Then in consequence, it would seem, of that profound scientific discovery he laid down that if a weak but brave man is arrested for assaulting a strong but cowardly one, whom he has robbed of his cloak or some other garment, neither of them ought to state the true facts; the coward should say that the brave man didn't assault him single-handed, and the brave man should contend that there were only the two of them, and then have recourse to the famous plea 'How could a little fellow like me have attacked a big fellow like him?' Upon which the C big fellow will not avow his own poltroonery but will try to invent some fresh lie which will probably supply his opponent with a means of refuting him.[3] And similar 'scientific' rules are given for other cases of the kind. Isn't that so, Phaedrus?

Ph. To be sure.

Soc. Bless my soul! It appears that he made a brilliant discovery of a buried art, your Tisias, or whoever it really was[4] and whatever he is pleased to be called after. But, my friend, shall we or shall we not say to him—

Ph. Say what? D

---

[1] 259 E.   [2] cf. Arist. *Birds* 471, οὐδ' Αἴσωπον πεπάτηκας.

[3] 'The impotent conclusion of these elaborate mystifications was not, we may presume, contemplated by Tisias, but is maliciously added by Socrates' (Thompson).

[4] Plato perhaps hints that the real discoverer was Corax, the reputed teacher of Tisias, who 'was pleased' to be called after a bird of prey (the crow).

Soc. This: 'In point of fact, Tisias, we have for some time before you came on the scene been saying that the multitude get their notion of probability as the result of a likeness to truth; and we explained just now that these likenesses can always be best discovered by one who knows the truth. Therefore if you have anything else to say about the art of speech, we should be glad to hear it; but if not we shall adhere to the point we made just now, namely that unless the aspirant to oratory can on the one hand list the various natures amongst his prospective E audiences, and on the other divide things into their kinds and embrace each individual thing under a single form, he will never attain such success as is within the grasp of mankind. Yet he will assuredly never acquire such competence without considerable diligence, which the wise man should exert not for the sake of speaking to and dealing with his fellow-men, but that he may be able to speak what is pleasing to the gods, and in all his dealings to do their pleasure to the best of his ability. For you see, Tisias, what we are told by those wiser than 274 ourselves[1] is true, that a man of sense ought never to study the gratification of his fellow-slaves, save as a minor consideration, but that of his most excellent[2] masters. So don't be surprised that we have to make a long detour:[3] it is because the goal is glorious, though not the goal you think of.'[4] Not but what those lesser objects also, if you would have them, can best be attained (so our argument assures us) as a consequence of the greater.

Ph. Your project seems to be excellent, Socrates, if only one could carry it out.

Soc. Well, when a man sets his hand to something good, it is good B that he should take what comes to him.[5]

Ph. Yes, of course.

Soc. Then we may feel that we have said enough about the art of speech, both the true art and the false?

Ph. Certainly.

---

[1] οἱ σοφώτεροι οἷον οἱ Πυθαγορεῖοι, says Hermeias rightly; cf. (with Thompson) the conception of men as κτήματα θεῶν at *Phaedo* 62B.

[2] For ἀγαθοῖς τε καὶ ἐξ ἀγαθῶν see note on 246A (p. 69).

[3] Referring to 272D, μακρὰν περιβαλλομένοις.

[4] I take the address to Tisias to end at οὐχ ὧν σὺ δοκεῖς, and follow Thompson in accepting Heindorf's ὧν for ὡς. 'The goal you think of' is τὸ ὁμοδούλοις (=τῷ πλήθει) χαρίζεσθαι. But (adds Socrates in an aside to Phaedrus) in the long run service to the gods proves to be the best means of affording true gratification to our fellow-men.

[5] *sc.* whether success or failure.

Except for its closing sentences, this section does little more than underline and sum up what has been said before of the deficiencies of existing rhetoric. So far as there is anything new, it is the substitution of the 'probable' (τὸ εἰκός) for the 'plausible' (τὸ πιθανόν) in the theorists' requirement, and Socrates's ridicule of this by an illustration taken from Tisias's own manual. Whether a speaker aims at probability or plausibility, he is, argues Socrates (referring back to 261 E ff.), relying on deceptive similarities, or making what looks something like the truth pass for the truth itself. Only dialectic, which includes both a desire for truth and a method for attaining it, can remedy this state of things. It is no light task, as Socrates admits, but the toil is justified by the goal, which is nothing less than doing the pleasure of the gods, our good and gracious masters.[1]

Thus the section closes with the sudden introduction of a religious note, and a momentary elevation of thought and language which is characteristically Platonic: ὥστ' εἰ μακρὰ ἡ περίοδος, μὴ θαυμάσης· μεγάλων γὰρ ἕνεκα περιιτέον, οὐχ ὧν σὺ δοκεῖς: these are moving words, and indeed the whole of the last dozen lines here cannot fail to remind us of a more famous and even more moving passage of the *Phaedo* (116C): ἀλλὰ τούτων δὴ ἕνεκα χρὴ ὧν διεληλύθαμεν, ὧ Σιμμία, πᾶν ποιεῖν ὥστε ἀρετῆς καὶ φρονήσεως ἐν τῷ βίῳ μετασχεῖν· καλὸν γὰρ τὸ ἆθλον καὶ ἡ ἐλπὶς μεγάλη.

[1] For the paramount importance of truth compare *Laws* 730C 1 ff.: ἀλήθεια δὴ πάντων μὲν ἀγαθῶν θεοῖς ἡγεῖται, πάντων δὲ ἀνθρώποις· ἧς ὁ γενήσεσθαι μέλλων μακάριός τε καὶ εὐδαίμων ἐξ ἀρχῆς εὐθὺς μέτοχος εἴη, ἵνα ὡς πλεῖστον χρόνον ἀληθὴς ὢν διαβιοῖ.

XXV

*It remains to decide under what conditions written compositions may be
deemed proper. Socrates prefaces the discussion with a myth of the
invention of writing by the Egyptian god Theuth (known to the Greeks as
Hermes) and its unfavourable reception by King Thamus. The grounds for
this disapproval are brought out, and the disadvantages of the written as
against the spoken word are developed, Socrates finally deciding that
though it may be useful by way of reminder to the author and to others of
what they know, it should be regarded as 'pastime' (παιδιά) rather than
as serious business (σπουδή); 'lucidity, completeness and serious importance' (278 A) belong only to the conclusions of dialectic, written not in ink
but in the souls of men.*

274 B   *Soc.* But there remains the question of propriety and impropriety
in writing, that is to say the conditions which make it proper or
improper. Isn't that so?

Ph. Yes.

Soc. Now do you know how we may best please God, in practice
and in theory, in this matter of words?

Ph. No indeed. Do you?

C   *Soc.* I can tell you the tradition that has come down from our
forefathers, but they alone know the truth of it. However, if we could
discover that for ourselves, should we still be concerned with the fancies
of mankind?

Ph. What a ridiculous question! But tell me the tradition you
speak of.

Soc. Very well. The story is that in the region of Naucratis in
Egypt there dwelt one of the old gods of the country, the god to whom
the bird called Ibis is sacred, his own name being Theuth. He it was
D   that invented number and calculation, geometry and astronomy, not
to speak of draughts and dice, and above all writing. Now the king
of the whole country at that time was Thamus, who dwelt in the great
city of Upper Egypt which the Greeks call Egyptian Thebes, while
Thamus[1] they call Ammon. To him came Theuth, and revealed his

---

[1] I accept Postgate's Θαμοῦν for θεόν in D 4.

ırts, saying that they ought to be passed on to the Egyptians in general. Thamus asked what was the use of them all: and when Theuth explained, he condemned what he thought the bad points and praised E what he thought the good. On each art, we are told, Thamus had plenty of views both for and against; it would take too long to give them in detail, but when it came to writing Theuth said 'Here, O king, is a branch of learning that will make the people of Egypt wiser and improve their memories: my discovery provides a recipe for memory and wisdom'. But the king answered and said 'O man full of arts, to one is it given to create the things of art, and to another to judge what measure of harm and of profit they have for those that shall employ them. And so it is that you, by reason of your tender regard for the 275 writing that is your offspring, have declared the very opposite of its true effect. If men learn this, it will implant forgetfulness in their souls: they will cease to exercise memory because they rely on that which is written, calling things to remembrance[1] no longer from within themselves, but by means of external marks; what you have discovered is a recipe not for memory, but for reminder. And it is no true wisdom that you offer your disciples, but only its semblance; for by telling them of many things without teaching them you will make them seem to know much, while for the most part they know nothing; and as men B filled, not with wisdom, but with the conceit of wisdom, they will be a burden to their fellows.'

Ph. It is easy for you, Socrates, to make up tales from Egypt or anywhere else you fancy.[2]

Soc. Oh, but the authorities of the temple of Zeus at Dodona, my friend, said that the first prophetic utterances came from an oak-tree. In fact the people of those days, lacking the wisdom of you young people, were content in their simplicity to listen to trees or rocks, provided these told the truth. For you apparently it makes a difference C

---

[1] If αὐτοὺς...ἀναμιμνησκομένους is to be kept we must take it as a sense-construction as though τοὺς μαθόντας ἐπιλήσμονας παρέξει had preceded. Alternatively αὐταῖς...ἀναμιμνησκομέναις, suggested to me by Dr Bury, might be read.

[2] The little myth of Theuth and Thamus is, like that of the cicadas, apparently Plato's own invention, though of course the personages belong to Egyptian history or legend. The inventor of writing in Greek legend was Prometheus; but he was unsuitable for Plato's purpose, since it would have been difficult to make anyone play against him the part that Thamus plays against Theuth. And in any case it was natural enough for Plato to go to Egypt for a tale of pre-history, just as in a later dialogue he goes to an Egyptian priest for his story of Atlantis.

who the speaker is, and what country he comes from: you don'
merely ask whether what he says is true or false.[1]

Ph. I deserve your rebuke, and I agree that the man of Thebes is
right in what he said about writing.

Soc. Then anyone who leaves behind him a written manual, and
likewise anyone who takes it over from him, on the supposition that
such writing will provide something reliable and permanent,[2] must be
exceedingly simple-minded; he must really be ignorant of Ammon's
utterance, if he imagines that written words can do anything more
D than remind[3] one who knows that which the writing is concerned
with.

Ph. Very true.

Soc. You know, Phaedrus, that's the strange thing about writing,
which makes it truly analogous to painting.[4] The painter's products
stand before us as though they were alive: but if you question them,
they maintain a most majestic silence. It is the same with written words:
they seem to talk to you as though they were intelligent, but if you ask
them anything about what they say, from a desire to be instructed, they
go on telling you just the same thing for ever. And once a thing is put
E in writing, the composition, whatever it may be, drifts all over the
place, getting into the hands not only of those who understand it, but
equally of those who have no business with it; it doesn't know how
to address the right people, and not address the wrong. And when it is
ill-treated and unfairly abused it always needs its parent to come to its
help, being unable to defend or help itself.

Ph. Once again you are perfectly right.

276 *Soc.* But now tell me, is there another sort of discourse, that is
brother to the written speech, but of unquestioned legitimacy? Can
we see how it originates, and how much better and more effective it is
than the other?

Ph. What sort of discourse have you now in mind, and what is its
origin?

---

[1] I follow Thompson and Robin, against Burnet, in putting a full stop, not
a question-mark, here.

[2] I take ὡς τι...ἐσόμενον to belong to ὁ τέχνην...καταλιπεῖν as much as to
ὁ παραδεχόμενος: for to speak of one who 'thinks he has left a written manual'
is, by itself, nonsense. This could be indicated by deleting the comma after
καταλιπεῖν and putting dashes before and after καὶ αὖ ὁ παραδεχόμενος.

[3] I accept Dr Bury's suggestion πλέον ποιεῖν οἰόμενος [εἶναι].

[4] The Greek word for 'painting' (ζωγραφία, etymologically a 'drawing of
living beings') is closely connected with that for 'writing' (γραφή).

Soc. The sort that goes together with knowledge, and is written in the soul of the learner: that can defend itself, and knows to whom it should speak and to whom it should say nothing.

Ph. You mean no dead discourse, but the living speech, the original of which the written discourse may fairly be called a kind of image.

Soc. Precisely. And now tell me this: if a sensible farmer had some B seeds to look after and wanted them to bear fruit, would he with serious intent plant them during the summer in a garden of Adonis,[1] and enjoy watching it producing fine fruit within eight days? If he did so at all, wouldn't it be in a holiday spirit, just by way of pastime? For serious purposes wouldn't he behave like a scientific farmer, sow his seeds in suitable soil, and be well content if they came to maturity within eight months?

Ph. I think we may distinguish as you say, Socrates, between what C the farmer would do seriously and what he would do in a different spirit.

Soc. And are we to maintain that he who has knowledge of what is just, honourable and good has less sense than the farmer in dealing with his seeds?

Ph. Of course not.

Soc. Then it won't be with serious intent that he 'writes them in water'[2] or that black fluid we call ink, using his pen to sow words that can't either speak in their own defence or present the truth adequately.

Ph. It certainly isn't likely.

Soc. No, it is not. He will sow his seed in literary gardens, I take D it, and write when he does write by way of pastime, collecting a store of refreshment both for his own memory, against the day 'when age oblivious comes', and for all such as tread in his footsteps; and he will take pleasure in watching the tender plants[3] grow up. And when other men resort to other pastimes, regaling themselves with drinking-parties and such like, he will doubtless prefer to indulge in the recreation I refer to.[4]

Ph. And what an excellent one it is, Socrates! How far superior to E

---

[1] A pot or window-box for forcing plants at the festival of Adonis.
[2] A proverbial phrase for useless labour.
[3] αὐτούς can only refer to κήπους, and seems to involve a confusion between the 'garden' and the seeds or plants growing in it.
[4] Reading ⟨ἐν⟩ οἷς λέγω with Heindorf.

the other sort is the recreation that a man finds in words, when he discourses[1] about justice and the other topics you speak of.[2]

Soc. Yes indeed, dear Phaedrus. But far more excellent, I think, is the serious treatment of them, which employs the art of dialectic. The dialectician selects a soul of the right type, and in it he plants and sows his words founded on knowledge, words which can defend both 277 themselves and him who planted them, words which instead of remaining barren contain a seed whence new words grow up in new characters; whereby the seed is vouchsafed immortality, and its possessor the fullest measure of blessedness that man can attain unto.[3]

Ph. Yes, that is a far more excellent way.

Soc. Then now that that has been settled, Phaedrus, we can proceed to the other point.

Ph. What is that?

Soc. The point that we wanted to look into before we arrived at our present conclusion. Our intention was to examine the reproach levelled against Lysias on the score of speech-writing, and therewith B the general question of speech-writing and what does and does not make it an art. Now I think we have pretty well cleared up the question of art.

Ph. Yes, we did think so, but please remind me how we did it.

Soc. The conditions to be fulfilled are these: first, you must know the truth about the subject that you speak or write about: that is to say, you must be able to isolate it in definition, and having so defined it you must next understand how to divide it into kinds, until you reach the limit of division; secondly, you must have a corresponding discern-

---

[1] Either there is a bad anacoluthon, or μυθολογοῦντος should be read, with Richards. Phaedrus is of course referring to *written* μυθολογία, and although the verb (like μῦθος itself) does not necessarily carry any sense of 'myth-making', yet we are doubtless meant to detect an allusion to the μυθικὸς ὕμνος of the present dialogue.

[2] ἄλλων ὧν λέγεις πέρι refers to c 3 above. It cannot mean 'other topics which you commonly talk about', for that would need the pronoun σύ.

[3] The words εἰς ὅσον ἀνθρώπῳ δυνατὸν μάλιστα are to be noted. Socrates is not here speaking of the felicity of the soul which is liberated whether temporarily or finally from the body, but of that attainable by an ἄνθρωπος, a compound of soul and body. The term ἀθάνατον is here only applied to the undying truth passed on from generation to generation, but it might equally well have been applied to the possessor of truth (τὸν ἔχοντα), for he does attain immortality so far as an ἄνθρωπος can; this we were told in a closely parallel passage of the *Symposium* (212 A) where the final words should especially be noted: τεκόντε δὲ ἀρετὴν ἀληθῆ καὶ θρεψαμένῳ ὑπάρχει θεοφιλεῖ γενέσθαι, καὶ εἴπερ τῳ ἄλλῳ ἀνθρώπῳ ἀθανάτῳ καὶ ἐκείνῳ. For the meaning of ἀθάνατος γενέσθαι see Bury, *Symposium*, p. xliv.

ment of the nature of the soul, discover the type of speech appropriate c
to each nature, and order and arrange your discourse accordingly,
addressing a variegated soul in a variegated style that ranges over the
whole gamut of tones, and a simple soul in a simple style.¹ All this
must be done if you are to become competent, within human limits, as
a scientific practitioner of speech, whether you propose to expound or
to persuade. Such is the clear purport of all our foregoing discussion.

Ph. Yes, that was undoubtedly how we came to see the matter.

Soc. And now to revert to our other question, whether the delivery D
and composition of speeches is honourable or base, and in what
circumstances they may properly become a matter of reproach, our
earlier conclusions have, I think, shown—

Ph. Which conclusions?

Soc. They have shown² that any work, in the past or in the future,
whether by Lysias or anyone else, whether composed in a private
capacity or in the role of a public man who by proposing a law becomes
the author of a political composition, is a matter of reproach to its
author (whether or no the reproach is actually voiced) if he regards it
as containing important truth of permanent validity. For ignorance of
what is a waking vision and what is a mere dream-image of justice
and injustice, good and evil, cannot truly be acquitted of involving E
reproach,³ even if the mass of men extol it.

Ph. No indeed.

Soc. On the other hand, if a man believes that a written discourse
on any subject is bound to contain much that is fanciful: that nothing
that has ever been written whether in verse or prose merits much
serious attention—and for that matter nothing that has ever been
spoken in the declamatory fashion which aims at mere persuasion
without any questioning or exposition: that in reality such compositions are, at the best, a means of reminding those who know the truth: 278
that lucidity and completeness and serious importance belong only to

---

¹ This is a new point. The manifold nature of soul, of which we heard at
271 A–B, is not the same as the ποικιλία which one particular soul may exhibit as
against the ἁπλότης of another.

² Socrates continues his sentence as though there had been no interruption.

³ I take ὕπαρ and ὄναρ not adverbially, but as real nouns: for ὕπαρ so used,
cf. *Pol.* 278 E and *Laws* 969 B. To suppose that writing can convey 'important
truth of permanent validity' is tantamount to an inability to distinguish between
ὕπαρ and ὄναρ: cf. ὀνειρώττουσι περὶ τὸ ὄν (*Rep.* 533 C). We were told above (276 A)
that the γεγραμμένος λόγος is no more than an εἴδωλον of the λόγος ζῶν καὶ ἔμψυχος,
and the present antithesis is a mere variant of that.

those lessons on justice and honour and goodness that are expounded and set forth for the sake of instruction, and are veritably written in the soul of the listener: and that such discourses as these ought to be accounted a man's own legitimate children—a title to be applied primarily to such as originate within the man himself, and secondarily B to such of their sons and brothers as have grown up aright in the souls of other men:[1] the man, I say, who believes this, and disdains all manner of discourse other than this, is, I would venture to affirm, the man whose example you and I would pray that we might follow.

Ph. My own wishes and prayers are most certainly to that effect.[2]

This section is in part the outcome of contemporary dispute between the rhetoricians on the comparative value of the extempore speech and that which is carefully prepared, written out and memorised before delivery. Isocrates, himself debarred by physical disadvantages from achieving distinction as a speaker, had had recourse to the essay in order to reach a public wider than that of his own school; but this novelty was distasteful to many of his professional brethren, whose spokesman in extant literature is Alcidamas. In his work *On Sophists*,[3] which is thought to have appeared not later than 380 B.C., Alcidamas adopts the same general attitude towards the written discourse that Plato here puts into the mouth of Socrates; and indeed the similarities of language[4] are such that, in view of the improbability of a common source, borrowing can hardly be denied. Chronology makes it likely that Plato is the borrower; but the point is of little moment, for the contemporary dispute of rhetoricians is no more than a handle for the introduction of a matter which touched and troubled 'Plato himself directly and personally, and perhaps had troubled him for many years past.

It will be obvious to anyone who reads these pages with perception that Plato is concerned to state and defend his own position in the matter of authorship. How could his writing of dialogues be of any value compared with the 'living word' of the master whom he por-

---

[1] In the clause ἐὰν εὑρεθεὶς ἐνῇ the emphasis falls on the participle. A man's legitimate spiritual children are primarily those truths which he himself has discovered by a process of dialectic, and secondarily those which, while logically consequent upon the former, are actually reached, again dialectically, by others. The distinction no doubt reflects the relation between the head of a school (such as Plato himself) and its members or disciples building upon his teaching.

[2] With these words Phaedrus's conversion to philosophy is signalised.

[3] περὶ τῶν τοὺς γραπτοὺς λόγους γραφόντων ἢ περὶ σοφιστῶν. Brzoska in Pauly-Wissowa, *RE*, dates it between 390 and 380, Christ-Schmid before 380.

[4] Collected by Friedländer, *Platon* I, pp. 129 f. I am greatly indebted to Friedländer's chapter 'Das geschriebene Werk' in interpreting the present section.

rayed in them, and who had shown his own estimate of writing by
never writing at all? How could one who persistently decried 'copies'
as against 'originals', representation (μίμησις) as against action, and
who had made a special application of the antithesis to dramatic poetry,
justify his own dramatic representations? How could he who, through
the mouth of Socrates, had twitted the orators with their long harangues,
comparing them to 'books which can neither answer questions nor put
them' (*Protag.* 329A), justify the composition of a work like the
Republic, with its long tracts of virtually unbroken didactic exposition?
We may perhaps believe that at first Plato stifled the protest of his
conscience by adhering as closely as possible to the Socratic βραχυλογία
and by carefully abstaining from positive conclusions: if he allowed
his Socrates to discuss and suggest, but not to teach or lecture, he was
not 'writing' in any real or reprehensible sense, but merely perpetuating
the master's activity. But such a self-justification, if it was ever made,
was of dubious validity from the first; and as 'Socrates' became
inevitably more and more Platonised it could not have been maintained. Yet Plato had undoubtedly an urge to go on writing—the mere
volume of his output guarantees that—and cannot have failed to be
conscious of literary power in such great works as *Phaedo, Symposium*
and *Republic*. On the other hand the coincident testimony of our
present section and of *Epistle* VII (341–4) reveals his deep distrust of
the written word as a medium of philosophy, whether moral or
metaphysical: it was always open to misunderstanding, it could never
express the whole mind of the writer, and it might do more harm than
good if it came into the hands of ignorant and unsympathetic readers;
moreover—and here again the two sources confirm one another—the
deepest truths can only be communicated through the long-lasting
association of a mature mind with one less mature, a 'sowing of the
living word in another's soul'. The σπουδαῖος, as the *Epistle* puts it
(344C), the serious philosopher, will not put what he deems σπου-
δαιότατα into writing, and he himself has never composed a manual of
his doctrine (341C).

It would be absurd to conclude from these passages that the content
of the dialogues was, in the eyes of their author, of little value; it is
surely plain that Plato writes for the most part in a vein of deep
seriousness, with a sincerity at times passionate. We may well believe
that his profoundest thoughts could not be set down: but we may also
believe that remembrance of the power of Socrates's spoken word—
a power which he describes so vividly through the mouth of Alcibiades
in the *Symposium*—together perhaps with the consciousness[1] of similar

---

[1] As may be inferred from the words which he imagines Dion addressing to
him, at *Ep.* VII 328D: σὲ μάλιστα ἠπιστάμην ἐγὼ δυνάμενον ἀνθρώπους νέους ἐπὶ τὰ
ἀγαθὰ καὶ τὰ δίκαια προτρέποντα εἰς φιλίαν τε καὶ ἑταιρίαν ἀλλήλοις καθιστάναι ἑκάστοτε.

power in himself, led him at times to underrate the value of all written philosophy, including his own. Moreover he probably felt to the end the dangers of dogmatism, and the desirability of the teacher's keeping himself always open to the suggestions, and even the corrections, of the pupil.

There was also of course the peril of δοξοσοφία (275 A–B): a reader tends, Plato thought, to imagine that he can absorb wisdom quickly by an almost effortless perusal of written words; but what is so absorbed is something neither solid nor permanent (hence the comparison to 'gardens of Adonis'); true wisdom and understanding, whether about God or the universe or the life of man, can only come by long study and reflection, aided normally by a teacher who is himself still learning, a guide rather than an authoritative exponent: then will knowledge come, point by point, as a flash of illumination: ἐκ πολλῆς συνουσίας γιγνομένης περὶ τὸ πρᾶγμα αὐτὸ καὶ τοῦ συʒῆν ἐξαίφνης, οἷον ἀπὸ πυρὸς πηδήσαντος ἐξαφθὲν φῶς, ἐν τῇ ψυχῇ γενόμενον (*Ep.* VII, 341 C).

Socrates's words at 276 E 4–277 A 4 should be compared not only with Diotima's at *Symp.* 209 B[1] but also with 249 A 1–4 and 256 A–B above. All these passages express, in their varying ways, the same fundamental thought: that the association of two kindred souls, the one guiding and the other guided, in the pursuit of truth, beauty and goodness, is the means to the highest human felicity. Although the language of our present passage is less erotic, the words ὅταν...λαβὼν ψυχὴν προσήκουσαν φυτεύῃ τε καὶ σπείρῃ μετ᾽ ἐπιστήμης λόγους mean just the same as παιδεραστήσαντος μετὰ φιλοσοφίας (249 A). And when we see this, we see also that this discussion of the merits and defects of writing, culminating as it does in the exaltation of the spoken words of dialectic, is no extraneous appendage to the main theme of the dialogue—the praise, to wit, of the philosophic life as Socrates and Plato understood it.

---

[1] Especially B 5 ff.: τά τε οὖν σώματα τὰ καλὰ μᾶλλον ἢ τὰ αἰσχρὰ ἀσπάζεται ἅτε κυῶν, καὶ ἂν ἐντύχῃ ψυχῇ καλῇ καὶ γενναίᾳ καὶ εὐφυεῖ, πάνυ δὴ ἀσπάζεται τὸ συναμφότερον, καὶ πρὸς τοῦτον τὸν ἄνθρωπον εὐθὺς εὐπορεῖ λόγων περὶ ἀρετῆς καὶ περὶ οἷον χρὴ εἶναι τὸν ἄνδρα τὸν ἀγαθὸν καὶ ἃ ἐπιτηδεύειν, καὶ ἐπιχειρεῖ παιδεύειν.

XXVI

278B–279C MESSAGES TO LYSIAS AND ISOCRATES

Phaedrus is now bidden to convey to Lysias the purport of the late argument: the writer of speeches, the poet and the lawgiver, if their writing conforms to the conditions developed in the last section, deserve a different name: the name of philosopher. But Socrates agrees that there is a message for his own young friend Isocrates too; this takes the form half of prophecy, half of hope, that he may use his considerable gifts for higher purposes than ordinary rhetoric.

The dialogue ends with Socrates uttering a short prayer, in which Phaedrus joins, for inward goodness, for spiritual riches together with such material wealth, but only such, as befits the wise and temperate.

Soc. Then we may regard our literary pastime[1] as having reached 278 B a satisfactory conclusion. Do you now go and tell Lysias that we two went down to the stream where is the holy place of the Nymphs, and there listened to words which charged us to deliver a message, first to Lysias and all other composers of discourses, secondly to Homer and C all others who have written poetry whether to be read or sung, and thirdly to Solon and all such as are authors of political compositions under the name of laws: to wit, that if any of them has done his work with a knowledge of the truth, can defend his statements when challenged, and can demonstrate the inferiority of his writings out of his own mouth, he ought not to be designated by a name drawn from those writings, but by one that indicates his serious pursuit. D

Ph. Then what names would you assign him?

Soc. To call him wise, Phaedrus, would, I think, be going too far: the epithet is proper only to a god; a name that would fit him better, and have more seemliness, would be 'lover of wisdom', or something similar.

Ph. Yes, that would be quite in keeping.

Soc. On the other hand, one who has nothing to show of more value than the literary works on whose phrases he spends hours, twisting them this way and that, pasting them together and pulling them apart,[2] E will rightly, I suggest, be called a poet or speech-writer or law-writer.

[1] The reference is probably not to the whole dialogue, but to the discussion from 274 A 6 onwards.

[2] Dionysius of Halicarnassus (*de comp. verb.* p. 208, Reiske) tells us that Plato continued throughout his life 'combing and curling' (κτενίζων καὶ βοστρυχίζων)

Ph. Of course.

Soc. Then that is what you must tell your friend.

Ph. But what about yourself? What are you going to do? You too have a friend who should not be passed over.

Soc. Who is that?

Ph. The fair Isocrates. What will be your message to him, Socrates, and what shall we call him?

Soc. Isocrates is still young, Phaedrus, but I don't mind telling you 279 the future I prophesy for him.

Ph. Oh, what is that?

Soc. It seems to me that his natural powers give him a superiority over anything that Lysias has achieved in literature, and also that in point of character he is of a nobler composition; hence it would not surprise me if with advancing years he made all his literary predecessors look like very small fry; that is, supposing him to persist in the actual type of writing in which he engages at present; still more so, if he should become dissatisfied with such work, and a sublimer impulse lead him to do greater things. For that mind of his, Phaedrus, contains an innate tincture of philosophy.

B   Well then, there's the report I convey from the gods of this place to Isocrates my beloved, and there's yours for your beloved Lysias.

Ph. So be it. But let us be going, now that it has become less oppressively hot.

Soc. Oughtn't we first to offer a prayer to the divinities here?

Ph. To be sure.

Soc. Dear Pan, and all ye other gods that dwell in this place, grant that I may become fair within, and that such outward things as I have c may not war against the spirit within me. May I count him rich who is wise; and as for gold, may I possess so much of it as only a temperate man might bear and carry with him.

Is there anything more we can ask for, Phaedrus? The prayer contents me.

Ph. Make it a prayer for me too, since friends have all things in common.

Soc. Let us be going.

his dialogues, and that at his death a tablet was found with numerous variants of the opening sentence of the *Republic*; cf. also Diog. Laert. III, 37. It is possible that the present sentence reflects the impatience of Plato the philosopher with Plato the meticulous literary artist.

The conjunction (278 c) of Lysias and other λογογράφοι with the poets (Homer) and legislators (Solon) takes us back to an earlier passage (258 A–C): here, as there, the purpose is to generalise the judgment passed upon 'composition'; in the earlier passage, however, the distinction between speaking and writing was latent: now it has been explicitly drawn, to the disadvantage of writing; nevertheless the fundamental distinction for Plato is between those, whether speakers or writers, who rest on a basis of dialectic, who possess the truth about that on which they speak, and the ability to uphold it, and those who do not. In short, the message to be delivered to Lysias by Phaedrus is essentially the same as that which earlier (261 A) the θρέμματα γενναῖα addressed to Phaedrus himself: ἐὰν μὴ ἱκανῶς φιλοσοφήσῃ, οὐδὲ ἱκανός ποτε λέγειν ἔσται περὶ οὐδενός. Lacking 'philosophy' (and we have learnt more fully since 261 A what that means) a man may be 'a poet, or speech-writer or law-writer', but no more; and he will not be even ἱκανὸς λέγειν, because philosophy alone can make him so.

We can, I think, detect now a deeper reason for bracketing the λογογράφος with the poet and the speech-writer. All three[1] claim, implicitly if not expressly, to prescribe to their fellow-men what they should do, how they should live their lives. Though not professed teachers of ἀρετή like the Sophists, they are open to the same criticism from Plato's standpoint: they do not know the moral εἴδη, nor do they even seek to know them; they are in that condition of ἀπαιδευσία which marks the prisoners in the cave;[2] in terms of the *Phaedrus* myth, they have forgotten what little their souls had seen in the supra-celestial region.

Lysias, with whom the whole conversation started, and who has been kept before the reader's mind throughout as the typical product of an unreformed, that is to say an unphilosophic, rhetoric, is beyond the reach of human warnings or messages when Plato writes. But Isocrates is not. There must be some point in the parallelism (279 B 1–3) of the two messages, and I do not see how it can be other than this, that what we cannot hope for from the dead we can from the living. I agree with Wilamowitz[3] that there is no trace of irony in what is said of Isocrates here; and the fact that he is favourably contrasted with Lysias in itself rules out the idea that he, personally and individually,

[1] The λογογράφος is here probably not thought of in the narrow sense of professional speech-writer for litigants, but in the broader sense given to it earlier, which would include the Lysias of the *Olympicus* and the *Epitaphius* (if genuine), and the epideictic speeches of which the ἐρωτικὸς λόγος of our dialogue purports to be an example.

[2] On the meaning of ἀπαιδευσία (*Rep.* 514 A) see H. W. B. Joseph, *Knowledge and the Good in Plato's Republic*, p. 26.

[3] *Platon* II, p. 122: 'Wahrlich ein hohes Lob: keine Spur von Ironie, nur der Wunsch, dass er die Begabung für Philosophie ausbilden möchte.'

has been the target of all the foregoing critique of rhetoric. The playfu
description of him as Socrates's παιδικά must imply that Socrate
knew and liked him as a young man; and that Plato should recal
this friendship, and should put into Socrates's mouth a prophecy
albeit a conditional prophecy, of future greatness with the purpos
of calling attention to its non-fulfilment, is in my judgment ver
improbable.

I should interpret the first half of the prophecy as already fulfillec
when Plato wrote; Isocrates's orations, notably the *Panegyricus* o
380 B.C., had already put all previous orators in the shade (whether w
ourselves agree is beside the point); the second half, the 'sublim
impulse leading to greater things' is as yet unfulfilled; but I do not se
why Plato should not still have hoped for its fulfilment. If Plato had
as he surely had, any hope of his proposals for a philosophic rhetori
being adopted, he must win over Isocrates to his cause. He may hav
been, probably he was, over-sanguine; but Isocrates in 370 B.C. was
though elderly, not necessarily impervious to argument.

There may be a second motive behind the message to Isocrates. The
passage of *Rep.* VI referred to above[1] had been taken by Isocrates a
meant for his address; and whether or not it was so, Plato may well have
wished to make a conciliatory gesture, an *amende* both for that anc
for anything in the present dialogue which might have been taker
amiss.[2] As we have seen, Isocrates must have been in Plato's minc
in much of the latter part of our dialogue; and even without being
conscious of having given offence, it may well be that he felt that
some kind words could do no harm; kind words they are, and sincerely
meant.

The closing paragraphs recall us to the scene in which the whole
dialogue has taken place, and remind us of the inspiration which
Socrates felt from the outset and ascribed to the local deities. The

---

[1] See p. 143, n. 2.

[2] cf. Wilamowitz, *op. cit.* II, p. 122: 'Versichern kann man nicht, dass der
Phaidros die Wunde heilen will, die der Staat geschlagen hatte; unmöglich ist es
nicht.' R. Flacelière (*Revue des études grecques* XLVI, 1933, pp. 224 ff.) regards the
encomium as seriously meant, yet combined with a touch of irony: Isocrates's
φιλοσοφία is only φιλοσοφία of a sort, and it is possessed φύσει instead of as the
result of dialectic. He thinks Isocrates is placed on the same level as the statesmen
of *Meno* 99 B ff., who possess right opinion θείᾳ μοίρᾳ.

That this last may be the case seems to me quite likely, but I do not think any
irony is thereby involved; nor do I think φύσει ἔνεστί τις φιλοσοφία τῇ διανοίᾳ
need mean anything different from φιλόσοφός πώς ἐστι τὴν φύσιν. The man,
suggests Socrates, has an innate love of whatsoever is καλόν and an innate hatred
of whatsoever is αἰσχρόν, finding the former οἰκεῖον and the latter ἀλλότριον like
the philosophic dog of *Rep.* 376 B; for all his scorn of scientific ethics, Isocrates is
on the side of the angels.

For the influence of Socrates upon Isocrates, Flacelière points (*inter alia*) to
ad Nicoclem (II), §§ 11–12.

closing prayer has no special connexion with the context of the dialogue, but is eminently characteristic of the real Socrates in its depreciation of external and bodily goods as compared with the goods of the spirit. And Phaedrus's last words, in their moving simplicity, show us once more that the devotee of clever but hollow oratory has become one in heart and mind with the lover of truth, the genuine ψυχαγωγός.

INDEX OF NAMES